MURDER ON THE INSIDE

MURDER ON THE INSIDE

THE TRUE STORY OF THE DEADLY RIOT AT KINGSTON PENITENTIARY

CATHERINE FOGARTY

BIBLIOASIS

WINDSOR, ONTARIO

FIRST EDITION

Library and Archives Canada Cataloguing in Publication

Title: Murder on the inside : the true story of the deadly riot at
    Kingston Penitentiary / Catherine Fogarty.
Names: Fogarty, Catherine, author.
Identifiers: Canadiana (print) 2020039147X | Canadiana (ebook) 20200391488 |
    ISBN 9781771964012 (softcover) | ISBN 9781771964029 (ebook)
Subjects: LCSH: Kingston Penitentiary. | LCSH: Prison riots—Ontario—Kingston.
Classification: DDC 365/.641—dc23

Edited by Janice Zawerbny
Copyedited by John Sweet
Text and cover designed by Ingrid Paulson

Title page: Old image of Kingston Pen, 1800s.
Queen's University Archives, V23-PuB-Kingston-Pen-15

Published with the generous assistance of the Canada Council for the Arts, which last year invested $153 million to bring the arts to Canadians throughout the country, and the financial support of the Government of Canada. Biblioasis also acknowledges the support of the Ontario Arts Council (OAC), an agency of the Government of Ontario, which last year funded 1,709 individual artists and 1,078 organizations in 204 communities across Ontario, for a total of $52.1 million, and the contribution of the Government of Ontario through the Ontario Book Publishing Tax Credit and Ontario Creates.

PRINTED AND BOUND IN CANADA

For my dad, Edward Charles Fogarty,
who instilled a passion for learning and a love for reading.

I love you and I miss you.

CONTENTS

The penitentiary will not be a place where the criminal can hide from the public and forget his responsibilities as a citizen. It will be a place where he will learn the skills and develop the self-control that he must have before he can expect to be accepted as a free member of the world.

—Commissioner of Penitentiaries A.J. MacLeod (1966)

INTRODUCTION

FIFTY YEARS AGO, on April 14, 1971, a small group of inmates at Kingston Penitentiary, Canada's oldest prison, overpowered unsuspecting guards and instigated what was to become one of the most violent and devastating prison riots in our country's history.

The early 1970s was a time of great political and social upheaval, and what was happening in our prisons reflected that change. Deteriorating prison conditions and the increasing awareness of basic human rights were creating a combustible penal environment both in Canada and south of the border. The civil rights movement of the 1960s had given rise to a new breed of inmate—politically aware young men with radical ideas of rights and freedoms. Prisoners wanted to be treated like humans instead of numbers, and they were demanding to be heard.

You have taken our civil rights, but we want our human rights, read a banner hanging outside the prison walls in Kingston during the riot. But what began as a rallying cry to the outside world for prison reform and justice quickly dissolved into a tense hostage taking, savage beatings and ultimately murder. For four terrifying days, prisoners held six guards hostage as they negotiated with ill-prepared prison officials and anxious politicians, while heavily armed soldiers surrounded the prison and prepared for an attack.

It was an insurrection, unprecedented in scope and savagery, but the deadly ingredients for the riot had been brewing long before that fateful night in April. The warden of Kingston Penitentiary had alerted his superiors in Ottawa that the prison was dangerously overcrowded and understaffed. Another aggravating factor was the recent transfer of inmates to a new penitentiary called Millhaven. Rather than welcome a chance to leave the aging structure they were in, Kingston Pen prisoners were terrified of the newly built super-maximum prison, which was rumoured to be even more repressive, with security cameras and hidden microphones monitoring inmates' every move.

But the danger signs were not heeded, and the years of mistreatment, bitterness and distrust ultimately created a human volcano inside the prison. Life inside the archaic jail was humiliating and dehumanizing. There was serious overcrowding, few rehabilitation programs, severe punishments and extreme isolation.

When the rebellion finally erupted, it made headlines around the world, as did another prison riot six months later in Attica, New York, where thirty-nine guards and inmates were killed by police fire. Fortunately, the Kingston Penitentiary riot did not end in the bloodshed of Attica, but it did cost the lives of two men and changed the lives of many more.

Like many long-forgotten stories, I found this one by chance. It was a brief mention in the *Globe and Mail*'s "This Day in History" column. Intrigued, I cut it out and added it to my ideas folder full of other scraps of paper. But there was something about this story that I was inexplicably drawn to, a desire to know more about what actually happened behind Canada's limestone fortress so many years ago. Six months later, that small piece of newsprint became the inspiration for my first foray into historical nonfiction. I can now say, five years later, that I really had no idea what I was getting myself into!

A few months into researching the story, I found myself driving to Kingston, the picturesque town on the shores of Lake Ontario where Canada's most famous prison opened in 1835. The original facility consisted of a single cellblock containing 154 cells. Designed to hold 500 inmates, its population grew every year as more and more desperate men found themselves locked away inside its walls.

I was heading into the "belly of the beast," having snagged a hard-to-find ticket for the Kingston Penitentiary tour. Since the penitentiary closed its doors in 2013, thousands have flocked to the notorious prison to finally get a look inside. But I wasn't just a curious tourist; I was a writer on a mission to find the true story behind the events of April 1971. I knew Kingston was the place to begin my research. After all, it was the birthplace of the Correctional Service of Canada, and Kingston Pen was one of the city's defining institutions. But by the time I drove back to Toronto twenty-four hours later, I was certain of only one thing: the ghosts of the 1971 Kingston Penitentiary riot were not going to be easily awoken.

Although the riot had occurred decades earlier, I soon discovered this was an event that few were willing to revisit. The Correctional Service of Canada, which controls all federal penitentiaries, was quick to ensnare me in red tape. Calls and emails would go unanswered for weeks. Every request led to more forms and more delays. The Canadian Penitentiary Museum, which is conveniently housed in the former Warden's Office across the street from Kingston Pen, informed me that they had little information about the riot. The Kingston Police also had no records dating back to 1971.

Multiple trips to the Ontario provincial archives required more paperwork, freedom of information requests and further appeals. When documents were finally received, they would often be heavily redacted. A trip to the Queen's University archives to obtain historical photos from the *Kingston Whig-Standard* led to even more frustration when it was discovered that someone had removed all of the photo negatives related to the four-day riot. But with each disappointment or closed door, I remained determined to exhume this story from behind prison walls.

Eventually, I was put in touch with a group of retired correctional officers. When I contacted the organizer of the group, she was more than willing to offer assistance in trying to find any officers who had worked at Kingston Pen during the riot, but she cautioned me that they might not want to talk. Once again I was up against a well-entrenched code. Prison guards, for the most part, like police officers, live behind a "blue wall" of silence.

A carefully worded email was distributed to over one hundred retirees, but my inbox remained empty. Then, a few weeks later, I received one short, cryptic note: "I was there, but I don't know how much I can tell you." Eventually, a few more emails trickled in. Soon, I was headed back to Kingston for several clandestine meetings in shopping malls and coffee shops. The retired prison guards I met were initially cautious and suspicious. The job had made them that way. These were strong men and women who had worked in an unforgiving environment. Their work for the most part was mundane, but potential violence lurked around every corner. Their only refuge was the camaraderie they shared with each other. They did not take their jobs home with them and they did not talk to outsiders.

But eventually some did talk, and the stories they told me were similar. Their recollections of the April 1971 riot were scarce. Many of them who had returned to duty during the riot had stood outside the prison walls for four days and nights, helpless while their six kidnapped colleagues remained inside. Most of what they knew had come from hearsay, rumours and news reports.

As they mined their memories and slowly revealed their stories, I was surprised to learn that many of them held an enduring respect and fondness for Kingston Penitentiary. It was Canada's oldest prison, archaic in its structure and systems, but the men who had worked within its walls felt part of a shared history and a connection to its memory. For them, there was no place like KP.

But many were angry. Angry with the bureaucracy they had worked for. "You give them thirty years and you don't get so much as a thank you in the end," said one retiree. At their biannual reunions at the local legion hall they now swap old stories and remember old friends. And just recently they had started talking about PTSD.

As I continued my research, I sought out others who might have been involved in the riot. I searched names that appeared in old press clippings, court records and news reports, but sadly, most inquiries led to an obituary. Undeterred, I contacted families to find out more about their loved ones and their recollections, if any, of the events of April 1971. Most family members had little to share due to the passage of time, but even the smallest detail about their husband, father or brother has helped me bring their loved ones back to life on the page.

Eventually, I found a few individuals who had lived through the riot and were willing to tell their side of the story. A 2013 CBC documentary led me to Kerry Bushell, who is the only living survivor of the six guards who were taken hostage. Nervous about calling him out of the blue and dredging up old memories, I sent him a letter explaining my book. Would he want to return to that nightmare forty-five years ago, when he and the other guards thought they would be killed? I wasn't sure. But he called back. Not long after that, I was able to meet Kerry and his wife, who were newlyweds at the time of the riot. Having survived the ordeal and its long-lasting repercussions, Kerry's voice is an important part of this story.

But there are other voices too—voices from a different perspective, but equally poignant in the retelling of this story. I interviewed inmates who took part in the riot, including one who was ultimately charged with murder. As a seventeen-year-old petty thief, Robbie Robidoux was thrust into a world where he learned how to fight in order to stay alive. Kingston Pen was the big house and every inmate lived by the convict's code. Stool pigeons and sex offenders were the lowest of the low, and to this day he has little remorse about killing one of them.

There have been many stories and a few books written about Kingston Penitentiary, but very few have touched upon its deadliest riot in any detail. Often relegated to a few sentences or a paragraph, it has been largely ignored. But there was one other book written about the riot. In 1985, former Kingston Penitentiary inmate Roger Caron published *Bingo!*, an intimate and harrowing story of his experience during the prison uprising. While many have questioned its veracity, no one can dispute the fact that Mr. Caron was there. His perspective and retelling of the story remains the only written eyewitness account.

Today, Kingston Penitentiary stands empty. Although slated for the mothballs many times, including after the 1971 riot, it wasn't officially closed until September 30, 2013. For 178 years the formidable fortress housed thousands, including some of Canada's most notorious criminals, and their many stories remain deeply embedded in its foundation.

Designated a National Historic Site of Canada in 1990, the federal government announced in 2012 that it would be closing the aging maximum-security prison due to its "crumbling infrastructure and costly upkeep." Now, for seven months a year, the St. Lawrence Parks Commission offers guided tours of the waterfront landmark. Tickets sell out months in advance and eager crowds line up outside the north gatehouse on King Street waiting to get a look inside. Young guides take you on a well-rehearsed tour of the aged facilities and retired correctional officers stationed at several points along the visit offer a more intimate account of working behind the ominous limestone walls.

When the tour reaches the central dome area of the penitentiary, where the riot took place, an officer tells each group about the four fateful days in April 1971 when rioting inmates kidnapped six guards and took over the prison. He talks about the brass bell that used to sit in the middle of the dome and governed every inmate's move, and how it was the first symbol of repression destroyed in the riot. And then the retired guard tells his captive audience about what happened in the dome on the last night of the riot, when a group of undesirable inmates were rounded up, tied in a circle and tortured until all of them were either unconscious or dead. Then the tour moves on.

What the Kingston Penitentiary tour doesn't talk about is what happened after the riot, when busloads of inmates were transported to the hastily opened Millhaven Institution a few miles away, in Bath. As the shackled prisoners stepped off the buses, they were met by a gauntlet of baton-wielding guards ready to take their pound of flesh. Inmates were injured, and charges were eventually laid against thirteen prison guards, a first in Canadian history.

After the riot, the federal government ordered a commission of inquiry into the disturbance at Kingston Penitentiary. The seventy-page Swackhammer Report condemned the system in place at the prison and made sweeping recommendations for improvements. The report also led to the creation of the Office of the Correctional Investigator in 1973 and the formalization of an internal grievance procedure for inmates.

Today, the Office of the Correctional Investigator looks into what is going on in Canada's correctional facilities. In his most recent annual report, in 2019, Ivan Zinger, the current Correctional Investigator, stated, "With present spending, investment and staffing levels, Canada should be outstanding in every aspect of correctional performance." But his report indicated that considerable improvement was still needed. Inmate assaults on each other and against staff are increasing, suicides are escalating, and prison homicides are at their highest numbers in a decade.

The year 2021 marks the fiftieth anniversary of the Kingston Penitentiary riot, and yet, as I learned, it remains a story few want to revisit. This story takes you behind the walls of the maximum-security prison during its deadliest siege, when men from all walks of life—convicts, lawyers, newsmen, politicians and prison administrators—were thrust together to try to bring about a peaceful resolution to a dire situation. Out of the fray emerged some unlikely heroes who saved hundreds of lives, including those of the kidnapped guards, while others sadly turned their rage against the weakest among them.

But half a century after the Kingston Penitentiary riot, an event where prisoners asked to be heard and demanded to be treated humanely, we have to ask, what have we learned? Our country still struggles with fundamental questions related to incarceration and basic human rights. Cruel injustices continue to happen in our prisons every day.

It is my hope that in re-creating this moment in our penal history, I have offered the reader a glimpse into a world that remains hidden from our view, a peek behind the curtain of a correctional system that is still deeply flawed in its philosophy and practices. The Russian writer Dostoyevsky once said: "The degree of civilization in a society can be judged by entering its prisons." But how are we to judge if we are still not even allowed to see inside?

1

TICKING TIME BOMB

Wednesday, April 14, 1971

BILLY KNIGHT SAT quietly at one of the folding card tables at the back of the gymnasium. With his dark-brown jacket, khaki-coloured pants, striped shirt and black boots, he resembled every other guy in the room as he glanced at the well-worn playing cards held by his nicotine-stained fingers and then up at the clock behind the tattered basketball net. He was contemplating his next move.

Two portable televisions stood in the centre of the cinder-block gym. Some television show was on. It could have been *Hawaii Five-O* or *The Mod Squad*, two current favourites amongst the group. Or perhaps it was a rerun of *Gunsmoke*. It didn't really matter because, with little else to do, the men were watching the screens impassively. This was a marked difference from the night before, during the fifth game of the quarter-final playoff series between the Toronto Maple Leafs and the New York Rangers.[1] The series was tied two-all. Popular Leafs players including Dave Keon, Paul Henderson and Darryl Sittler were up against fellow Canadians Tim Horton and Mike Robitaille on the Rangers. The guys sitting in the gym lived for *Hockey Night in Canada*. It was the one thing that took them away from the deadening routine of prison life. But it was frustrating when games went into overtime and they couldn't stay to watch. The televisions were turned off at precisely 10:30 p.m. no matter what. That was the rule.

In total, seventy-eight men from range two were gathered in the prison gym that night.[2] William (Billy) Knight, prisoner #6622, was one of them. Everyone at KP, as the Kingston Penitentiary was nicknamed, knew Billy Knight. As the prison barber, he interacted with most of the inmates. Cutting hair was a trade he had picked up over the years while incarcerated. Strict adherence to personal grooming was one of the basic rules on the inside. Hair had to be short, and beards and moustaches were not permitted.[3] When inmates came out of the "hole," or solitary confinement, they were immediately handed off to Knight for the removal of any unruly hair growth. Fancying himself a fashionable guy despite his less than stylish surroundings, Billy's hair was always meticulously groomed into a high 1940s pompadour, each strand of hair wet-combed to stand out in a high front wave above his forehead.

A well-liked, mouthy type, Knight never backed down from an argument. He was a strong advocate for exposing conditions within the prison and was always making impassioned speeches to anyone who would listen. If someone had a grievance with the administration, as many did, they knew to talk to Knight about it. He was a natural leader among the inmates. He was even writing a book, called *The Walking Dead*, an autobiography and exposé of prison life. He claimed it was going to revolutionize the system.

Knight was only twenty-eight, but he had already spent more of his life behind bars than on the outside.[4] The fourth of eleven kids, William James Knight was born on March 17, 1943, and lived his early years on his grandfather's farm in Don Mills, Ontario. His parents were poor and uneducated. Young Billy quickly learned the ways of the street and developed an early skill for petty theft. He would often steal groceries from the local A&P to help feed his family. Physical abuse from his parents and older siblings was common, but when his six-year-old brother Jimmy was hit and killed by a drunk driver on his way home from school, the family dynamic got much worse. Billy resorted to skipping school and running away from home. At fourteen he was arrested for shoplifting and sent to the county jail. At fifteen he stole his first car and was sent to Guelph Reformatory for a year.

For the next ten years, Knight bounced in and out of jail and in and out of jobs. He had developed a problem with alcohol that constantly got him into trouble. At eighteen he got married, and he continued stealing to support his new family. In 1966 he broke into a Salvation Army thrift store in Windsor, Ontario, to steal clothing. Sentenced to three years for break and enter, he attempted to run from the courthouse. This would be the first of many escapes for Knight. In 1969, while out on parole, Knight smashed a store window in Kingston and stole some cigarettes. Because of his previous record for theft, he was sentenced to three more years. In the winter of 1970 he got out on a day pass from Collins Bay penitentiary and took off. He stole a 1963 Ford in Ottawa and headed north. In Wawa, Ontario, the car finally ran out of gas, and Knight ran out of luck. Running from the police through snow-covered fields with no winter clothing, he was soon caught by the cops. Still, he was determined not to go back to jail. When the police took him to the hospital in Sault Ste. Marie for frostbite on his toes, he bolted again, only to be recaptured a few blocks away.

Knight's wild Wawa adventure cost him seven more years in the penitentiary. He was also charged ninety-six dollars for walking away with a prison-issued uniform, which was deducted from his canteen fund. For the second time in his criminal career, Knight landed in Kingston Penitentiary—the big leagues of Canadian federal prisons. Being a small, wiry guy, Knight knew that in order to survive in a place like Kingston Pen he had to be smart. Make one bad move or piss off the wrong con and your life belonged to someone else.

AS THE EVENING of April 14 wore on, Knight continued playing cards. Scattered throughout the smoke-filled gymnasium were six other inmates he had recruited to help with his plan. Robert Adams and Allan Lafreniere sat at Billy's table. Charles Saunders and Emanuel (Manny) Lester were at the next. And over by one of the television sets, Brian Dodge and Leo Barrieault appeared glued to what was on the screen, but in reality they were watching the guards.

That night, there were ten officers on duty in the main cell block. Three were in the gym and another was stationed in the gun cage that overlooked the entire room. Outside the gym, two guards were on the ground floor of the main dome, which contained a maze of metal stairways and circular galleries. Fanning out from the dome were eight cellblocks with more than six hundred cells. Four officers stood in the passageways around the perimeter of the dome. They were stationed at their respective posts in preparation for the inmates leaving the gymnasium to walk back to their cells.

The night keeper, or senior guard on call, was Edward (Ed) Barrett. At fifty-seven he had worn the uniform for close to thirty years, and it showed in the deep wrinkles and red veins on his face. Working alongside him were Douglas Dietrich and Donald Flynn, a loud, overly confident man. William Babcock was another hard-line screw, and it was his job to maintain order and discipline in the gymnasium. Also working that night were Terrance (Terry) Decker, Douglas (dad) Dale and Joseph Vallier. Completing the group was young Kerry Bushell. At twenty-four, he was the rookie on staff and still in training. At Kingston Pen you learned on the job, and you learned quickly.

In 1971, Kingston Penitentiary had 359 employees, including administrators, support staff, medical personnel and guards.[5] The relationship between the inmates and the guards at Kingston Pen was constantly strained, but in the weeks and months leading up to the night of April 14, 1971, the atmosphere inside the ancient stone prison had become downright volatile. The inmates were at war with the guards and the guards were at war with the prison administration.[6] Backed by a powerful union, the Public Service Alliance, the guards wanted more money, more authority, more training and more protection. The administrators, in turn, were up against an inflexible bureaucracy called the Canadian Penitentiary Service. In one way or another, everyone was doing time.

Guards, for the most part, came from the same poor, working-class backgrounds as many of the convicts they watched over. They received little formal training and were expected to learn on the job. Fish screws (new guards) were quickly faced with the contradiction between their limited training at the staff college, which emphasized a new rehabilitation concept, and the harsh attitude of the old guard once they arrived at the prison.[7] They had to either conform to the rigid stance of the experienced staff or be ostracized. New recruits learned to abide by the code or find a new career. You didn't communicate with an inmate other than to tell him what to do, and you were never to show respect or kindness to any prisoner. To do so would lead to the instant label of con-lover.

Clinging to an archaic military system of strict order and discipline, seasoned guards revelled in punishing inmates for the smallest infraction. Shirts had to be buttoned and tucked at all times; hands had to be removed from pant pockets when walking; and there was no talking past 8 p.m. The penitentiary rules stated an inmate could speak with the officer in charge of him only in matters connected with his work. He had to approach the officer in a respectful manner, address him as Sir and stand at attention. Step out of line and you could lose hard-earned privileges or, worse, you went to the hole.

There was little pride or feeling of accomplishment associated with being a prison guard. It was the "occupation of last resort," the job you took if you couldn't get anything else. Poor public attitudes towards the many prisons in the Kingston area also contributed to a lack of respect for guards in the community. Guards did not wear uniforms out in public and their families kept to themselves in the city.[8] They worked a lot of overtime because of constant staffing shortages, but they knew where to get a cold beer when their shift was done. The Portsmouth Tavern, or "the Ports," in the adjoining village was the place you went to drink if you worked at KP.[9]

The job of a prison guard was dangerous, tough work. New recruits were hard to find and even harder to keep once they got a taste of Kingston Pen. As a result, the prison was often severely understaffed. And on the night of April 14, 1971, that was a situation Billy Knight planned to take full advantage of.

2

A NEW APPROACH TO INCARCERATION

They are not to gaze at visitors passing through the prison nor sing, nor dance, whistle, run, jump nor do anything which might disturb the harmony or contravene the rules of the prison.

—1836 prison regulations

IN 1826, HUGH CHRISTOPHER THOMSON, a member of the Legislative Assembly for Kingston and editor of the weekly journal the *Upper Canadian Herald*, recognized that crime rates in British North America were on the rise due to the increase in immigration from the British Isles.[10] He believed that the district or common jails operating in Upper Canada did not deal with any form of rehabilitation and prisoners sat idle until their release. Thomson, who was born in Kingston in 1791 to Loyalist parents from New York, travelled south to well-established penitentiaries in the United States to study and recommend a new approach to incarceration. In his report to the Legislative Assembly of Upper Canada in February 1831, he stated that a penitentiary should be

a place which by every means not cruel and not affecting
the health of the offender, shall be rendered so irksome
and so terrible that during his afterlife he may dread
nothing so much as a repetition of the punishment, and
if possible, that he should prefer death to such a contin-
gency. This can all be done by hard labour and privations
and not only without expense to the province, but possibly bringing in revenue.

In 1832, the government of Upper Canada paid a modest one
thousand pounds for fifteen acres of land on the shores of Lake
Ontario overlooking Hatter's Bay to build British North America's
first penitentiary. The location was two miles beyond Kingston's
western border on West Street. The location also afforded easy
water access for the transport of goods, and the area had an abun-
dance of limestone found in the local quarries that could be used
in the construction of the facility.

The city of Kingston is situated at the eastern end of Lake
Ontario midway between Toronto and Montreal. It is one of the
oldest settlements in Canada. The War of 1812 resulted in a significant military and naval presence at Kingston and stimulated the
local economy and population growth.[11] In 1832, the completion
of the Rideau Canal, a 125-mile-long waterway, linked Bytown
(later Ottawa) to Lake Ontario and the St. Lawrence River at
Kingston. This development reinforced Kingston's commercial
function and its strategic military significance. Kingston was initially the largest town in Upper Canada and was the capital of the
new Province of Canada from 1841 until December 1843.

Kingston offered a potential market for convict goods and the
necessary supplies to operate the prison. But the proposed penitentiary was met with strong local resistance. Resident business
owners were concerned about the free forced labour in the prison

and the number of items that would be produced and sold into the local economy. It was generally acknowledged that prison-made goods could be produced in higher quantities and sold more cheaply than those manufactured by independent tradesmen. Local workers also felt the penitentiary would represent unfair, government-funded competition. Pointing to the experience of their fellow craftsmen in upstate New York, where the Auburn Prison had virtually destroyed the shoemaking trade, Kingston workers denounced the establishment of the penitentiary in their city. A petition was drafted deploring "the labour of rogues in competition with honest men."[12] In 1835, before the arrival of any convicts, a public meeting in Kingston passed a resolution outlining the trades that the penitentiary should avoid at all costs.[13] There was even a suggestion to move the penitentiary to Marmora, sixty miles north-west of Kingston. But despite fervent opposition, the government went ahead with building the new penitentiary in Kingston.

Originally called the Provincial Penitentiary of the Province of Upper Canada, the grey stone fortress was constructed in 1833–34. Deputy Keeper William Powers and master builder John Mills from the Auburn Prison in New York were hired to oversee the construction of the complex. Hugh Christopher Thomson, who was responsible for bringing the penitentiary system to Canada, was chosen to be the first warden, but poor health and a weak heart led to his premature death at age forty-three in 1834.

THE ORIGINAL SOUTH WING of the penitentiary was a single, large lime-stone cellblock with 144 cells. The three other wings of the main building were completed by the 1850s, and the circular rotunda that connected the four cellblocks was added in 1861. The "dome," as the rotunda came to be known, was the prison's nerve centre. Circular in construction, it was more than one hundred feet high and about seventy feet across. The large skylight of German glass that illuminated the top of the dome became a famous landmark when viewed from water or land.[14] All of the cells opened onto narrow iron catwalks or galleries leading to stairwells down to the floor of the rotunda. Eight cellblocks lettered A to H branched off from the circular dome. One former prisoner described it as a "human honey-combed beehive," and continued: "Fresh air was at a premium. Open the dirt-splattered windows on the cellblock walls and a damp, shivering, dungeon-like cold would envelop your body like a shroud. Close the windows and the air would become stiflingly difficult to breathe."[15]

One of the most prominent exterior features of the prison, the North Gate, was completed in 1845 and still stands on King Street West.[16] According to local historians, the gates, which were designed by William Coverdale, have some symbolic meaning: the two limestone pillars that flank the door represent the pillars of justice, and the gates were constructed to remain constantly in shadow.

THE PRISON OFFICIALLY opened with the arrival of six inmates on June 1, 1835. Mathew Tavender was the first.[17] Sentenced to three years for grand larceny, he was put to work as a stonecutter on his second day. Like most of the original inmates, he worked in the limestone quarries until his release three years later. Convict work gangs were a common sight along the rural roads outside Kingston well into the twentieth century as uniformed inmates went to and from the local quarries. By 1845, there were 450 inmates, including women and children. Susan Turner, Hannah Downes, and Hannah Baglen were the prison's first female inmates, sentenced on Aug. 28, 1835 for grand larceny.[18]

Although a women's prison had been included in the original design of Kingston Penitentiary, it was not considered a priority. Female inmates were confined in a walled-off section of the prison. Their quarters were cold, cramped and crawling with bugs. By

1846 the vermin problem had become so acute that the women refused to work.

The two most common crimes for which both men and women were imprisoned were larceny (stealing money) and theft of animals. Stealing a pig or cow could get you a year in the penitentiary, while a horse or ox could get you five. For more serious crimes, Canada had the death penalty. In 1859, the offences punishable by death included murder, rape, treason, poisoning, injuring a person with intent to commit murder, and mistreatment of a girl less than ten years of age. By 1869, only three offences were punishable by death: murder, rape and treason.

In 1867, the government of Canada became responsible for the maintenance and management of the Kingston Penitentiary by virtue of section 91 of the British North America Act. The penitentiary was authorized to receive offenders sentenced to terms of more them two years who mainly came from the provinces of Ontario and Quebec. The Penitentiary Act of 1868 established a federal Penitentiary Service under the jurisdiction of the federal Department of Justice.

The lakeside compound renamed Kingston Penitentiary became Canada's first federal prison, and according to its warden all convicts residing within its walls were "devoid of rights and were to be regarded as dead to the outside world." In its early years, "the Big House," as it came to be known, was open to visitors for the sum of one shilling threepence for men and half that amount for women and children. One famous visitor by the name of Charles Dickens made mention of the institution in his book *American Notes*: "There is an admirable gaol here, well and wisely governed and excellently regulated in every respect."[19] Dickens knew prisons well, having visited his father in an English gaol, where the elder Dickens had been imprisoned for debt in 1836. When Charles Dickens visited Kingston Penitentiary in May 1842, he noted that the men were employed as shoemakers, rope makers, blacksmiths, tailors, carpenters and stone-cutters, while the female prisoners were occupied in needlework. Dickens even took notice of one particular female inmate, a beautiful girl of twenty who had been incarcerated nearly three years already for horse stealing. "She had quite a lovely face, though as the reader may suppose from her history, there was a lurking devil in her bright eye which looked pretty sharply from between her prison bars."

In 1901, Warden J.M. Platt finally cancelled tours of the prison, saying his institution was not a "zoo or a menagerie."

MODELLED AFTER THE PRISON in Auburn, New York, the new Canadian jail espoused a philosophy of order, discipline and punishment. As the word *penitentiary* implied, "it was to be a place to lead a man to repent for his sins and amend his life." It was the Quakers of Philadelphia who had originally introduced the concept of the penitentiary, in 1789.[20] They felt it was possible to make offenders "penitent" and put them back on the straight and narrow by seg-regating them through imprisonment and offering them opportunities for labour and reflection. The concept of long-term imprisonment then spread to England as an alternative to exiling offenders to the penal colonies.

Combining the features of solitary confinement and group labour, Kingston Penitentiary was a place where inmates worked in total silence thirteen hours a day, six days a week, at a variety of trades. Hard work, strict rules and religion permeated the pris-oners' lives in the nineteenth century. It was thought that intense manual labour would encourage "clean living" and help the reha-bilitation process. Inmates were forbidden to speak at any time, as it was believed that silence would promote a monastic, religious environment. It was only on Christmas and New Year's Day that the ban on silence would be lifted. Incredibly, this rule continued until 1935 and was strictly enforced.[21]

Adjusting to the strict prison regime was not easy. Daily life was a numbing routine of roll calls, work and sleep. There was no recreation or allowance for private hobbies. Education was considered a great privilege and only well-behaved prisoners could attend evening classes after their long workday. An inspector's memorandum from 1867 referred to lamps being introduced in the west wing of the prison to allow for the accommodation of reading. This was considered an indulgence, along with allowing prisoners to walk in the yard for half an hour on Sunday afternoons. But the administration hoped both privileges would prove an incentive to good conduct.

In the nineteenth century, a coarse diet was also considered to be part of the punishment. Kitchen keepers usually bought the cheapest supplies available, and fresh vegetables, milk and butter were luxuries seldom served. Cooks were often untrained and most of the food was steamed in big boilers, which made everything soggy and flavourless. In 1899, inspector Douglas Stewart admitted in his report that "frequent loathing is produced by the continuous and monotonous round of soups and boiled meats and the unbroken absence of roast and relish." But prisoners found their own clever ways of supplementing their rations. Pigeons became a perennial favourite. They were considered a delicacy and often ended up in the stewpot.

At night, inmates were confined to sleeping cells with no windows. Stacked four storeys high, each cell measured thirty inches wide and eight feet deep. The tiny cells contained only a bed, a Bible, a small bucket for drinking water—called a "piggin"—and a bucket to use as a toilet.[22]

At the back of each cell was a peephole that allowed guards to patrol what they deemed the "hidden avenues of inspection." Prisoners were allowed to bathe only once a month, and the stench emanating from the cellblocks wafted out between the iron bars of the prison windows. Disease spread quickly amongst prisoners in their dirty, cramped quarters and many suffered from dysentery, scurvy, malnutrition and lice.

The staff at the nineteenth-century prison included a warden, a deputy warden, a clerk, a chaplain, a physician, eleven keepers and sixteen guards. Many of the employees came from Portsmouth village, immediately to the west of the penitentiary, since one of the conditions of employment at Kingston Pen was that officers had to live within the sound of the penitentiary bell. The bell was rung twice daily, at the start and close of the day, as a signal that staff could leave and to give assurance to the local community that all was well. For the villagers, the afternoon bell meant that all of the convicts were accounted for and were secure in their cells for the night. The symbolic practice of ringing the bell at the begin-ning and end of the day continued until the prison closed in 2013.

The first warden was Henry Smith, who took his responsibilities seriously—especially those that called for strict discipline in the enforcement of silence and hard labour. According to the *Kingston Chronicle*, "Mr. Smith's habits of industry and active vigilance make him peculiarly fit for this responsible office." From the start, Warden Smith set about imposing a severe regime of hard labour and disci-pline. Convicts could not speak to, look at, wink at, laugh with or nod to anyone. Anything that might disturb the silence of the institution was forbidden. Physical punishments such as whippings were often imposed on prisoners with absolute brutality. An inmate in violation of the rules would be brought to the keeper's hall, where he would be stripped naked and buckled face down to a strapping table at his ankles, waist and wrists. The convict would be fitted with dark goggles to prevent him from identifying the guards administering the beating. Smith also had prisoners chained up in their cells with no light or put in the "box," a kind of vertical oak casket with air holes.[23] Prisoners would be put in the coffin-like structure until the warden deemed them repentant. If those punishments were ineffective, there was the water bath. A convict's arms and legs would be secured in wooden stocks and a small barrel would be placed over his head. A water pipe was connected via a larger barrel and the barrel encasing the prisoner's head would slowly fill with water. This form of torture was eventually discontinued when an American prisoner died, but not before Kingston Pen officials had used it over three hundred times.

Life inside Kingston Penitentiary during the nineteenth century was humiliating and dehumanizing, and many reformists were critical of the Smith regime. Within months of taking the position, Smith had succeeded in raising his own salary, had put two of his relatives on the payroll and was demanding kickbacks from the Kingston merchants that supplied the penitentiary.[24] He even allowed one of his sons to use prisoners as target practice with his bow and arrow.

Smith's cruelty eventually proved too much for the penitentiary physician, Dr. James Sampson. He laid charges against Smith, which ultimately resulted in an investigation. Just thirteen years after the opening of the Provincial Penitentiary at Kingston, the first commission of inquiry into its operation was convened. The commission's secretary was George Brown, founding editor of the Toronto *Globe* (today's *Globe and Mail*) and lifelong rival of Kingston native and politician John A. Macdonald. The Brown Report, issued in May 1849, was a scathing attack on Henry Smith's administration of the institution.[25] It painted a picture of barbaric, dehumanizing conditions in which physical abuse was used repeatedly and indiscriminately. The commissioners were appalled by the practice of corporal punishment, particularly as it was applied to child convicts and women. Elizabeth Breen, a twelve-year-old girl, was flogged five times in a three-month period, and ten-year-old Peter Charbonneau was publicly lashed fifty-seven times for the repeated offences of winking and laughing. Antoine Beauche was given a three-year sentence at Kingston in 1845, when he was eight.[26] Beauche and his two brothers had been convicted for picking pockets on a steamship. According to the Brown Commission: "This eight-year-old child received forty-seven corporal punishments [the lash] in nine months, and all for offences of the most childish character." Another child, eleven-year-old Alec Lefleur, was lashed on Christmas Eve in 1844 for speaking French.[27]

It would not be until the passing of the Juvenile Delinquents Act of 1908 that any significant change would be made regarding the incarceration of young people.[28] During the same year, the Act Respecting Prisons for Young Offenders was also enacted to provide separate prisons for youth.

One of the main messages of the Brown Commission was that prisons should be more about reformation than punishment. Its recommendations were aimed at both ending corporal punishment and improving the physical conditions (diet, sanitation, medical treatment) of prisoners. It also suggested separating different types of prisoners: men from women, youths from adults, and the criminally insane from the sane. This idea established a strategy that has been used ever since with classifying inmates.

The Brown Report resulted in Warden Smith's immediate resignation, and it became the first in a series of inquiries that would stretch well into the twentieth century, all of them highly critical of the penitentiary and its procedures. Corporal punishment, though reduced in frequency, continued for more than a hundred years after the Smith regime, and was not formally abolished until 1972.

In 1853, a women's ward was finally built at the penitentiary in Kingston. Floggings diminished, but females were still chained, submerged in ice water, put in a dark cell, or kept on bread and water. The more rebellious female inmates would be humiliated by having their heads shaved. In 1913, the women at Kingston finally got their own building. But life behind the walls of Kingston Penitentiary, the oldest pen in the country, would remain repressive and inhumane for all of its occupants.

3
CANADA'S TOUGHEST TEN ACRES

They call this place just west of hell.
You'll make no friends, that's just as well.
A cold, sad and angry place,
say the wrong thing and you'll lose your face.
That's why they call this place just west of hell,
You'll make no friends, that's just as well.

—Kingston Pen inmate

NORMAN RIDDIOUGH, the director of information for the Solicitor General, stated that the general public was the last group that should be told what went on in Canadian prisons.[29] In its early years, Kingston Pen played a vital role in the growth of Kingston. The prison brought prosperity, and along with the other prisons being built in the area, it created an impressive local economy. The Pen was the ultimate symbol of "institutional Kingston," a city that survived in large part on the government payroll. By the early 1970s Kingston had the largest concentration of correctional facilities in Canada and was dubbed "Penitentiary City" by locals.

Apart from Kingston Penitentiary, there were nine additional federal and provincial institutions and minimum-security farm camps within a forty-kilometre radius of the city. Kingston was also the home of Canada's only federal penitentiary for women, which opened in 1934.

In the spring of 1971 there were 641 inmates at Kingston Penitentiary.[30] It was where Canada's most dangerous offenders went to serve out their life sentences. Well-known as the "decrepit home of diddlers and rats," according to a former inmate, it provided a protective custody environment for inmates who wouldn't survive in other institutions. KP was a prison filled with the lowest of the low and was looked down on by inmates in other prisons.

"As soon as you walked in, you had a sense that society has crushed and defeated you," said Rob Tripp, a freelance journalist who wrote about KP for more than twenty years. "It was a human warehouse of death, decay and horror. Many inmates died of murder and suicide within its walls."[31]

Kingston Pen was considered the toughest ten acres in Canada and in many respects it was like a small, walled-off inner city. It had its own government, police force, hospital, school, churches and industries. Its citizens for the most part obeyed its rules and laws, but adherence to the inmate code was the only thing that counted and an inmate's true standing was determined by his fellow prisoners, who would classify him as a wheel, a solid guy, a tough guy or, if they thought he was an informer, a rat. Basic tenets of the code were never trust or support a screw or the prison administration, never squeal on a fellow con, never steal from another inmate and never enter another man's cell unless invited. "The inmate code was really a guidebook on how to succeed in prison by not really trying to reform," wrote former inmate Roger Caron.[32] "In order to gain acceptance, one must follow the code to a fine degree." Basically, you were to mind your own business and do your time. Don't be a fly on the wall, wise cons would advise. Instead, be the wall. Violate the code and your life became a living hell.[33]

At the prison heart of the city was the dome, and in the centre of the dome was a hefty brass bell that had ruled over the prison population for decades. It was Warden Ponsford in the 1920s who believed he could simplify the management of the prison by using a bell, similar to keeping a school on schedule.[34] From the guards' point of view, the bell kept the inmates in line, but for prisoners it was an abomination, a hated symbol of repression. The bell controlled the inmates' every move. It rang to wake them up, to send them off to work, to announce every meal and to send them to bed. By the end of each prison day, the bell had rung over one hundred times. About the hated gong, Roger Caron wrote: "To the cons it was an object of repugnance and outrage, an unjustifiable punishment. A brass monster that we were convinced had been designed solely to shatter our nerves with its loud and strident ringing. For the prison staff it was the golden cow."

The central dome was a simmering beehive of more than 640 cells stacked four storeys high, making up thirty-two ranges. The cells or "drums" were narrow, damp and cold. The only pieces of furniture in each cell were an iron bunk fastened to the wall by a short chain, a table, a folding chair, an open-mouthed toilet and a metal sink with cold running water. Below the sink was a small water bucket to collect hot water in the evenings. Attached to the bars at the front of each cell was a square box into which earphones could be plugged in order to listen to one of three radio channels provided, two in English and one in French.

Inmates also valued books, mostly for reading but also for stacking on top of their toilet lids to prevent rats from crawling out of the latrines in the night. The maze of sewers below the prison was also home to feral cats that fed off the bloated rodents.

The only opening in the cell was a barred gate, thirty inches wide, set in a concrete arch that was three feet thick. The cells could be locked or unlocked by spinning a windlass—two spoked wheels outside the locked barrier at the end of the range. Above the cells was a vertical locking bar with a protruding horizontal handle. Every morning and night an inmate tapper was assigned to race down the range raising each handle—tap, tap, tap, until all cells were opened. The tappers were also responsible for passing out hot water at night for the guys to shave.

Within his cell, a prisoner was only permitted to sleep, listen to the radio and read. Inmates could also write two authorized letters a week to relatives on the outside, but all incoming and outgoing mail was censored. Telephone calls were only allowed under exceptional circumstances and usually brought news of a family tragedy. Visitations were permitted twice a month. Approved family members would communicate across a counter divided by a glass panel with a small screen to speak through.

While serving his sentence, an inmate could engage in a hobby craft if he could financially afford it. A prisoner could buy tools and materials to do woodwork or leather work in his cell between supper and lights out. Inmates were also strictly limited in how they could decorate their cells. Any personal item such as a photo or memento, no matter how insignificant, for which an inmate did not have a prison-issued licence was considered contraband and subject to seizure.

When prisoners arrived at the penitentiary, they were issued two bath towels, two hand towels, a pocket comb, a metal mirror, one bar of soap, toilet paper, a toothbrush and tooth powder. They were given ten minutes to shower once a week in a giant horseshoe-shaped ring of showers otherwise known as the car wash. Inmates would deposit their dirty uniform into a slot in the wall, shuffle around the horseshoe, which contained sixteen shower nozzles, and then pick up a clean uniform on the way back to their cell. Two guards regulated the water and it was up to them whether the showers were hot or cold.

For inmates deemed troublemakers by the guards, there was the hole, an escape- proof cellblock located in a concrete bunker between the north and east wings. There were twenty metal doors, each with a peephole and a food slot. Behind each door an inmate was confined twenty-three and a half hours a day, with one half-hour of exercise in a small segregated yard. Each cell consisted of a concrete platform for a bed, one thin, spongy mattress and two army blankets. Sheets and pillows were not permitted. Inmates were fed a restricted diet of bread and water for breakfast and dinner and a regular meal for lunch, but there was no gravy, dessert or hot beverage. A single bright light encased inside a screened box on the ceiling illuminated the prisoner's bleak surroundings: cinder-block walls covered in dried blood and angry carvings from former tenants. The light was never turned off.

Serving time at Kingston Pen was a life of despair and oppression, but time in the hole was a nightmare that few recovered from. Not surprisingly, many resorted to self-harm and suicide as a way out. "I am not sick nor crazy," wrote Auréle Rozen on February 28, 1967. "I cannot bear to be locked up for twenty-three hours a day. My morale is low, and I am disgusted with life. Thank you and adieu." Guards found his body in a segregation cell later that day. Rozen had hanged himself.

In his award-winning memoir on prison life, *Go-Boy!*, Roger Caron recounted his anguish while confined to the hole for over a year. "The cell pulsated with bad vibes from those who had suffered there before me and especially from those who could not go on and had hung themselves with a blanket. All sense of reality was lost and the will to go on was quickly extinguished in both the weak and the strong."

For Caron, his only way out was going on a hunger strike. After twelve days with no food, he was transferred to the psychiatric ward, where many of the prison's most dangerous inmates resided. In the loony bin, tranquilizers were apparently handed out like candy and patients such as Caron were forced to undergo electroconvulsive therapy. Refusing meant being sent back to the hole.

LIFE INSIDE KINGSTON PEN was monotonous. Control came from the dreary and predictable fact that everything happened day after day in the exact same way. The prison population consisted of groups of inmates in separate, segregated ranges who were tightly contained and never brought together in one place. A Toronto *Star Weekly* reporter who was granted a rare look inside in 1960 wrote: "Old timers and first offenders, the vicious and the harmless, the illiterate and the genius, the notorious and the unknown, all are thrown together to make up this strange community inside the walls."

Every day involved the sequential manoeuvring of each range of inmates through the same routine.[35] The morning began at 6:45 a.m. with the ringing of the bell. After the first head count, inmates were released from their cells for "jug up." They would proceed single file to the kitchen to obtain their iron breakfast trays, which were then taken back to their cells. Unlike prison scenes in Hollywood movies, there was no central dining hall; every meal was consumed in a cell. Breakfast might consist of dry toast, margarine, jam, porridge and a mug full of steaming chicory coffee.

The food service was a constant source of complaints and dissatisfaction but working in the kitchen was one of the most sought-after jobs in the prison. It meant you were trusted and given more freedom. And you were allowed to wear kitchen whites instead of the standard-issue prison uniform.[36] For some it also offered the chance to smuggle out food and ingredients to make homebrew. Nutmeg, mouse poison, gasoline, shoe polish and aftershave lotion were all in high demand as ingredients for the mind-altering concoctions that were prepared in secret.[37]

After each meal, another prison count would be done before inmates were allowed to proceed to their assigned workshops. Inmates were paid a wage for their work that averaged twenty-five cents to fifty-five cents per day depending on their pay grade. Inmates would return to their cells at 11 a.m. to begin the lunch-time rotation, and again at 3:45 p.m. to begin dinner. Beef was served more than pork and chicken, and turkey was served at least once a month. "A great many inmates were never so well fed in their private lives as they are during their incarceration," an internal memo to the Solicitor General once noted.

The supper service was completed by 4:45 p.m., after which the inmates would stay in their cells until they were called for "gym up," indoor or outdoor recreation depending on the weather. The desolate outdoor yard was situated in the southeast corner of the prison. Under the watchful gaze of the guards in the gun towers, groups of prisoners paced up and down or found a place to sit in the shade and smoke. After recreation, inmates would return to their cells. Every day was the same and every night ended with the same thought, as prisoners lay awake in their bunks wishing they were anywhere but inside Kingston Penitentiary.

LIFE INSIDE KINGSTON Pen hadn't always been so dreary. In the post-war period of the late 1940s and early 1950s, penal reform focused on education and training for inmates so they could improve their skills and increase their hopes of gainful employment upon release. By 1957, there were over 257 educational and training programs available to inmates, including typing courses, plumbing and heating, barber training and bookkeeping.[38] The inmates also organized and participated in a wide variety of sports, including boxing, floor hockey, basketball and soccer.

In the mid-1950s, Kingston Pen even had its own baseball league. There were six prison league teams and an all-star team, the Saints, that played in the Kingston area league. Local teams would be invited to play at the penitentiary diamond as hundreds of inmate fans cheered on their team. The Sunday afternoon games were broadcast on the local radio station with the sounds of screaming convicts shouting, "Murder the bums!"[39] Large sums of money were wagered every weekend with the prison bookies, and from time to time inmate and staff games were also scheduled.

The penitentiary also ran an annual or biannual sports day, which was planned and organized by an inmate committee. It was regarded as one of the highlights of the year and greatly improved the morale of the whole prison. The warden at the time, Richard Allan, felt that recreation and sports released tensions in men who would otherwise have brooded about real or imagined injustices.

There were musical groups too. *Kingston Penitentiary Is On the Air* was a half-hour variety show that was broadcast throughout Ontario on Saturday nights in the summer months, featuring musicians like the Solitaires, an eight-piece inmate orchestra. There was a large choir that would practise twice a week in the Protestant chapel, and a correspondence course in music was available in which inmates could learn musical theory and technique.

For those who weren't musically inclined, there were chess and bridge clubs.

In the fall of each year, inmates would set up a Santa's workshop. Bicycles, cars, dolls and many other toys would be repaired and distributed to needy Kingston families at Christmastime.

Prisoners also produced a monthly penal magazine called the *KP Telescope*, which was Canada's first prison publication beginning in 1948.[40] Each volume included a prison update from the warden and several other columns of interest. Prisoners could submit creative writing and poems for publication, and sports updates were always included. Subscribers across Canada paid a dollar a year to receive it, and Coca-Cola advertised on the back cover.

But by the mid-1960s the character of the inmate population began to change. The civil rights movement gave rise to more outspoken, politically active inmates who began demanding more rights. In addition, the number of drug convictions in Canada exploded, and this led to serious overcrowding. And once incarcerated, drug dealers and gang members often continued their enterprises.

In a memo written to the Solicitor General in 1966, the Commissioner of Penitentiaries, A.J. MacLeod, stated there was a significant change in the types of inmates being sentenced to imprisonment for two years or more. "They are younger, more vicious, more aggressive, more hostile, more irresponsible, and therefore more dangerous than ever before."[41] According to the Commissioner, this new "type of inmate" caused a higher number of serious incidents in federal prisons, including escapes, assaults, hostage takings and murder.

As a result, Kingston Penitentiary became more repressive and security oriented. Recreational programs were curtailed, family visits were electronically monitored for fear of drug smuggling, and prison lockdowns occurred on a regular basis. The last edition of the prison magazine was published in 1969, and by 1971 most recreational programs had been cancelled altogether. For those seeking to better themselves through education, classroom instruction was limited to reading, writing and math, but only up to grade eight.[42] Inmates could only attend school for two half days per week. Correspondence courses through Queen's University were available, but inmates were responsible for purchasing their own textbooks.

With fewer education and rehabilitation programs and limited contact with the outside world, inmates spent sixteen hours a day locked in their dark, poorly ventilated cells, just as they had been in 1938. The claustrophobic confinement wore on the emotions of many men. "Men literally became grunting, growling creatures in cages," said Dr. Scott, the prison psychiatrist, in 1971. "Inmates whether mentally well or sick, intellectually capable or moronically stupid, all pass through the same prison gates to the same prison cells, the same jobs and the same rehabilitative training." Scott estimated that 20 percent of Kingston's inmates suffered from "a definable degree of mental illness." But due to a shortage of psychiatrists willing to work in a prison, few inmates had access to any mental health services.

ARTHUR JARVIS WAS the seventeenth warden of Kingston Penitentiary, a position he had held since 1967. He was a handsome man in his mid-fifties, with a boxer's physique and sharp, chiselled features. He had a taste for well-tailored suits, red ties and solid, thick-soled shoes. Originally from Collingwood, Ontario, he had joined the Penitentiary Service in 1938.[43] His first job had been as a scout, which required him to spend long hours on horseback patrolling the Collins Bay penitentiary grounds. He was a well-liked warden who had a reputation for firmness and fairness, but he had dealt with his fair share of problems. He often found himself frustrated by the politics and bureaucracy of the prison service and recently had been struggling to hire a new deputy warden for KP, a position that had been left vacant for months.

As 1971 began, Warden Jarvis knew there was trouble brewing at Kingston Penitentiary. There had already been one serious incident. Two violent offenders stoned on homebrew and armed with homemade knives had attacked three staff members in the carpenters' shop and held them hostage.[44] They then demanded asylum to Cuba.[45] The hostage taking ended twenty-four hours later, with the guards overpowering one of their captors.

After the kidnapping, Jarvis detailed his concerns in a letter to the Commissioner of Penitentiaries and the Regional Director of Ontario.[46] In his three-page letter, dated January 18, 1971, he stated, "There is a high degree of tension at Kingston Penitentiary at this time. In fact it appears to be almost at the point of explosion." Jarvis blamed the volatile atmosphere on staff shortages, serious overcrowding, and widespread anxiety over the transfer of inmates to a newly built maximum-security prison on the outskirts of Kingston. Mature and experienced staff were also being transferred to Millhaven, leaving Jarvis with new, inexperienced guards incapable of managing an overloaded prison. He also noted that the penitentiary's psychiatric facilities were insufficient, resulting in inmates with mental conditions being released before they were ready. At the same time, the segregation and dissociation cells were at full capacity. Jarvis knew something had to give.

> This population at Kingston Penitentiary exceeds by far the number of the type of desperate inmates that we should have in a maximum-security institution. We have almost seven hundred of the most difficult inmates in the country to deal with. God knows what will happen if one of us breaks down under the pressure. I don't. Unless some immediate action is taken, I expect many serious incidents to occur in the very near future.

This was the second such letter Jarvis had sent to the Commissioner of Penitentiaries. In a letter dated November 24, 1970, he had outlined his concerns about the position of deputy warden, which had been vacant for some time. As a result, the assistant deputy warden had been filling in, and his workload had doubled.

I know that the amount of work is more than enough for two men and in a short time his health will break down owing to the strain. There is no doubt in my mind that Kingston Penitentiary will continue to operate for the next four years and the inmate population will not deplete to less than 350 from our present count of 680.

With the inmate population steadily increasing, the maximum-security institution required a full complement of senior staff.

Warden Jarvis's letters were never answered. In the next two months, there were three prisoner suicides and thirty-five attempts.[47]

FOR YEARS, KINGSTON Penitentiary had been considered an obsolete institution in both its design and its function. Along with five other federal prisons across the country, it had operated as a multi-classification facility, accommodating all inmates from the best to the very worst; but with the introduction of minimum- and medium-security institutions in 1959, the archaic limestone fortress now functioned as a purely maximum-security facility. The physical infrastructure at KP was outdated and inadequate for such a large and volatile group.

In 1956, the Fauteux Committee investigated Canada's correctional system and reported that overcrowding in federal penitentiaries was a matter of grave concern. The committee made special mention of the situation at Kingston Penitentiary and recalled that Collins Bay Institution had been built in 1930 to relieve the population pressure on Kingston at that time. The committee recommended that no penal facility in Canada should contain more than 600 inmates. In 1956, the year of the Fauteux Report, Kingston Pen housed 959 prisoners.

Finally, in the early 1960s, the Canadian Penitentiary Service initiated a ten-year construction plan to build six new maximum-security institutions to replace Canada's aging prisons. A new facility called Millhaven would replace Kingston Penitentiary. The maximum-security facility would cost $11 million to build and would house 1,350 prisoners, including 450 maximum-security cells. One of the main design criteria for all the new correctional facilities was to provide an environment that would, as far as possible, eliminate increasing hostility between inmates and staff. This meant creating physical barriers between prisoners and guards.

But before construction began on any of the new institutions, the government was bombarded with vociferous condemnation over the new designs. Critics called the new plans obsolete, oppressive and out of step with modern penology. Instead of building more old-style fortress-like prisons that maintained punitive measures by separating inmates from staff, opponents of the government's plans felt the new penitentiary designs should place more emphasis on rehabilitation and support. New prisons didn't need more clanging bars and barriers, they needed fewer. In a telegram to Prime Minister Lester B. Pearson dated April 28, 1967, J. Mooney, the president of the John Howard Society, said the decision to build Millhaven was illogical and unreasonable.[48] Its physical structure would result in professional staff being too far away from inmates and its rigid design would be completely out of step with modern penology.

As a result of the fervent criticisms, a special Senate–Commons committee on penitentiaries was set up to investigate concerns over the new designs, and the start of construction was delayed. The resulting seventeen-page report criticized the rigid and repressive nature of the proposed design for Millhaven but said it should be built as planned because prison space was so urgently needed. It would take too much time to produce new designs. Millhaven received the green light in October 1968, almost three years behind schedule.

ON THE MORNING of April 14, 1971, the first twelve inmates from Kingston Penitentiary were transferred to Millhaven. Additional transfers of forty inmates per month were to begin even though the prison was still under construction and not fully staffed. The new multi-million-dollar super-maximum-security institute — "the Haven," as it came to be known — was located eighteen miles west of Kingston. The state-of-the-art prison was constructed in the form of an octopus, low to the ground with tentacles forming a network of escape-proof cells. The four security control centres were accessible through a 225-foot tunnel from outside the prison, making them virtually impenetrable. Eight gun towers were located outside the barbed wire perimeter, from which powerful telescopic military rifles were pointed at the exercise yard. Two twenty-foot chain-link fences topped with rolls of razor wire encircled the entire complex. Specially trained attack dogs and their handlers patrolled between the fences.

Prisoners would be housed in individual, rubber-carpeted cells, each with its own toilet, desk and steel cot. Each cell had an iron door with a look-through window, controlled by a guard who sat in a bulletproof booth. The cells were L-shaped, ten feet deep and seven feet wide.

For Kingston Pen inmates, the prospect of transferring to Millhaven was terrifying. Everything connected to its imminent opening was shrouded in mystery, sending the prison rumours flying. Prisoners were hearing about an extensive electronic bugging system that would monitor and record every conversation, and cameras in every cell that would eliminate the little privacy they currently had.[49] Kingston Pen may have been a hellhole, but it was one they knew well. They feared Millhaven would be much worse.

But the inmates at KP were not leaving without a fight. There had been talk in the cellblocks for weeks, whispers and rumours of riots and breakouts, every scheme more salacious than the last.

There was even chatter about grabbing hostages, but most of the prison population ignored such rumblings. For some of the cons, particularly those with only a little time left on their sentences, any kind of prison upheaval would damage their chances for parole. Action by a few could mean punishment for all. They knew any attack on the institution would tighten security measures even further, and retribution from the guards would be severe. Still, no one informed the staff of any potential rebellion.

FOR THE STAFF at Kingston Pen, April 14 was an ordinary day, nothing out of the normal routine. It was still too cold to head outside to the recreation yard, so the evening would be spent in the gym. The first group of seventy-eight inmates were in the rec hall between the hours of 6 and 8 p.m. The second group of seventy-eight from range two arrived in the gym at 8:30 p.m. The next evening, the two other ranges would have their turns in the recreation hall. This routine ensured that no more than a quarter of the prison population was ever in the same place at the same time. The only exception to this was on weekends, when half the inmates were allowed into the exercise yard.

At precisely 10:30 p.m., senior guard Ed Barrett rang the bell. The maddening sound signalled a return to the cells. Billy Knight, like every other inmate, hated the ringing instrument. In his prison manifesto, he wrote: "It has no heart, it has no feelings; disobey its brassy orders or curse it for its pain inflicting callousness and it will drag you to the dungeon for a lesson in respect."

In the gym, the televisions were turned off and the folding chairs and tables restacked. Knight held back a little and watched as the inmates fell in line. As the guards began to corral the inmates out of the gym, down a long corridor past the hobby shops and towards the dome, Knight motioned for his gang to take their well-rehearsed places in the lineup. Inmates Charles

Saunders and Brian Dodge quickly moved to the front of the group of cons, while Robert Adams, Allan Lafreniere and Leo Barrieault held back.

The officer in charge, Donald Flynn, was standing in the corridor between the dome and the gym. He unlocked the gate to the main cellblock passageway and passed the key to 27-year-old Terry Decker. Decker walked up the hallway towards the gym, where he waved to William Babcock in the recreation hall. Babcock blew his whistle and the men from range 2-H lined up to start their march back to the cells. No more than twenty inmates would be sent through at a time. Guards Douglas Dale and Joseph Vallier waited on the range, where Dale, with the spin of a large iron wheel, opened the cell doors. Vallier was preparing to lead the men down the cell corridor, where he would spin the wheel again, moving the travelling bar almost two hundred feet in length so each lock fell into place at the same time.

As the uniformed inmates from 2-H shuffled past guard Terry Decker, he failed to notice that something wasn't right.[50] There were six imposters in the line. Knight's men had traded places with other inmates. But Decker did notice an exposed shirttail on one of the prisoners. The institution's dress code was to be adhered to at all times. Pointing his finger directly at Knight, the cocky young guard yelled, "Tuck that shirt in!"

Knight froze. This was not part of his plan. There were twenty male convicts moving through a narrow steel-encased corridor. He could feel their eyes on him. This was the moment, the point of no return. He swung his body around and, with all his might, punched Decker in the stomach. As the unsuspecting guard crumpled to the floor, Knight shouted, "That's the last fucking order you're going to give!" The Kingston Penitentiary riot had begun.

The dome, 1800s.

Convicts working in the yard. *Canada Illustrated News*, 1873.
Courtesy of Canada's Penitentiary Museum

View of Kingston Penitentiary looking east along King Street.
Queen's University Archives, V23-PuB-Kingston-Pen-7

Tim Buck, 1942. General Secretary of the
Communist Party of Canada.
Toronto Star *Archives, 1942*

Agnes Macphail.
Public domain

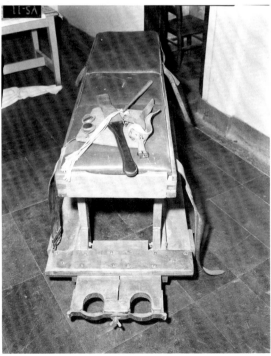

Strapping table.
Toronto Telegram *fonds, York
University Libraries, Clara
Thomas Archives and Special
Collections,* ASC07586

Guard ringing brass bell to move inmates during mealtime, 1957.
Toronto Telegram *fonds, York University Libraries, Clara Thomas Archives and Special Collections,* ASC07588

Inmate in his cell, 1957.
Toronto Telegram *fonds, York University Libraries,*
Clara Thomas Archives and Special Collections, ASC07590

The KP Saints Baseball Team, 1953.
Courtesy of W.D. Jordan Rare Books and Special Collections, Queen's University, Kingston, Ontario

The KP Saints playing a baseball game at Kingston Penitentiary.
Queen's University Archives, George Lilley fonds, V25_5-13-45_2

The KP Saints playing a baseball game at Kingston Penitentiary.

Queen's University Archives, George Lilley fonds, V25_5-13-45_2

Inmates repair toys for needy children in the local area.
Courtesy of W.D. Jordan Rare Books and Special Collections, Queen's University, Kingston, Ontario

John Maloney, Regional Director of Penitentiaries, shows press the homemade knives used in the kidnapping of three guards at Kingston Pen in January 1971.
Queen's University Archives, Kingston Whig Standard, V142-8-107

4

BINGO!

Bingo: prison slang for riot

Wednesday, April 14, 1971

ON THE NIGHT of April 14, Terry Decker was working the four-to-twelve shift. He hadn't been scheduled to work, but he had agreed to switch shifts with a fellow officer who wanted the night off. After a three-year stint in the army, Decker had joined the Penitentiary Service and was making an annual salary of $4,200.

Now he lay winded on the floor from Knight's sudden punch. He hadn't seen it coming. And before he could get up, another inmate, Charles Saunders, pushed him back down and ripped the keys to the recreation hall out of his left hand, tearing the nerves in his fingers. Then two other inmates pulled him up and dragged him towards the dome.

While Decker was being attacked, four other inmates—Brian Dodge, Leo Barrieault, Allan Lafreniere and Robert Adams—ran towards the dome. It was critical they reach the dome barrier before the guards realized what was happening and locked it. Officer Babcock, who was still in the gymnasium, did not realize anything was wrong until he saw Decker's cap lying on the floor next to the open gate.[51] Guards were never seen without their hats and could be disciplined for removing them. "Take the gate," he yelled to his colleague Raymond Pattinson. "Don't let anyone through." Babcock ordered all of the inmates to line up against the wall in the gym. Confused, the prisoners complied.

Guarding another gate farther down the corridor, Officer Flynn didn't see anything before inmate #6363, Brian Dodge, ran towards him and knocked him to the floor. "Finish him off and lock him up in F-block," shouted Knight as he ran past the two men struggling on the ground.

At the same time, three unsuspecting guards were waiting for the prisoners in the dome area. Standing beside the dreaded brass bell was senior guard Ed Barrett. With him were Joseph Vallier and Douglas Dittrich. Without warning, inmate #3141, Allan Lafreniere, grabbed Barrett by the shirt and shoved him toward the north wall of the dome. As Barrett struggled, inmate Robert Adams grabbed a foam fire extinguisher and threatened to spray it into Barrett's face if he didn't back down. Barrett relented.

Then Brian Dodge grabbed Dittrich. Guard Joseph Vallier stood motionless. He wasn't sure what to do. Knight approached him and told him he was outnumbered. Not knowing how many prisoners were involved in the riot, Vallier decided he wasn't going to be a hero at that moment. He surrendered.

Two additional guards, Douglas Dale and Kerry Bushell, were stationed one level up on the rotunda, on range 2-H, in order to supervise the movement of inmates back to their cells. "Throw down your keys," yelled an inmate from below. Realizing something was terribly wrong, Dale ran to lock the range, but before he could get to the gate, another inmate grabbed him. At the same time, inmate Leo Barrieault, who had climbed up the side of the tier, grabbed Bushell from behind. "Don't try anything or I'll break your neck," yelled Barrieault. Bushell had been on the job only six months. He did not resist and threw the keys down to the dome floor.

Then Dale had to make a quick decision. He also had other keys in his possession, keys that could open the entire second tier locking device, freeing all the prisoners on that range. As the inmates pushed him down the stairs towards the dome, Dale threw the keys behind an inaccessible gate leading to the keeper's hall. At least some of the inmates would stay locked up, thought Dale.

Six guards—Barrett, Vallier, Flynn, Dale, Bushell and Decker— were now locked inside the corridor of 1-F block, effectively cut off from the dome floor and the telephones. The inmates demanded their watches, rings, cigarettes and money. Night keeper Ed Barrett handed his wallet to an inmate. "Look after this," Barrett said, "and don't forget, I'll remember who you are."[52]

Billy Knight and his gang had just instigated a prison riot, and with the dome in control of the inmates, the prison was effectively immobilized. But this wasn't the first time Canada's most notorious prison had fallen into the hands of its dissatisfied residents.

THE FIRST MAJOR uprising at Kingston Penitentiary happened on October 17, 1932. Canada was in the depths of the Great Depression, which left millions of Canadians unemployed and homeless. Desperation led many into a life of crime, and the country's prisons overflowed. Kingston Pen, built to house 564 inmates, had over 900 men housed within its walls. "The prisons are seething volcanoes," said writer and political activist D.M. LeBourdais in 1933. "They are now crammed to the roofs and unless something is done and done speedily, the tops will blow off every one of them."[53]

In the 1930s, prisoners were still subject to archaic means of punishment, including wearing a ball and chain while they worked or being dunked in a trough of ice and slush as a cure for mental deficiencies. Fed up with the way they were treated, Kingston's prisoners finally decided to stage a peaceful demonstration to bring their complaints to the attention of the administration. Their demands included better food, increased recreation time, more family visits, and cigarette papers to go with their penitentiary-issued tobacco. The previous warden, John Ponsford, had banned cigarette papers when convicts were caught using them to record gambling bets.[54]

Upon learning of the impending protest, acting warden Gilbert Smith locked the inmates inside their workshops. Prisoners in the mailbag shop climbed out the window and quickly unlocked the other workshops. The freed inmates then gathered in the dome area and addressed their complaints to Warden Smith. Smith ignored their request to contact Ottawa with their grievances and instead called in the military.

Late in the day, as high winds and rain swept across the penitentiary grounds, three batteries of the Royal Canadian Horse Artillery arrived at Kingston Penitentiary under the command of Colonel J.C. Stewart. Stewart and his troops quickly surrounded the dome on all four sides. Then military trucks arrived with blankets and overcoats for the soldiers, suggesting they expected an all-night siege. The story made headlines across the country, with the *Ottawa Citizen* reporting, "Excitement runs high among the thousands of spectators huddled in the rain and cold as police and soldiers force the onlookers back from the prison gates."

Once the inmates realized the army was on site, they panicked. They took officers hostage and retreated back to the mailbag shop. From there the situation quickly escalated. Shots were fired into the mailbag room and much of the equipment was destroyed. Several hours later Warden Smith met with a committee of inmates and finally agreed to take their complaints to Ottawa. The insurrection ended without injury and the warden believed he had quelled the riot. But a few days later, when the warden had not followed up on their requests, disgruntled inmates began destroying their cells.

Among the inmates at the time was famous activist Tim Buck, leader of the Communist Party of Canada. A mild-looking man with blue eyes and wispy hair, he had led the Communist Party since 1929. Buck, along with eight other known Communists, was serving a five-year prison sentence for sedition under section 98 of the Criminal Code.[55] Section 98 made it a crime to belong to any political party that advocated change by the use of "force, violence, or physical injury." It was a time of great social unrest in the country and the government used the sedition law to silence any suspected agitators.

Warden Smith was fed up with the rioting prisoners. He called the army back to the penitentiary on October 20, and the prison guards on duty were issued shotguns. They were then ordered down the narrow duct-ways between the ranges, where they fired into the cells through peepholes. One inmate was hit and lay bleeding in his cell. Then eleven shots were fired into Tim Buck's cell. Buck, who had a small physique, managed to dive under his bunk for cover. A fellow inmate who years later wrote about his life in Kingston Pen described the attack on Buck and called it a cold and deliberate attempt at murder. "When darkness fell, shot after shot of rifle fire was poured into the cell of the leader of the riot. Only by miracle was the intent defeated."[56]

Four days later, Warden Smith was unceremoniously relieved of his duties, and Tim Buck and his comrades were paroled one year later. Buck's imprisonment ended up helping the Communist cause in Canada. Many citizens hit hardest by the Depression were sympathetic towards the party and indignant towards the treatment he had received. Buck's first public appearance after his release from jail was held at Maple Leaf Gardens in Toronto, where seventeen thousand people showed up to listen to his emotionally charged speech. From there he went on a cross-country speaking tour and attracted even greater numbers to the party.

In 1935, the new Liberal government repealed the section of the Criminal Code under which Buck had been imprisoned. The Communist Party of Canada was declared legal in 1937.

The 1932 riot resulted in immediate calls for prison reform. Agnes Macphail, the first woman elected to Canada's House of Commons (in 1921) and a member of J.S. Woodsworth's Co-operative Commonwealth Federation, was among those demanding change. In 1935 she went to Kingston Penitentiary to see the conditions for herself. At the gate, she was told no ladies were allowed inside. "I'm no lady, I'm an MP," Macphail protested, and she became the first woman to tour the penitentiary. What she saw appalled her. She witnessed men strung up, blindfolded and beaten with thick leather paddles, and deplorable living conditions.

Agnes Macphail realized the penal system was not designed to reform prisoners but to punish and socially isolate those convicted of a crime. To change this, she introduced a resolution calling for a meaningful program of prison labour. She argued this would save the government thousands of dollars a year and give prisoners a chance to learn trades and feel useful while serving their time. Her office soon became a centre for ex-prisoners who had nowhere else to bring their grievances, as well as a meeting place for reformers. She distilled their thoughts into recommendations that she brought before the House.

Macphail pushed for reduced use of corporal punishment, mandatory education for illiterate inmates, and an increase in inmates' exercise and outdoor time. But her most challenging proposal for reform was to end military and political appointments to senior penitentiary positions. She wanted to appoint wardens and superintendents with penology training and medical doctors with psychological training, and to implement a system of training for guards and officials in the prisons.

Macphail was met with a great deal of resistance to her recommendations. As the first and only female Member of Parliament, her male colleagues expected her to be quiet and ladylike, and to only discuss issues related to the home and family values. Instead, Macphail irritated the other Honorable Members by stepping outside her sphere and raising the debate on prison reform, a topic considered utterly unsuitable for a woman. Press reports at the time labelled her a "hysterical sob sister" and "sentimentalist."

On April 5, 1935, the *Ottawa Journal* reported that Prime Minister R.B. Bennett's minister of justice, Hugh Guthrie, was not prepared to take recommendations from Miss Macphail after her visit to Kingston Penitentiary. Guthrie stated in the House of Commons, "Miss Macphail's judgment would be more respected on the woman's prison, but on issues related to Kingston Penitentiary I am inclined to place more weight on the word of a man." Guthrie also tried to discredit her by claiming her information about prison conditions came from a notorious sex offender in Kingston Pen.

Prime Minister Bennett's Conservatives were defeated in 1935, and a year later the new Liberal government under William Lyon Mackenzie King announced the creation of a Royal Commission to investigate the penal system of Canada. Mr. Justice Joseph Archambault was appointed to head the new inquiry on penal reform, and the commission's 1938 report was a landmark in Canadian corrections. The committee noted that while there had been ongoing criticism of prison practices in the hundred years since the opening of Kingston Penitentiary, most recommendations and inquiries had remained largely ignored. Violence and punishment were still the main hallmarks of the prison experience.

Archambault firmly believed that if prisoners were provided with the opportunity for rehabilitation, the rate of recidivism would decline substantially. Under the system in place at the time, Archambault did not feel prisoners were provided with an opportunity to reform their behaviour while incarcerated. Among the commission's recommendations was the complete revision of penitentiary regulations to provide "strict but humane discipline and the reformation and rehabilitation of prisoners." The primary objective of the reforms was to focus on treatment within prison walls through more educational and vocational training. The report also noted that a guard working in a Canadian penitentiary in 1938 earned a lower wage than a Toronto street cleaner.[57] As a result, the job attracted men with little education and minimal skills. The report recommended that a training school be built for the Penitentiary Service, where new recruits could be trained, and ongoing education would be offered throughout a correctional officer's career. The Correctional Staff College would not be realized until twenty-six years later, opening in October 1964.

But by far the most important and far-reaching of the Archambault proposals was for a prison commission that would have full authority over the management of penitentiaries and act as an independent federal parole board.

Macphail was finally vindicated. Justice Archambault sent her a copy of the 418-page report with the inscription: "To Miss Agnes Macphail, M.P., courageous pioneer and untiring worker on behalf of prison reform in Canada."

While acknowledging the work of Miss Macphail, the Archambault Report reflected an increasingly widely held preference for rehabilitation over retribution. But when Canada declared war on Germany in September 1939, the priorities of a nation at war superseded penal reform, and many of the Archambault Report's recommendations were put on indefinite hold.

When the war ended in 1945, the push to change Canada's prisons resumed. The country's first Prison Commissioner, Major General R.B. Gibson, was committed to prison reform. He implemented more than a hundred of the Archambault Report's recommendations. New penitentiaries were built, including separate facilities for young adult male offenders. Rules and regulations were softened and there was new hope for rehabilitative treatment. It seemed that attitudes were shifting and new approaches to corrections might finally be put into action.

But by the early 1950s, prisons throughout North America were once again filled to capacity, and violent disturbances were becoming more frequent. Although more recreational and rehabilitative programs were introduced after the Second World War, rising crime rates resulted in massive overcrowding. Kingston Penitentiary was teeming with more than a thousand inmates living under the weight of oppression and routine. Eventually, tensions boiled over.

5

THE EMBERS OF DISCONTENT

ON THE AFTERNOON of Friday, August 13, 1954, a group of Kingston Penitentiary prisoners attacked a prison guard in the exercise yard. Local papers reported that officer Robert Wylie had been hit by a baseball bat while the inmates were playing a morning baseball game. He managed to escape, but the prisoners then began setting fires in the prison with their cigarette lighters. Inmates were not allowed to carry matches. Shouting, "Burn the hellhole to the ground," small gangs of rioters ran through the east and north wings and then towards other buildings south of the main cellblock.[58]

The fire destroyed the iconic cupola of the main dome that had been part of the Kingston skyline for more than a hundred years.[59] The fire was eventually contained, but two days later inmates set more fires, destroying many of the shops and the historic horse stable. Fortunately inmates were able to save the eight horses inside the stable.

The *Whig-Standard* reported that more than 160 armed soldiers were keeping guard against a possible prison breakout. The Kingston Police chief at the time, T.J. Truaisch, said that the entire city police force had been called to the prison, while the Royal Canadian Mounted Police patrolled the harbour.

Once the fires were controlled and the prisoners were returned to their cells, guards found an assortment of baseball bats, chisels and knives littering the exercise yard. A hundred-foot rope with a large steel hook on the end was also discovered. Inmates interviewed after the riot confirmed that the fires were set as a diversion for a mass escape attempt, but not a single inmate had even tried to get over one of the thirty-foot walls of the prison.

The riot lasted ten hours and caused over $2 million in damage to the prison. The inmates were quickly put to work repairing the extensive destruction of the main cellblock and shops. In a 1954 *Maclean's* article about the riot, a former prisoner who was released the following day described the event as a senseless act initiated by a small, aimless gang of convicts determined to destroy all they could. But having spent six years in KP, he understood why riots happen. "A prison is an active volcano, churning and bubbling under the pressure of monotony and routine," wrote ex-con #1604. "I think prisoners riot because they can't help it. It is natural reaction to an unnatural existence."

THE UPRISING AT KINGSTON PEN coincided with another federal investigation into the correctional system. The Fauteux Committee established a year before, in 1953, determined that prisons could not just fulfill a custodial role, but needed to begin addressing the behaviour and attitudes of inmates. Prisons needed to adopt programs designed to tackle the root causes of crime while also providing vocational training, pre-release programs and aftercare support. The report redefined the goals of corrections as the reform and rehabilitation of offenders, rather than merely their custody. The Fauteux Report recommended hiring better-trained personnel with professional qualifications in criminology, psychiatry, psychology, social work and law.

The report also examined the field of remission and parole. A key recommendation was to create a national board of parole that would extend to all federal offenders and replace the archaic Ticket of Leave System (TLA) that had been in place since 1899. Under the Ticket of Leave, offenders could be granted early leave from a penitentiary at the discretion of the Governor General, but wardens in each institution also had the power to make arbitrary parole decisions. A new parole act *was* passed in 1959, creating the National Parole Board, the first independent decision-making tribunal in Canada.

After the 1954 riot, Kingston Pen did not experience any more fires, but the embers of discontent continued to smoulder for seventeen years, until Billy Knight and a small group of disgruntled inmates reignited the sparks of rebellion.

6

SHAKE OFF THE SHACKLES

Wednesday, April 14, 1971

WITHIN MINUTES of the guards being attacked, word of the riot spread throughout the cellblocks. With the dome now under the control of the inmates, the prison belonged to them. Knight and his team rushed to the nearby tiers to free the rest of the prisoners still locked in their cells. Knight knew he needed additional manpower fast if he was going to control the takeover. Smashing a wall safe behind the keeper's desk in the dome, he grabbed all the keys and passed them out. He started running from wing to wing, shouting orders like a general. "Brothers!" he yelled with authority. "Our time has come to shake off the shackles. We've taken control of the dome and we've got six hostages. You will all be released from your cells." Prisoners still behind bars began yelling for their freedom. Raging inmates looked for anything they could use to pry open the cell doors. Someone from Knight's group opened the plumbing supply room. Now armed with four-foot pipe wrenches and lengths of steel pipe, inmates pounded and pulled at the locking mechanisms above the cells until they opened. Soon the inmates were in control of the main cellblock and began smashing everything in sight.

It didn't take long for the emancipated prisoners of Kingston Penitentiary to turn their wrath towards the most hated symbol of their oppression: the repugnant brass bell in the centre of the dome. Using chairs, pipes and anything else they could find, they smashed away at the gong until a final blow from a fire extinguisher shattered it into pieces.

Other rioters had more practical needs on their minds and wanted to break into another area of the prison. The entrance to the well-stocked kitchen was directly between B and C blocks. A group of inmates rushed at the heavy oak door, but before they reached the entrance—boom! A blast from a shotgun rang out from inside the kitchen, shattering the small window in the door. The charging inmates dropped to the floor as glass shattered on top of them.

Crawling on his hands and knees, Billy Knight moved away from the damaged kitchen door towards the radio room. He immediately called the warden. "If there are any more shots fired, we'll start cutting off some fingers," he yelled.[60] Jarvis could hear someone else yelling in the background. "Tell him we'll drop a finger out the window for every shot," said Manny Lester. "We've got to be firm."

Inmates standing along the railings above the dome floor began throwing debris and calling out threatening insults. The guard who'd fired the shot through the kitchen door had just put his kidnapped comrades in grave danger.

INMATE BARRIE MACKENZIE was sitting in his cell on range 3-B listening to the outbreak below him when someone opened his range with a key. As soon as he was freed from his cell, he let others out, including his friend Brian Beaucage. Soon a group of guys regarded as solid cons were standing on the range wondering what their next move was. They didn't know who or what had instigated the riot, but they weren't going to let anyone fuck them over.

As pandemonium continued to spread throughout the cell-blocks, another gang of inmates quickly designated themselves guardians of the six hostages. As inmate Roger Caron later reflected, "They knew the value of healthy pawns, knew that without them the authorities were certain to machine-gun their way inside the main cellblock, a dreadful outcome that would have left a lot of people dead."

Holding the guards in cellblock 1-F, the inmates knew their hostages were too exposed and the angry mob could turn on them at any time. The screws had to be moved. They herded the guards into a service corridor—a dark, narrow duct behind G and H blocks. They shut the door and wired it shut from the inside. "No one will get you; we'll protect you," Vallier would remember them saying. The guards could see out the door and saw prisoners running and smashing everything in sight. It seemed as though the inmates were trying to protect them, but how long would they remain safe?

One of the members of the inmate police force, as they came to be called, was Wayne Ford. Inmate #2778 was serving a life sentence for the murder of his mother, a crime he committed on May 16, 1963, when he was sixteen. After a heated argument one day, he bludgeoned his mother, Minnie Ford, to death with a baseball bat and left her sprawled on the kitchen floor while he returned to his grade ten afternoon class at Earl Haig Secondary School in Toronto. The following Victoria Day holiday weekend, he convinced two of his best friends to help him dispose of her corpse in Lake Couchiching, where the family had a cottage.[61] The sudden disappearance and search for Mrs. Ford, the wealthy widow of a respected Toronto businessman, was front-page news and the story captivated the city. Wayne told police his mother met a man and had moved to Fort Myers, Florida, where the family owned property, but investigators could find no trace of the woman from Willowdale. She had simply vanished.

With his mother gone, the handsome Wayne Ford had no one to answer to. He turned the family home into a brothel and went on a crime spree, robbing banks and selling guns. It was only a matter of time before Ford's arrogance and recklessness became his undoing.

In the fall of 1966, the badly decomposed body of Mrs. Ford floated to the surface of Lake Couchiching. Wayne Ford was charged with capital murder. For the police, he wasn't hard to find since he was already serving time in Kingston Penitentiary for escaping from Burwash Reformatory.

Labelled a dangerous, non-treatable psychopath by the judge at his trial, Ford was sentenced to life behind bars and was returned to serve out his time at Kingston Penitentiary. He was twenty-one years old.

For the cold, unrepentant murderer, life behind bars was easy. At six foot three and 285 pounds, Ford had earned a healthy respect amongst the inmate population at Kingston. He lifted weights, held various jobs in the prison workshops and kept to himself. "I'd been a criminal most of my life," said Ford in an interview with the *Toronto Star* in 2013. "You don't walk into the prison and say, 'hey everybody, you fuck with me and I'll kill you.' But you spread the word. You let it be known." Ford was considered a monster, an unredeemable psychopath, and no one was going to challenge him.[62]

FORD WAS LOCKED in his cell on the fourth tier when the riot began. He watched as other inmates ran past him, destroying everything in their wake while yelling and screaming. He wanted out. Then someone smashed open his cell and he ran down to the dome floor. Ford grabbed a three-foot length of two-inch pipe and began running towards 1-F. He knew some guards had been taken hostage and he hoped they weren't already dead. Any chance of getting out of the riot alive would be gone if the guards were killed. They were their only insurance against an all-out attack.

Running down the cellblock, under the overhang so nothing would land on his head from the ranges above, Ford found the guards huddled in the service corridor behind G and H ranges. A few other inmates Ford recognized were protecting them. The guards looked at him in terror, their faces lined with anxiety. He lowered the pipe in his hand. "I'm not here to hurt you," he told them. Ford told the guards to follow him to a safer location. "Don't look at anybody, don't run. Just walk normally," he said.

The hostages were quickly moved through the throngs of hostile inmates. At first Ford tried to lock all six guards in the plumbing area on the ground floor, but he decided it wasn't safe. They were too visible and too vulnerable. As they made their way up the winding metal stairs, inmates began shouting at them. When they finally got to the fourth floor of B-block, someone in the angry mob below suggested that a few of the screws should take a plunge off the fourth-tier balcony. The crowd cheered.

Ford had to act fast. He pushed three guards into one cell and three into another. One of the other inmates had found a chain and padlock. With all of the locking mechanisms destroyed, it was the only way they could secure the two cell doors. Once the guards were locked up, Wayne Ford turned to them and said, "Now take off your clothes."

SOON AFTER THE RIOT BEGAN, Billy Knight summoned the prison population to the dome. Standing on range three overlooking the dome floor and brandishing a short iron club, he was relishing his moment of glory. "We've got hostages, men," he shouted. "We're not going to release them until our demands are met, and that, my brothers, will take days of hard talk."

The inmates pounded the metal railings with their crude weapons. Knight was now king of the limestone castle and he wanted to assure his comrades that past injustices would be rectified.

"Have courage, my brothers, and remember when people have nothing to lose but themselves, only a coward would deny them the right to rebel." Surrounded by a captive audience, Knight outlined his reasons for the riot. "By sunrise we'll have direct communication with the outside world," he told the prisoners. "Either we get penal reform or else we turn this shithouse into a parking lot!"

"Let one of the screws do a nosedive off the balcony and the pigs will get the message," yelled an angry voice from the dome floor.

"Brothers! Brothers!" replied Knight. "Let's not give the pigs the satisfaction of finding a reason to label us as animals to the world. We need the public's support and we won't get it by creating a bloodbath."

Knight continued to stress the need for non-violence, but some of the men in the excited crowd were not happy. Billy Knight had instigated a riot that was putting all of their lives in jeopardy. One of those individuals was Brian Beaucage, a 23-year-old convict from London, Ontario, who was serving an eight-year prison sentence for manslaughter. He had recently been returned to Kingston Pen after attacking a prison instructor with a sledgehammer at Collins Bay penitentiary. A well-known motorcycle gang member, Beaucage was short on talk and fast with his fists. An early intake report stated: "Beaucage is an intelligent person who resorts to assaultive, aggressive behaviour without much remorse and provocation. He is considered to be a very manipulative and potentially dangerous person." Brian Beaucage did not like Billy Knight.

Beaucage was a loner, but he had befriended a young kid in Kingston Pen by the name of Robbie Robideau. Only seventeen when he was sent to Kingston, Robideau was a product of the system. From the age of seven he had been a ward of the state, and the state had not treated him well. From group homes he ended up in training schools, and from training schools he ended up in the reformatory. As he made his way up the prison ladder, Robideau learned how to survive. "If you didn't fight, you were dead. They tried to knock the aggression out of me with shock treatments, but it didn't work. It just made me worse." Now he was prisoner #6897 in Kingston Penitentiary.

Just before the riot, he had been released from solitary confinement, where he had spent thirty days for striking a guard. "In the hole, you were locked in your cell for twenty-three and a half hours a day," Robideau would recall years later. "We got bread and water and a full meal every twenty-one days. They took away your mattress every morning and gave it back to you at night. The only thing they left you was a bible."

As the riot unfolded, Robideau felt a sense of freedom he hadn't experienced in a long time. As other inmates smashed up their cells and anything else they could get hold of, Robideau and his friend Brian Beaucage had a different sport in mind. They were heading towards 1-D, the protective custody unit, where they knew they would find some easy prey.

AFTER HIS IMPASSIONED speech to the inmate population, Billy Knight left the dome area and ran towards the gymnasium to free the rest of the inmates who had been left behind. The gym was a large, rectangular, high-ceilinged building. On the north side was a stage where inmates had put on shows and concerts in years past. There was a doorway to the yard at the southwest corner of the gym and an elevated gun cage in the southeast corner.

When he entered the gym, Billy could see the confused inmates lined up against the south gym wall. It was deathly quiet. There were sixty-four men in total and three remaining guards. The guards stood defensively in front of the gun cage, located across from the entrance to the gym. Ken Garrett was the guard locked in the gun cage. Garrett, whom the other guards called Ponderosa Pete after he bought a hobby farm, was a well-respected senior officer. He had started his career at KP in 1961, and as a former Second World War vet he knew how to handle a gun. He had his rifle pointed directly at the inmates. If they attacked, his plan was to take out as many as he could before he ran out of ammunition. Hidden below in the gun cage, out of sight but within his reach, was a Smith & Wesson thirty-eight revolver. Garrett knew, if he started shooting, he might not reach the thirty-eight in time. In a decision that would later result in a reprimand from his superiors, he passed the thirty-eight revolver through the gun cage to guard Bill Babcock. Now there was a loaded gun within reach of over sixty desperate inmates. Years later, Ken Garrett reluctantly retold the story to his son, Spencer, who had also become a corrections officer at Kingston Pen. "I wanted the guards in the gym to have a fighting chance," he explained. "They were sitting ducks and I didn't care if they fired me."

When Knight walked back into the gymnasium, he didn't expect one of the officers to be armed. Babcock, also known as "Killer Bill," pointed the revolver he had just been handed towards Knight. Witnesses later recounted the exchange between the riot leader and the armed guard:

"Let's talk," said Knight to Babcock.

"Anything I've got to say to you will come from the mouth of this gun," replied Babcock.

"We've got full control of the dome and six hostages. I want you to release my brothers. Let them join me in my peaceful protest."

Shaking his pistol at Knight, Babcock wasn't backing down. "We have the artillery, so why should we move?"

Knight then suggested that if the gymnasium was emptied, it could be used as a rendezvous point between himself and the administration to negotiate a peaceful resolution.

Throughout his twenty-two years of service, Babcock had never imagined or trained for this moment, but he still wasn't prepared to give in. "Go away, just go away," he told Knight.

Knight didn't respond. Babcock then watched as Knight suddenly turned and left the gym, locking the last barrier behind him. The inmates left stranded in the gym weren't sure what would happen next.

As soon as Knight retreated from the gymnasium, Ken Garrett grabbed the phone located in the gun cage and called the emergency operator stationed inside the front gates to tell him there was a riot going on in the main cellblock. As administrative protocol dictated, the operator in turn called the assistant deputy warden, Doug Chinnery, at his home across town to advise him of the situation. A mild-mannered man who would later play a significant role in the crisis, Chinnery was at first skeptical about what he was hearing.

"They've taken over the dome," stated the emergency operator.

"Aw, c'mon," Chinnery laughed, thinking it was a joke.

He soon realized it wasn't.

ON APRIL 14, 1971, Warden Arthur Jarvis was working late in his office to catch up on a backlog of work. As usual, he had informed the north gate officer that he would be in his office for a few hours in case he was needed. It was a chilly spring evening. The Warden's House, situated directly across from the penitentiary, was an impressive limestone structure built entirely by convict labour. In 1873, John Creighton became the first warden to live in the house.[63] In the late nineteenth century the residence became known as Cedarhedge, after the extensive and well-manicured hedges that once lined the driveway. Now, in the early spring, flower gardens waiting to bloom filled the front lawn overlooking the penitentiary.

Jarvis could see the main gate of the penitentiary from his window, although he had chosen to have his desk face into the room. In the time he had occupied the front room of the Warden's House, he had done little to change its decor. A framed picture of John Diefenbaker's Bill of Rights hung on one panelled wall, and an autumn landscape painting hung on the opposite one. Brown manila files littered his desk, which was devoid of any personal mementoes or photos. On the warden's bookshelf sat a piece of whimsical sculpture, a small man looking up at a bird on his hand. The inscription read, "Go ahead, everybody else does."[64]

At eleven o'clock, Jarvis received a call from the gate officer, telling him the inmates had taken over the central dome area of the prison. A second call from Assistant Deputy Warden Chinnery confirmed the initial report. In his twenty years with the Correctional Service, Jarvis had dealt with numerous situations— it came with the job. But he had never been faced with a full-scale prison rebellion. He had warned his superiors that something serious was going to happen, but no one had responded to his letters. Kingston Penitentiary was a ticking time bomb, and it had just exploded!

THERE WAS NO specific riot plan for staff to follow, but Warden Jarvis immediately ordered all off-duty guards back to the prison. The penitentiary armoury located within the north gate was unlocked, and as the guards returned to the prison, they were armed with rifles and posted around the perimeter of the main cellblock. Jarvis then notified the duty officer of the Canadian Forces Base at nearby Barriefield and requested the army be put on standby.[65] The base commander advised Jarvis that 45 troops would be ready to move on twenty minutes' notice and 120 more with one hour's notice.[66] More infantry from Petawawa could be sent in by helicopter if necessary.

Jarvis had to notify his superiors. He contacted the Regional Director of Penitentiary Services, John Maloney, and the Commissioner of Penitentiaries in Ottawa, Paul Faguy.

John Maloney wasted no time getting to the prison. He arrived just after eleven thirty and proceeded to the keeper's hall, where he received a preliminary report from Jarvis. The administration knew little about what was happening inside the prison, but staff still had control of the keeper's hall, the hospital, the dissociation cells and the kitchen.

Maloney was a tall, distinguished man with a long career in corrections. Joining the Penitentiary Service in 1957, he had worked his way up from a guard's position. Maloney had served as a warden at British Columbia Penitentiary and Matsqui Institution in Abbotsford, BC. He had extensive experience in dealing with inmate populations, but Kingston Penitentiary would prove to be an event he would never forget.

SHORTLY AFTER MIDNIGHT, Warden Jarvis received a phone call from guard Ken Garrett in the gymnasium. Garrett told the warden an inmate wanted to talk to him. Jarvis wasn't sure what to do. Who was the prisoner and what did he want? Was it a trap?

Jarvis walked over to the gym, not knowing what he would encounter when he got there. When he entered the gun cage where Garrett was stationed, he could see all of the inmates lined up against the gymnasium wall. They were quiet and under control. But soon his attention was diverted to the exit gate, where he heard a key turning the lock. Another prisoner walked into the gym alone. Jarvis recognized Billy Knight, the prison barber.

Turning towards the other prisoners, Knight gestured to them with a peace sign. Ignoring guard Bill Babcock, who had a revolver pointed directly at him, Knight approached the barred gun cage to speak to the warden. He assured the warden that a peaceful demonstration was intended, and they didn't want to see anyone get hurt. But, he added, the presence of additional armed officers surrounding the building was agitating the inmate population.

"What exactly do you want from us?" asked Jarvis.

"For a start, we want positive results in our desire for decent living conditions," said Knight.

Knight then requested the guards be removed from the gun cage and the gymnasium so the remaining inmates could return to their cells.

Making a decision that would later be called into question, Warden Jarvis agreed to Knight's request. He was in a no-win situation. He knew the prison had been taken over by hundreds of hostile inmates, and six of his officers had been kidnapped. They could be in serious danger. He hoped if he complied with Knight's request, the insurrection would end quickly and without bloodshed.

Jarvis and the three guards left the gymnasium. The inmates in the gym followed Knight back to the dome, adding sixty-four more discontented prisoners to the growing rebellion.

7

INTO THE NIGHT

Wednesday, April 14, 1971

AS THE NIGHT of Wednesday, April 14, wore on, Warden Jarvis, Regional Director Maloney and other senior penitentiary officials sat in the keeper's hall, attached to the north wing cellblock. The air in the room was thick with cigarette smoke. There was little conversation as they waited for news from inside the prison. There was one phone in the room, and they were to keep Paul Faguy, the Commissioner of Penitentiaries, apprised of the situation as it developed. But they still weren't entirely sure what the situation was. Did the inmates have weapons? Were they planning a large-scale escape? Were they going to kill the guards? Whatever the prisoners were organizing, the men sitting in that room were ill-prepared to respond. They had no riot plan. There was no riot squad, and there was no hostage negotiator. Other than ordering all off-duty guards to return to the prison and putting the military on standby, the prison administration had no clear plan. "There isn't much we can do," said Maloney to the gathering press. "All we can do is wait and hope to communicate."

The prison administrators also lacked direction as to who should be in charge, the warden or the Regional Director. The

Canadian Penitentiary Service had a long history of conflict between its centralized administration and local prison personnel. The authority of wardens in dealing with matters pertaining to the day-to-day functioning of their institutions was often delayed or nullified by prison inspectors or superintendents, who rarely visited the prisons.

In 1938, the Archambault commission noted numerous examples of the centralized control of trivial matters that resulted in wardens spending most of their valuable time buried in paperwork versus the day-to-day management of their prisons. At the time of the commission, any expenditure over one dollar had to be approved by the superintendent, along with other requests such as hinges for storm windows and typewriter repairs. On one occasion, guards were prevented from buying a wreath for the deceased wife of a fellow officer because it would have been necessary to secure the approval of the superintendent in a timely manner.

Although the Archambault Report revealed that a great deal of time was wasted, prison bureaucracy remained relatively unchanged over the next three decades.

This only added to the confusion and tension in the keeper's hall on the night of April 14, 1971. Warden Jarvis was responsible for the management of Kingston Penitentiary and for the safety of every person behind its walls. He knew the prison and its population best. But with Regional Director Maloney on site, Jarvis had lost independent authority; Maloney would have to get everything approved through Ottawa now. However, Jarvis and Maloney did agree on one thing: They could not regain control of the main cellblock without risking the lives of the hostages. Their only course of action was to wait.

THE SIX KIDNAPPED guards waited as well. They had no idea what time it was or how long it had been since the riot began. Did their families know what was happening? Had their wives been notified?

Crouched in their padlocked prison cells, they listened to the sounds of hundreds of convicts rejoicing in their sudden freedom. Metal smashed against metal, followed by loud cheers. The noise was deafening, but at least it meant the inmates were focused on something other than the hostages. Most of the lighting on the ranges had been knocked out, so the men could not see beyond the shadows of the inmate police force protecting them. The group looked to be about thirty strong.

The guards, now dressed in inmate clothing to help them blend in, were almost indistinguishable from their captors. But their new uniforms did not protect them from the bitter cold that had snuck into the cellblocks since many of the windows in the prison had been smashed. The guards said very little to their abductors for fear of setting them off. Donald Flynn, who had a reputation as a loud and assertive screw, sat quietly with his colleagues, reassuring them the riot would likely be over by the morning. He didn't want them to know what he was really thinking: they weren't going to get out of the prison alive.

Joseph Vallier was panicked. As the father of five kids, he didn't know how his wife, Doris, was going to cope if something happened to him. He'd only been on the job for six months, but at forty-seven he didn't have a lot of options and his family needed the steady income.

Terry Decker clutched his swollen hand. He couldn't feel two of his fingers since the keys had been ripped away from him. He kept reliving the moment the inmates attacked him. Was this whole situation his fault? Why hadn't he noticed the imposters in the lineup coming out of the gymnasium?

Kerry Bushell, the youngest in the group, prayed silently. He had always attributed his good fortune to his strong Christian faith, and he knew his current fate was in the hands of God. He thought about the many nights he had worked in one of the guard towers overlooking the prison yard. He hated it. It was a lonely job, but he would sneak in a transistor radio to keep him company. And there was the owl—a snowy-white owl that would perch on the tower. Kerry would throw it some of his sandwich for entertainment. If only he'd been working in the tower this night.

Newly married, Kerry and his wife, Elaine, were anxious to start a family. He touched the pale band of skin that encircled his finger. Everything of value had been taken from the guards, including his wedding ring. Tomorrow was his twenty-fifth birthday and he prayed he would get home to spend it with his wife.

Senior guard Ed Barrett had not missed a day's work in his thirty years on the job. He never wanted to let the other guys down. But now he was worried that he might not be able to protect his brothers when they needed him the most. What the other guards didn't know was that Ed had a weak heart, and he wasn't sure he was going to make it out alive.

WHILE HUNDREDS OF inmates spent their first night of freedom roaming the cellblocks, destroying everything in their path, fourteen others remained locked up. They had no desire to be released, for freedom most certainly meant death. They were the inmates in 1-D, the wing of the prison that housed the "undesirables." This was the term used by inmates and staff to describe sex offenders and informants—the two types of inmates who ranked lowest on the prison's social ladder. In jailhouse slang, a child molester was a diddler or a skinner, and an informer was a rat or a stool pigeon.[67] Both were shunned and despised by other inmates. They were the pariahs of the prison system. Their segregation on the bottom tier of D-block, where they had their own workshop and exercise yard, was for their own protection. They ate alone and spent more time locked in their cells, which were the smallest in the prison. Attacks on undesirables were common occurrences if they were let out into the regular prison population.

Sex offenders were hated inside prison, and child molesters ranked the very lowest on the inmate hierarchy.[68] Treatment of sex offenders at the time involved behaviour modification, ranging from simple sex education to shock therapy to discourage aberrant sexual fantasies. The most sophisticated aversion therapy involved a penometer, a metal band that encircled the penis and measured sexual arousal. When the prisoner reacted to slides depicting rape scenes, he received an electric shock. The aim of the treatment was to create negative associations with the inmate's deviant impulses.[69]

The Solicitor General's department had recently authorized a study on dangerous sex offenders to determine their treatment needs.[70] Cyril Greenland, a professor of social work at McMaster University, was working with seventeen so-called dangerous sex offenders but found most to be non-violent.[71] He described the inmates as a pathetic group of socially and sexually inadequate individuals made up of older homosexual pedophiles, exhibitionists and mental defectives. He also noted they were living in conditions of appalling degradation. "Sexual offenders are spurned by the larger prison population," said Greenland. "They are subject to considerable personal humiliation and verbal and physical abuse." As one of his subjects had told him: "the inmates hate the guards, the guards hate the inmates and together they hate the sex offender."

But not all prisoners housed in 1-D were sex offenders or informers. One young inmate had been sent to the range at his own request because he had refused the sexual advances of other inmates and consequently his life had been threatened. Homosexuality was tolerated in prisons, but it had to appear to be consensual. Rape went against the general code of inmate behaviour. "After all," said Roger Caron in his book about prison life, "how could prisoners justify torturing skinners (child molesters) and diddlers for their nefarious crimes and yet condone rape amongst themselves?"

But some of the tougher cons would try to "persuade" some of the younger inmates to be their friends. In prison, a con looking for a sexual outlet with a younger con, known as a sweet kid, was called a wolf. A wolf was normally straight on the outside but engaged in sexual activity with other men while incarcerated. A wolf would try to buy a sweet kid's affection and loyalty with gifts and favours. If the sweet kid accepted items from the wolf, he would be indebted to the con.

Robbie Robidoux was seventeen when he arrived at Kingston Penitentiary in January 1971.[72] He was starting a three-year sentence for robbery. As the new guy, he was called a fish. When he entered his cell for the first time, a box of goodies was waiting for him on his bunk. Cigarettes, chocolate bars and potato chips temped him, but he knew if he took the goodies, he'd be owned. He was straight and he wasn't going to be beholden to a queer. He asked around and soon found the older inmate who had left the gifts. Robidoux beat the shit out of him. He had to do it—to let that guy and the other wolves know he wasn't for the taking. Any sign of weakness was an open invitation. For his defiance, Robidoux was put in the hole for thirty days.

Other young inmates who couldn't fight off the wolves had to be locked up in the segregation unit for their own protection. Still, regardless of why you were there, 1-D was the last address any inmate at Kingston Pen wanted to have.

SOON AFTER THE RIOT BEGAN, Billy Knight secured the keys to 1-D. He knew the fourteen undesirables would be in immediate danger and he had told them earlier to hide under their beds. But some of the more violent inmates were already circling. Hoping to keep control over the rebellion, Knight reiterated to the inmates gathered in the dome that any bloodshed would be detrimental to every-thing they were fighting for. But not everyone was interested in Knight's platitudes.

Inmate James Ball was locked in 1-D. He had switched off his cell light and was hiding under his bed. He knew he was in danger. A few days before the riot, he had talked back and insulted some of the cons on the tiers above him. He had violated the inmate code that demanded the lowest of the low defer to other prisoners. Suddenly something loud crashed against his cell door. Ball screamed. Two inmates armed with three-foot metal bars were smashing at the lock on his door. They didn't need the keys. "Come out from under the bed, we're here to kill you," witnesses reported hearing them say. "God have mercy on me," Ball cried. Within seconds the inmates were dragging him out from under his cot. Calling him a rat and a stool pigeon, they began beating him. As Ball lay cowering on the floor, three more inmates arrived. They attacked Ball again. The other prisoners in 1-D listened to his screams and prayed they weren't next.

After the second attack on Ball, another group of cons pulled a fire hose through the barrier at the end of the range. They turned on the powerful hose and began spraying into the cells of the other undesirables. The tormentors laughed and taunted the men as they scrambled beneath their bunks for protection.

Knight heard the screams coming from 1-D and rushed to try to stop the attack. Looking into the cells, he saw terror in the eyes of the men, who were soaking wet and cowering. Then he found James Ball lying in a large pool of blood. He wasn't moving.

Knight rushed back to the phone in the dome to dial the prison hospital. "We have an emergency situation here. An inmate is bleeding to death."

Ball had slit his wrists in a desperate bid to take his own life rather than be attacked a third time. He was moaning and crying out in pain. Knight had to get him to the hospital right away, but their access to the other buildings on the prison grounds had been cut off. If they carried Ball out, the armed guards might ambush them. Knight called the administration building and demanded to speak to the warden.

Warden Jarvis knew the men in 1-D were vulnerable to attack, but he hadn't anticipated a suicide attempt. He agreed to allow two inmates to carry Ball out of 1-D and deliver him to the hospital located in the east wing cellblock.

Knight had saved Ball's life, but no one knew at the time how Ball's own desperate actions may have saved him from the much worse fate still awaiting the other inmates of 1-D.

IN THE EARLY HOURS of the riot, violence was not limited to the unde-sirables. After Knight had arranged the release of prisoners from the gym, inmate Ralph Lake proceeded cautiously back to his cell. Lake was a thin, wiry guy in his late twenties. It was common knowledge amongst the prison population that he was in for rape. Lake was the clerk in the mailbag department, and according to his co-workers he was generally disliked. He had managed to sur-vive in the general population because he had a wolf protecting him—a big bad wolf named Harold St. Amour. He was the pens' resident bookie and a valuable friend to have on the inside. He wasn't the kind of guy you wanted as an enemy.

As Lake walked back from the gym towards the central dome area, he didn't get far before he was struck on the head with a pipe wrench. "Stoolie," the attacker yelled. Lake stumbled but managed to get away. He ran to St. Amour's cell on the top tier. Armed with a homemade shiv, St. Amour strung blankets across the front of his cell and defied anyone to come in. Two other inmates, Gary McCorkel and Melvin Travis, were also hiding in St. Amour's cell. Over the next few days there would be a lot of scores to settle, but for the time being Ralph Lake and the others were safe.

AT TWENTY-SIX, BRIAN ENSOR, inmate #9370, had already spent eight years in Kingston Pen. Nicknamed "the Camel" because of his height and the way he stooped over, he was serving time for assaulting two young girls in Hamilton, Ontario. At his trial, two psychiatrists testified that he had below-normal intelligence and was unable to control his sexual impulses.[73] In their opinion, if he were allowed to remain free, he would likely reoffend. As a result, he was in preventive detention, which meant he would be kept in prison until a parole board judged him safe to return to society. His case would be reviewed every three years.

Ensor was working with Professor Greenland from McMaster in his study of men who had been labelled dangerous sex offenders. In his research, Greenland described Ensor as a man with subnormal intelligence who had a history of convictions for non-violent sexual approaches to little girls. The professor also noted that Brian Ensor had not received the benefit of legal counsel at his trial.

Ensor worked in the machine shop and kept a low profile. He knew how the other inmates felt about him. He had already survived several beatings and a stabbing in the arm a few years earlier, but he stubbornly refused to be housed in protective custody. He didn't want to live with the other diddlers on 1-D. But now, with the riot under way, he knew he was a marked man.

Ensor was hiding in his cell on the fourth tier in E-block when two burly convicts appeared wielding metal pipes. He could not escape. The attackers dragged him out of his cell. A third attacker, Robbie Robidoux, who hated Ensor, soon joined in. Robidoux delivered hot water to the inmates every night so they could shave in their cells. But one guy on his rounds gave him the creeps. Ensor would stare at him and lick his lips. Now Robidoux had a score to settle.

The three cons pulled Ensor into the corridor towards the railings. He screamed and kicked and struggled to get away. He knew what they were trying to do. Ensor grasped at the metal as his attackers tried to push him over the railing to his death. Ensor tightened his grip and yelled out, begging for his life. Robidoux bit and kicked at Ensor's fingers to release his grip, but Ensor hung on. The attackers finally gave up and dropped him on the floor, where they continued to punch and kick at him. Eventually they stopped and left him curled up in a ball.

Months later, at their trial, when the inmates were asked why they had changed their minds about throwing Ensor over the balcony, they replied, "Because he was screaming too much."

Billy Knight and another inmate by the name of Barrie MacKenzie were planning an early morning meeting with the warden when they got word of the attempt on Brian Ensor's life. MacKenzie had been guarding the hostages. The two men rushed to Ensor's cell, where they found him huddled in terror. "Why me? Why me?" he cried out. He had been badly beaten. His eyes were swollen shut and his face was bleeding from several deep cuts.

Knight realized they had to move Ensor for his own protection. He knew that it was only a matter of time before his attackers would return. MacKenzie suggested moving Ensor to the protective custody range. Ensor refused. He didn't want to be locked up with the undesirables. He knew they were high on the extermination list. In spite of his resistance, Knight and MacKenzie dragged a struggling and screaming Ensor down three flights of stairs to the bottom tier. Brian Ensor was now locked in a cell on 1-D.

Knight was furious. He called for a general assembly in the dome area. Visibly shaken, he told the inmates the attack on Ensor was precisely the sort of thing they didn't want to happen. It made the inmates look like animals and would seriously jeopardize their chances of negotiating with the administration. He ordered an immediate stop to any harassment of the undesirables. Knight returned to 1-D and assured the terrified inmates that no further harm would come to them.

It was a promise he would not be able to keep.

WITH THE HEAT OFF the undesirables for the time being, the free-roaming gangs turned their attention towards another hated bastion of the institution, the religious chapels. Kingston Pen had three places of worship: the Catholic and Protestant chapels and a synagogue. The chapels were situated on the north side of the west wing. Most of the inmates despised the religious orders of the institution and hated the fact that they had to attend church services on Sunday mornings or be locked in their cells. "There were many gripes against the religious institutions," recalled Roger Caron. "The Catholic Church had a narrow-minded position on the censorship of our reading material, and we were refused subscriptions to *Playboy* magazine. They thought it would rot our minds and lead to masturbation." But the religious chapels hadn't always been so reviled. In the 1960s inmates at the prison had produced a booklet called *A Year in the Life of the Chapel at the Top of the Stairs*.[74] For inmates at that time, the chapel had become more than a house of worship. It was a sanctuary for troubled minds, a meeting place for lively discussion and a library that contained over 350 books.

Knight secured the keys to all three chapels. Realizing they could use some of the heavy oak benches and marble slabs to reinforce barricades, Knight handed over the keys to two brothers who were both serving life sentences for the brutal murder of a rival motorcycle gang member. Rumour had it they had quartered the guy by tying chains to his legs and driving off in opposite directions.

Knight told the brothers to round up a crew and haul the heavy oak benches down the metal staircases to reinforce the barricaded entrances around the dome. But the brothers had a different kind of renovation on their minds. Soon a strange reverberating sound could be heard from the upper entrance to the chapels. As other inmates looked up, they saw the wheels of the mahogany church organ rumbling across the hardwood floor on the top tier. The prisoners below scrambled for cover as it careened across the floor, smashing through the railing and shattering into pieces on the concrete floor of the dome. A shrill scream sounded from above as one of the brothers hung perilously from the top railing, clinging to the bent metal. His brother quickly pulled him to safety.

With the church organ obliterated, the inmates then turned their rage towards anything else they could damage or break. In the Catholic chapel nothing was left intact. The wooden pews were smashed, as was the marble altar. The floor was littered with torn bibles, candles and prayer books. Three stained glass windows lay in pieces and a marble statue of the Virgin Mary was unceremoniously decapitated. Inmates later testified that inmates were running around wearing priest robes and laughing while they were destroying the chapels.

Warden Jarvis and the others sitting in the keeper's hall heard music and singing coming from the chapel area. But then the sounds suddenly turned to shouting and the smashing of furniture. Soon after, a prison guard reported that something had been thrown over the railings near the chapel area. Helpless to do anything, Warden Jarvis prayed it wasn't a body.

When Knight saw the destruction of the religious areas of the prison, he declared the chapel area off limits and the barrier at the top of the stairs was deadlocked. Knight wasn't a religious man, but he knew the inmates were going to pay for the destruction of the chapels one way or another.

8

IN THE LIGHT OF DAWN

Thursday, April 15, 1971

BY EARLY THURSDAY MORNING, a subdued silence had descended on the prison. Many inmates had retreated to the safety of their cells. Others gathered around small fires they had built to try to stay warm. Blankets were at a premium. As the first rays of sunlight penetrated through the broken windows, the reality of the damage was illuminated for all to see. Anything that could be destroyed had been. The walkways along the cells were littered with smashed furniture, torn mattresses, bedsprings and plumbing fixtures. Water seeped into the corridors from broken water pipes. Graffiti was scrawled all over the walls, and the locking systems on each of the cellblocks lay in heaps of crumpled metal. In some places, debris was piled five to six feet high.

The peculiar calm that engulfed the prison brought a new reality to Knight and his men. The standoff might last days, and the prisoners would need food and water. Some would need medication. Knight knew that when hundreds of cons stumbled out of their cells in a few hours, he would have to answer their immediate demands.

WARDEN JARVIS and Regional Director Maloney were still sitting and waiting in the keeper's hall when they received a call from Knight in the dome. Knight wanted food and coffee to be brought in and he wanted medication for the inmates who needed it.[75] There were a number of diabetics who required insulin shots. Thinking he could resolve the standoff quickly, Jarvis refused. But a demanding and arrogant Knight would not back down. He told Jarvis the safety of the kidnapped officers was on his shoulders. Jarvis finally agreed to coffee and medication. "Coffee is being prepared and I'll send an orderly from the hospital with prescribed medication," he told Knight. Injections for diabetics could be given through the inner barrier at the keeper's hall.

But as an act of good faith, Jarvis also wanted to speak to one of the kidnapped guards on the telephone. He wanted to hear from one of his men first-hand that they were all safe. While Jarvis stayed on the phone with Knight, he could hear other inmates yelling and shouting in the background for a guard to be brought to the dome. He wondered if he had just put one of his men at more risk with the angry mob.

Guard Ed Barrett was lying on the bunk in his locked cell. His captors had dragged a few mattresses inside for the guys to take turns getting some rest, but no one had slept. It was cold. He had lain awake in the night listening to the screaming and the cries for help coming from deep within the limestone walls. As a senior guard, he was well aware of the pecking order in the prison and he knew the weaker inmates would be prey. It was the law of the jungle, and Kingston Penitentiary housed some very predatory animals.

As thin shafts of daylight reached the darkened cell range where the guards were being kept, Barrett heard the familiar sound of metal banging against metal. It was coming from the dome area. The cons were gathering again. Suddenly the bars swung open on the cell. "Barrett, come with us," said one of the inmates protecting them. Barrett stumbled to his feet. He was stiff from the cold and paralyzed with fear, but he said nothing. The other guards looked on, helpless to prevent their colleague from being taken away. Why were they taking Barrett? And more importantly, would they be bringing him back?

BARRETT WAS HASTILY BLINDFOLDED and led out to the top tier of B-block. Wayne Ford and another inmate held him on either side as he was guided down the winding stairs. Barrett could hear the inmates banging a steady rhythm on the metal rails in the circular dome. He felt his legs give out beneath him. The inmates laughed and taunted him about his new uniform—a baggy, ill-fitting prisoner's jacket and pants.

Still unable to see anything, he was led across the dome floor and handed the wall phone. The voice on the other end asked him to identify himself. Barrett recognized he was speaking to Warden Jarvis. Then a woman's voice came on the line. It was Barrett's wife. "No, it's really me," Barrett said, trying to convince her over all the noise in the background. Crying, she told the caller he was lying. "You've killed my husband," she yelled hysterically.

Standing beside Barrett, Wayne Ford heard the guard trying to convince his wife that it was really him on the phone.[76] "We just painted our daughter's room blue and there's a giraffe hanging in it," he told her. Ford heard the woman scream, "My husband's alive!"

The phone was handed back to the warden. In a voice cracking with emotion, Barrett told Jarvis that he and the other hostages were unharmed, but he believed their circumstances could change if the inmates' demands were not met. Hearing those words, Knight snatched the receiver from Barrett's hand. "Think about what you have heard," Knight said. And he had one other demand. "We want the armed officers removed from their positions surrounding the prison. They are too close." Then he hung up the phone.

It was a critical moment for Ford and the others. The administration now knew they hadn't hurt any of the guards. They were telling the truth. Ford knew they needed to keep the guards alive and in good shape as protection. If anything happened to the guards, they would all be murdered.

As Barrett was led away, the inmates resumed their familiar beat, the steady pounding of the railings with their iron bars. The prisoners were preparing for their first full day as liberated men. They were now in charge.

ON APRIL 15, THE RESIDENTS of Kingston woke to a pleasant spring morning. The forecast called for a sunny day with temperatures ranging from seven to twelve degrees Celsius. There was a chill in the air and the grass glistened with a fresh blanket of frost. Early morning motorists drove along King Street, passing the famous stone fortress that stretched along the south shore next to the idyllic Portsmouth Harbour. Several uniformed guards stood out front of the north gate smoking, but otherwise nothing seemed out of the ordinary. The prison was a defining institution in Kingston, but before the day was over, it was going to be the talk of the town.

GERRY RETZER WAS FAMILIAR with Kingston Pen. As a popular news reporter on staff at CKLC, Retzer had covered numerous stories about the prison for the local Kingston radio station. He had grown up in the Kingston area, and like most locals he revelled in stories of convict escapes or notorious criminals being transferred to the Pen.

On April 15, Retzer was covering the morning news beat. That day, Prime Minister Pierre Trudeau was in Tobago on his official honeymoon with his young bride Margaret, and Jimmy Hoffa, the famous US Teamsters president, had been sent back to prison for jury tampering and mail fraud. The trial of three men accused of kidnapping and murdering Quebec labour minister Pierre Laporte had been postponed, and rioting in Belfast, Northern Ireland, was escalating. On top of all that, news outlets everywhere were gearing up for the forty-third annual Academy Awards, to be broadcast that night.

Just after 11 a.m., the radio station received a call for Retzer. The man on the line said it was urgent. When Retzer took the call, an unfamiliar voice said he was calling from inside Kingston Penitentiary. "We've taken hostages," he declared. Years later Retzer recalled the bizarre conversation. "I had never received a call quite like that before," he said. "I was fairly new, and I would get calls about an accident on Highway 401 or a barn burning down. Frankly, it scared me. I didn't know what to make of this guy on the other end of the line."

The man on the phone told Retzer the inmates were ticked off about a lot of stuff and they wanted to hold a news conference to air their grievances. The caller said his name was Knight and he wanted Retzer to attend the news conference. "We want TV cameras and tape recorders," he added. Knight then assured Retzer that the hostages were unharmed and were being protected by an inmate police force.[77]

Knight passed the phone to another inmate, #7136, Manny Lester. Lester told Rezter that he had been elected by the inmate population to be their legal adviser. Lester, an imposing figure with thinning brown hair and a face ravaged by acne scars, was a 45-year-old American stockbroker who was serving time for fraud. In his new role as jailhouse attorney, Lester informed Retzer that a newly elected inmates' committee wanted to meet with a citizens' committee so the prisoners could present their grievances. He then gave Retzer a long list of prominent citizens in the media and in political and legal circles, hoping that some of them would agree to come to Kingston. "They wanted lawyers and

reporters from Toronto," Retzer recalled. "But they were also asking for Paul Newman, Mickey Rooney and Muhammad Ali.
Newman had just starred in that film *Cool Hand Luke*, so I think
that's why they were asking for him." More practical names on
their list were *Toronto Telegram* columnist Ron Haggart, national
NDP leader Tommy Douglas, civil liberties lawyer Alan Borovoy,
Dr. Morton Shulman and Toronto lawyer Arthur Martin.

Retzer agreed to come to the prison. He jumped in his car and
headed down to the penitentiary, not knowing what he might find.
When he got to the warden's office, a prison official stopped him.
"We have nothing to say to you," the official told Retzer. Not sure
what to do, Retzer drove back to the radio station and called his
news director, Conn Stevenson. "Go back, stick with it, and knock
at the door again," said Stevenson. "And so I did," recalled Retzer.
"Eventually, they let me in."

BY MIDDAY, WORD THAT something was going on at Kingston Penitentiary had quickly spread. Local media were already on site
trying to find out what was happening inside the prison, and eager
reporters from Toronto and Ottawa had hit the road, heading
towards Kingston.

Billy Knight was succeeding in getting his message out. He
wanted the entire world to come to the infamous Kingston Penitentiary and take a look inside. He wanted them to see how the
forgotten were treated and how they lived. The only problem was
that while Knight and a handful of inmates were focused on a
non-violent protest and the airing of their grievances, others were
intent on revenge and mayhem. By the time the world did get a
peek inside the penitentiary, the prison floor would be stained
with blood.

9
TAKE A LOOK INSIDE

The old-time prison administrator says he doesn't believe in coddling prisoners.

No one advocates the coddling of prisoners. All that we insist upon is that the prisoner be treated as a man, having still in him the potentialities of a good citizen. To strengthen, to encourage, to restore to a true appreciation of his own manhood and self-respect is surely not coddling a prisoner.

—letter to the editor, Maclean's, May 1916

Thursday, April 15, 1971

KNIGHT HAD DEMANDED a press conference and he was getting one. At 10:45 on Thursday morning, eight men were sitting in a whitewashed boardroom in the prison's hospital. The group consisted of William Baird and Sheldon MacNeil from the *Whig-Standard*, Gerry Retzer from CKLC radio station, Henry Champ from CTV News in Toronto and Graham Cox from the Canadian Press wire service.[78] Also sitting at the conference table were Regional Director John Maloney, Warden Arthur Jarvis and acting deputy warden Douglas Chinnery.

Fifteen minutes after the agreed-upon meeting time, three Kingston Penitentiary inmates sauntered into the room. All eyes and flashing cameras were suddenly on Billy Knight, Charles Saunders and Manny Lester. Knight and Saunders were dressed in their blue-grey denim inmate uniforms, while Lester had curiously added a black blazer to his prison ensemble.

Taking the lead, a confident Knight informed the reporters and prison officials that the prisoners were protesting against the inhumanities and the soul-destroying effects of incarceration they faced on a daily basis. Their actions were meant to represent a peaceful demonstration by an oppressed group whom the average citizen had chosen to ignore. "We're sick of being zombies," said Billy Knight. "This is our last-ditch stand against the inhumanities the prisoners will face upon a forced transfer to Millhaven."[79] He went on to describe the majority of the inmates as kids who had come from poverty-stricken or broken homes and who had spent most of their youth in orphanages or reform schools. They had been rejected, deprived, shit on and bounced around all their lives. Many of them, he claimed, were emotionally immature and illiterate. "You warehouse a man and you destroy him but show that same individual direction and you can contain him," extolled Knight. "Most of these kids shouldn't even be in here, for Christ's sake," he added.

Knight also declared they were rioting against the brutality of the guards and spoke about the two inmates named Jacks and Turner who had taken hostages in January. Knight claimed they had been severely beaten after their surrender. "That's not true," said Maloney. "Those inmates were armed with knives and were injured in a fight with the guards." Maloney went on to say that Mrs. Redmond, the Native social worker, had visited the inmates after the incident and was satisfied they had not been handled too roughly.

Knight stated that the prisoners' decision to overpower the guards and take hostages had been prompted by the transfer of twelve inmates to Millhaven Institution on Wednesday afternoon. The inmates at Kingston Penitentiary wanted to address their grievances before they were all forced to move to the high-tech prison, where they felt their treatment and living conditions would worsen. They had heard rumours the new penitentiary was bugged with electronic listening devices. "This is a once-in-a-lifetime chance for us," continued Knight. "If we fail to get the changes we want, we go into Millhaven with a worse system than exists now inside Kingston."

Reporter Sheldon MacNeil from the *Kingston Whig-Standard* sat across from the three convicts. He scribbled down notes as Knight spoke. He later wrote about the tension in the room escalating as the riot leader continued to air the prisoners' concerns in front of the prison administration. Knight was putting on a show of confidence and was taking full advantage of his captive audience. The ashtrays on the table filled quickly as the inmates bummed cigarettes from the willing reporters. Occasional sounds could be heard outside the room, where dozens of other prisoners were pressed against the cellblock windows trying to catch a glimpse of what was happening in the meeting.

Knight said they had 100 percent support for the riot amongst the inmate population and they wanted immediate penal reform. He assured the administrators that no convicts intended to escape, nor did they intend to harm any of the guards.

"You threatened to cut off their fingers if any more shots were fired," said Warden Jarvis.[80] He was clearly frustrated by Knight's rhetoric.

"We could chop off heads instead of fingers," Knight replied, staring directly at the warden before carrying on with his rant.

ONCE KNIGHT LAID OUT the prisoners' general dissatisfaction with life behind bars at Kingston Penitentiary, he went on to air other grievances regarding the new parole act and charges of police brutality.[81]

Before Maloney or Jarvis could respond, the reporters quickly barraged the inmate representatives with questions. Ignoring them, Lester pushed a piece of paper across the table. He informed the group he had written down five demands and the inmates would not answer any further questions.[82] The first demand referred to the need for food:

> Since we will take care of the guard hostages and also the undesirable misfits of 1D, we insist on having control of the kitchen. We will give you a daily list of our needs and will keep it to a minimum.

The demand gave instructions on where the food was to be left each day. It continued:

> We have plenty of food, candy, pop, and potato chips that we could make last for several months if need be. However, if we do not get control of the kitchen we will not feed the guards or the undesirables any food or water whatsoever.

It was later discovered that some of the inmates had been stock-piling food from the canteen, contradicting Knight's assertion that the riot had been a spur-of-the-moment decision.

The inmates' second demand related to medication:

> We want medicine needed by any inmate or hostage. Some men need their daily medication and some need special diet foods. We would like some basics such as aspirin, laxatives etc. It would be helpful if an inmate named Ralph Lundrigan be put in charge of all the medication and that he is free to come and go into the dome area.

Ralph Lundrigan, #7020, was a well-known inmate who worked in the hospital. In his late forties, he was serving a life sentence. He was a well-respected and trusted con amongst the inmate population.

Their third demand stated:

> *We cannot get through to the people in the prison adminis-*
> *tration. Therefore we are requesting the formation of a*
> *citizens' committee to negotiate a peaceful settlement. For*
> *further negotiations we must wait until at least four members*
> *of the noted people we asked for will agree to meet with us.*

Their fourth point addressed the selection of the prisoners' committee:

> *We wish to inform you that any of the inmates that will do*
> *the meeting and negotiating or who will form the inmate*
> *committee have been asked to do this by all of the inmates*
> *and are not doing this on their own.*

Their final statement was clear:

> *If any guards try to force their way into the dome from any*
> *place, they will do so at the peril of the hostages. We do not*
> *wish to harm anyone, our only desire now is to be heard.*

"We want the guns out of our faces and we want food," said Knight. "Then the men will be as quiet as babies."

"The guys are calm now," interjected Lester. Both Knight and Lester urged Warden Jarvis to remove the armed guards who surrounded the prison. "Every time there's a shot, you've got panic," said Knight. "Somebody's going to get killed."

Regional Director Maloney did not like the way the meeting was progressing. He felt the inmates were trying to manipulate the media and he needed to put a stop to it. He took off his horn-rimmed glasses and glanced down at the piece of paper in front of him. He told the three inmates their written demands would be considered. He then left the room, followed by the two other prison officials. The meeting had lasted seventeen minutes.

Following the meeting, Maloney raced back to the warden's office to contact Ottawa. He needed to discuss the inmates' request for a citizens' committee. Approval for such a group was going to have to come from the Commissioner of Penitentiaries, Paul Faguy. In turn, Faguy had to get approval from Solicitor General Jean-Pierre Goyer, the federal minister responsible for prison affairs. Goyer and his wife were already on their way back to Ottawa after cancelling their Caribbean vacation.[83] Goyer would assume overall command of the situation.

Faguy immediately refused the inmates' request for a committee.[84] He recognized some of the names on the potential list and knew they could escalate the situation even further if allowed access to the prisoners. Instead, he suggested sending two citizens of his choice to meet with the inmates. Maloney contacted Knight on the prison phone and relayed the message he had received from Ottawa. Hoping for a quick resolution to the matter, Maloney suggested that Knight take the proposal to the inmate population for a general vote. Knight said no and hung up the phone. They were at a stalemate.

But while communication was going back and forth between Kingston and Ottawa, radio announcer Gerry Retzer had made good on his promise to contact a list of prominent citizens, hoping some of them would agree to be part of an impartial citizens' committee. In fact, three distinguished men from Toronto were already en route to Kingston Penitentiary.

AS THE RIOT'S first full day wore on, the feverish atmosphere of the previous twenty-four hours had eventually died down. Many of the inmates lay awake on their beds, listening to the eerie silence that now engulfed the cavernous cellblocks. Others were sleeping off serious hangovers from homebrew. The most popular prison drinks were made from yeast cakes and tomato juice or potatoes and sugar, but without access to the kitchen, their current supplies would not last long.[85] Some guys were relying on prescription Valium, often supplied to the prisoners by medical staff, to calm their nerves. Pills were a valuable commodity on the inside and could easily be traded for other contraband. All the cell doors were now open, and inmates had the freedom to roam around looking for fun. The night before, according to witnesses, some of the resident drag queens had put on a show. Wearing colorful robes stolen from the Catholic and Protestant chapels, each drag queen strutted across the dome floor to the catcalls and cheers of the prisoners watching from above.

Guards and prison officials patrolling the outside of the main cellblock reported very little movement from within the dome area. However, every few hours, in a show of strength, the inmates could be heard pounding the railings that circled the dome. "The frightening sound brought a chill to my spine," said former inmate Roger Caron, writing about the events years later. "We were too hoarse to holler anymore, and our bodies sagged from fatigue and hunger. Sleep for more than an hour was impossible because of the enforced participation in the drumming," Caron recalled. "The riot leaders didn't want our silence to be interpreted as weakness."

Warden Jarvis was still refusing to allow food into the prison. He thought lack of food might hasten the end of the riot, but he failed to take into account how his decision might affect the hostages.

The six captured guards were feeling the strain of a lack of sleep and hunger. As they entered their first day as hostages, they had no knowledge of what the administration was doing to try to gain their freedom. The guards wrote notes to the warden saying they were doing well and that they wanted their families notified so they wouldn't worry. But they had no way of knowing if their messages were getting out.

The inmate police force had taken turns protecting them throughout the night, but the quiet of day seemed to bring a laxer approach to their security. Other inmates began roaming past their locked cell on B-block, laughing at the imprisoned guards and making wisecracks. The guards said nothing back. Then suddenly, without warning, two of the guys supposedly protecting them turned on them. The inmates unlocked the guards' cell. They grabbed guard Donald Flynn. Flynn began kicking and screaming as the cons dragged him along the top tier towards the railing. "It's the deep six for you, pig," the inmates were overheard saying to the terrified guard.

Flynn had worked at the prison for twenty-three years.[86] He and his wife, Katherine, had one son, who was still in high school. Flynn had never been involved in a prison riot. Now he was in grave danger.

"Out of the way! This pig is going to make a big splash!" yelled one of Flynn's captors to the other inmates. Their plan was to throw the guard over the railing to his death on the cement dome floor.

"Where's he going?" asked Barrie MacKenzie, a member of the inmate police force who had run back to the area when he heard the screaming.

"Into the pool," said the inmate as the other one tried to loosen Flynn's grip on the railing.

"We just drained the pool," replied a seemingly calm MacKenzie.

At the same time, other members of the inmate police force reappeared. Wayne Ford and Brian Beaucage moved carefully towards the two inmates. Realizing they were outnumbered and outmuscled, the one inmate turned to the other. "It's true," he said. "Ain't no water down there."

"Okay," replied the other. "We'll wait until the tide comes in."

There was an unspoken pecking order amongst the inmate population and Ford, Beaucage and MacKenzie were on top. They were powerful, natural leaders according to Roger Caron. Regarded as solid cons doing their time and staying out of other people's business, they weren't to be fucked with.

A distraught Flynn was taken back to his cell. Ford and the other inmates reinforced the door with a second chain and padlock. MacKenzie put the keys in his pocket, making himself the unofficial chief of the inmate police force. The range where the guards were being held was now completely off limits to other prisoners.

LATE THURSDAY AFTERNOON, Knight announced that a television reporter from Toronto would be entering the prison to talk to the hostages and report on the situation inside. Knight had requested the reporter. He wanted a member of the press to tour the prison to dispel any false rumors that might be circulated to the media by angry guards standing outside the prison.

Henry Champ was a handsome 34-year-old news director at CTV in Toronto. Originally from Hartney, Manitoba, Champ started his journalism career as a sportswriter at the *Brandon Sun* in 1960.[87] A large man with a booming voice, Champ was a serious newscaster with an aggressive approach to getting the story. He had attended the first news conference with the inmate committee, and when he heard they were looking for someone to go into the prison, he volunteered right away. He would be the only reporter with a first-hand exclusive on the prison uprising. It was dangerous and the inmates were unpredictable—but he knew he had to go.

10

THE CITIZENS' COMMITTEE

Thursday, April 15, 1971

BEFORE HENRY CHAMP could change his mind, armed prison guards were escorting him down a narrow sixty-foot corridor. At the end of the long passageway, he climbed over a barricade of wet mattresses and other debris piled more than six feet high. Soft drink cans, broken glass and bedsprings littered the walkway. When he reached the other side of the barrier, he was met by a middle-aged convict he recognized from the earlier meeting. It was Manny Lester, the prisoners' unofficial legal counsel. Lester shook his hand and led him towards the central dome.

As Champ entered the rotunda, an unforgettable sight met him. Hundreds of men, all dressed in prison greys, were lined up around the circular tiers directly over his head. They stood in silence, staring down at the newsman. If they decided to attack, he was trapped. Had he been set up? Then a single sound rang out. It was one of the inmates hitting an iron pipe against the railing. Others followed suit. The rhythmic sound grew louder and louder, a symphony of metal hitting metal. Somehow Champ knew this was a signal, a sign of approval. They were okay with him being there.

Champ walked through the destroyed prison and spoke to inmates, many of whom expressed a desire to end the siege peacefully.[88] But Champ wanted to see the hostages. Where were they being kept and what was their condition? He knew that the prison administrators and the families of the guards would be desperate for any information. Knight wouldn't take him to where the guards were being kept but agreed to bring one of the hostages down to meet with him inside the radio room. A cocky Knight also told Champ he could ask the guard any questions he wanted to.

Not long after, Ed Barrett was led into the room. He was blindfolded, with his hands tied behind his back. He was wearing a prisoner's uniform. Barrett looked nervous, unsure of the situation he found himself in. He was introduced to Champ. The senior guard told the reporter he and the others were being treated well and had not been harmed.[89]

After meeting with Barrett, Champ moved freely through the cellblock, speaking to more inmates and listening to their complaints. They quickly warmed up to the congenial outsider. Many of them grumbled about being bored and having little recreation time in prison. They asked him to do what he could to inform the public of their conditions. One guy even asked Champ to tell his wife that he was okay.

Champ's visit inside the prison lasted just over two hours. When he returned to the administrative building, he told Jarvis and Maloney the inmates had treated him well. "It was like a school without teachers," he said. "The convicts would flash me a peace sign, pat me on the back. I even watched TV with them." He said the inmates were acting in a democratic manner and had organized committees. He did not know what the food supply was like, but he had noticed some inmates scurrying around with bread and jars of peanut butter.

Champ said the inmates had set up a security detail to protect the undesirables—the stool pigeons and the sex offenders. He had spoken to some of them and most said they were not afraid, except for one inmate who was hiding under his bed. He told Champ he was going to hang himself and pleaded with the newsman to get him out.

Champ also reconfirmed to the warden and the other administrators that the spark that had ignited the riot was the transfer of some inmates to Millhaven the day before. They knew living conditions and the way they were treated at KP was bad, but they feared Millhaven would be far worse.

Before he left the prison grounds, some of the local reporters asked Champ how he felt as the only civilian allowed inside the prison. The seasoned reporter admitted he was scared. The atmosphere inside was intense. "I don't know how you people would have handled it," he said, "but I didn't ask those guys too many personal questions."

AT 5 P.M. ON THURSDAY AFTERNOON, three men in dark suits arrived at Kingston Penitentiary and were escorted to the deputy warden's office. They had arrived from Toronto to be part of the newly formed citizens' committee the prisoners had requested.

Professor J. Desmond Morton was a feisty Irishman and a well-respected lawyer. He was familiar with the prison as he had several clients in Kingston Pen, including inmate turned author Roger Caron. He was a member of the Faculty of Law at the University of Toronto and a popular commentator in the field of criminal law. He was recovering from a recent heart attack but had still agreed to come to Kingston after hearing his name announced on the radio. An Ontario Provincial Police helicopter had transported him directly to the prison.

Ron Haggart was a renowned investigative journalist and columnist who worked for the *Toronto Telegram*. Born in Vancouver in 1927, he began his journalism career at the University of British Columbia. He then worked at the *Vancouver Sun* before moving to

Toronto. A tall, distinguished man with a distinct stutter, he was a strong advocate for civil rights. "He was a fierce spokesman for those who could not speak for themselves," wrote Pierre Berton of his friend. "He got things done and he got laws changed." When Haggart found out the inmates had requested him, he didn't hesitate. He wasn't afraid of anything.

Haggart called on his friend Aubrey Golden to accompany him. Golden was a barrister and solicitor with extensive experience in labour relations and mediation. He wrote a column on legal issues for the *Toronto Daily Star* and was a frequent speaker on issues involving constitutional reform, collective bargaining, public affairs and censorship. Haggart and Golden had just co-authored a book called *Rumours of War*, which took a critical stand against the Trudeau government for violating civil liberties during the October Crisis of 1970.[90] The proclamation of the War Measures Act, under which hundreds of citizens were arrested and held without trial, was an outrage to Haggart. "He was totally inflamed by the injustice of it," said Golden many years later. "He would stay up all night writing and in those days we used typewriters and they were pretty noisy." The two friends who had just written about one famous Canadian crisis were now back together to try to negotiate the resolution to another.

THE WARDEN AND REGIONAL DIRECTOR met with the three men to brief them. No restrictions or limitations were given, as all of the men were still uncertain about the actual role of the citizens' committee. Plus, the Solicitor General's office had not officially sanctioned their participation in the situation. However, they did understand that the committee had no authority to bind the prison administration or government to any course of action or settlement. Their role was to exercise their best judgment in doing everything that was reasonably possible to bring the riot to a speedy termination and prevent loss of life or injury to the guards and the prisoners.

After their meeting, the prison officials and the three members of the citizens' committee proceeded to the hospital wing. There, the five men stood at a green steel door, the last barrier between the outside world and the main cellblock. They were speaking to Manny Lester and Billy Knight through a small, smashed-out window. Behind the two inmates, Haggart and the others could see a precarious barricade of benches, boards and other junk the prisoners had hastily piled together.

"You have asked us to come here to help you and we are here for that purpose. Now what can we do for you?" asked Desmond Morton.

Lester, who was a little more polished and articulate than Knight, told them that no one wanted to escape and assured them the hostages were safe. "All the men want is a fair hearing and investigation of their grievances." Lester also said the inmates had submitted several hundred notes outlining grievances. "We're processing them now," said Lester.

"We just want this whole farce exposed," Knight added. "We want the outside world to know what they are doing to us in this festering hellhole."

After the brief meeting in the corridor, the prison administrators sensed that the inmates were going to take their time presenting their grievances. Warden Jarvis realized the situation they found themselves in was not ending any time soon. He had to make a critical decision, and he had to keep the welfare of the hostages at the forefront. Jarvis announced that the prisoners would receive sandwiches and milk providing the hostages were given their share of the food.

KNIGHT WAS ANXIOUS to spread the good news: food was on its way. This was progress for Knight, who was beginning to lose credibility within the prison population. Factions were already starting to form against him and he was going to have to show stronger leadership to win them back.

True to his word, Jarvis had food delivered within the hour. The prisoners were ecstatic. Some inmates later recalled how long tables draped in bedsheets with candles from the chapels were set up in the centre of the dome area. It was only sandwiches, but the inmates were going to dine in style.

The prisoners formed a food committee to oversee and organize the fair distribution of the rations. In charge of the committee was inmate #6657, Dave Shepley, a normally gregarious guy in his early twenties who was serving a twelve-year sentence for armed robbery. Shepley had a long criminal record dating back to when he was a teenager. Growing up with eight siblings and an abusive, alcoholic father, he left home when he was fifteen and never returned. At eighteen, brandishing a gun, he robbed Peerless Dairy Store in Windsor, Ontario. He was caught with $187 in a pillowcase and was sentenced to five years in prison. After the dairy store robbery his crimes continued to escalate, and his rap sheet included assault, attempted rape and assaulting a peace officer. For all his time in and out of prison, he had developed a reputation as a strong-willed leader and had earned a healthy respect from other inmates.

Now, standing in the centre of the dome with a megaphone, Shepley monitored the long line of guys waiting to receive their food. It was one bologna sandwich each. No more, no less. When Shepley spotted a prisoner by the name of John McBride in the line a second time, he stopped him. McBride tried to explain that he was picking up a sandwich for his friend Ziggy, who was still passed out. Shepley refused to give him another sandwich. As dozens of inmates looked on, McBride punched Shepley in the jaw. McBride was quickly subdued by two of Shepley's friends.

"Let the kid go!" yelled Brian Beaucage, who was watching the altercation unfold from the second tier of the dome. McBride was released, but the blow had fractured Shepley's jaw in two places. With the warden's permission, he was sent to the hospital. Dr. Amodeo, the penitentiary physician, examined Shepley and suggested he stay in the hospital, but Shepley refused and signed himself out. He wanted to return to the dome to be with his friends.

Days and months later, Shepley's prison associates would relive the bologna sandwich incident. Something had drastically changed in Shepley when he returned to the dome. He was angry. Was it the pressure of the riot that was affecting Shepley's temperament, or was it the punch to the jaw? Regardless, before the riot was over, his change in mood would have fatal consequences.

AT 9 P.M. ON THURSDAY, the first full citizens' committee meeting was held in the hospital treatment room. Two other men from Toronto had joined Aubrey Golden, Desmond Morton and Ron Haggart. Arthur Goldwyn Martin was considered one of the top criminal lawyers in Canada. A graduate of Osgoode Hall Law School, he had been practising criminal law for thirty-three years and was treasurer of the Law Society of Upper Canada. As an advocate of legal reform, Martin had never lost a case in over sixty murder trials he had defended. The fifth committee member was William R. Donkin, a barrister and solicitor and the director of legal aid for York County.

When Knight, Saunders and Lester entered the room, two more inmates, Norman MacCaud and Barrie MacKenzie, joined them. MacCaud, inmate #7622, had been in and out of prison since he had taken part in a grocery store robbery in 1957. He was currently serving three years for forgery and possession of stolen goods. A well-read and opinionated convict, MacCaud had written a 30,000-word brief to the parliamentary committee on penitentiaries in 1967 detailing his experiences at Kingston Pen and what he believed was wrong with prison life.[91] MacKenzie, inmate #5106, was serving time for robbery and assault on a prison guard. Originally from Hamilton, he was another product of the system. As a kid, he had lived in fourteen foster homes before eventually getting caught for stealing and being sent to a reformatory. From there, prison was the next step on the criminal ladder. In 1968, MacKenzie and three other prisoners escaped from Halton County Jail in Milton, Ontario, after beating a guard unconscious with a crutch belonging to one of the escapees. They were all recaptured half an hour later.

As the five convicts settled into their seats for what would be a critical first meeting with the citizens' committee, the rest of the prison population was crowded into the recreation hall to watch the hockey game. It was do or die for the Toronto Maple Leafs in the playoffs against the New York Rangers, and no one would be turning the TV off before the end of the game.

The citizens' committee requested that the first full meeting not include any prison officials. They wanted to hear the inmates' grievances directly and without any input from the administration. As a well-trained journalist, Ron Haggart volunteered to take detailed notes.

The inmates' initial complaints were directed at the administration of the criminal justice system, including the operation of the courts, the police, the punitive nature of sentencing and similar matters. Knight told the attentive men sitting across the table from him that there were dozens of guys in the prison who would swear they were convicted on the basis of lies by the police. "Others will swear they were forced to talk by having their testicles nailed to a chair," he told the committee.

The second list of grievances related to the administration of the penitentiary system in general and Kingston Pen in particular.

The inmates spoke of mass punishments, whereby "the privileges of all would be reduced because of the abuse of a few." For example, if one inmate assaulted a guard, the entire prison might be locked down for days, meaning no recreational activities. They complained about the overuse of solitary confinement in the prison system, lack of meaningful work, manhandling of prisoners by custodial staff and extreme isolation. They also discussed the effects of long sentences and the difficulty of adjusting to society upon release from the penitentiary. Knight reiterated his points about life in the penitentiary being dehumanizing and degrading. He claimed that at least sixteen inmates had committed suicide in the past year, including Brian Hachey, who had deliberately set fire to his cell the preceding Christmas Eve.[92] The nineteen-year-old had only been in Kingston Pen one day when he set his clothing and furnishings on fire and burned to death.

Knight went on to say the prisoners believed the riot was their only means of letting the world know how they were suffering behind prison walls. They were also concerned about mass physical reprisals if and when the insurrection came to an end. Their jailers would want revenge.

At the end of the meeting, the inmates handed over another list of demands they declared would have to be met in order for the protest to come to a peaceful end:

. *Signed assurance from the Commissioner of Penitentiaries that no charges would be laid against any of the prisoners for their actions during the protest.*
. *The inmates to be returned to their cells under the watch of the citizens' committee.*
. *Their grievances to be presented to the administration with the citizens' committee present at a meeting to occur on Friday, April 16, at noon.*

. *The citizens' committee to observe the transfer of inmates to Millhaven.*

. *Prisoners not to be transferred outside Ontario.*

. *Priority in all transfers to be given to younger prisoners, who would be transferred first.*

. *Millhaven to be visited and observed by both the inmates' and citizens' committees under appropriate security.*[93]

The inmate representatives had spoken and the citizens' committee had listened. The five men from Toronto couldn't make any promises or guarantees, but they told the inmates if any harm came to a hostage after the original seizure, those responsible would be fully prosecuted. Knight assured them once again that they desired a non-violent resolution to the riot. The meeting ended just before midnight. The warden agreed with both committees that they would reconvene the following morning at nine.

WHILE THE MEETING was taking place inside the prison, more press and curious onlookers were gathering outside in the dark. Television and radio stations were reporting on emergency negotiations happening behind the walls of Canada's oldest prison. Journalists desperate for any update on the crisis approached weary guards and prison staff as they left the prison. One anonymous guard quoted in the *Kingston Whig-Standard* declared, "It's the do-gooders who got us into this mess, all those damn reformers and civil rights people who seem to forget that we're not dealing with boy scouts, that this is a maximum prison filled with killers and thieves." The guard went on to say, "Rehabilitation? We'll rehabilitate them, but we might just have to hurt a few of them a little bit."

The early press coverage wasn't going to elicit any public sympathy for the rioting inmates. The front page of the *Whig-Standard* carried pictures of the six guards being held captive in the prison.[94]

Underneath their images, one headline read, NO BIRTHDAY STEAK FOR MAN HELD BY REBELLIOUS CONVICTS. Kerry Bushell was spending his twenty-fifth birthday as a hostage instead of being at home celebrating with his 21-year-old bride of eighteen months, Elaine. They were planning a quiet dinner at a restaurant downtown; Elaine told the reporter. "Kerry likes steak, so I guess that's what he would have had," she added. Described as an attractive brunette, Elaine was staying with her parents while waiting for updates on the radio. Earlier in the day she had received a personal telegram from the Solicitor General of Canada: "I wish to express my deepest regret over the present situation at Kingston Penitentiary and I readily understand your concern. I can assure you that every possible action is being taken to effect the release of your husband unharmed."[95] Jean-Pierre Goyer's words did little to alleviate the fears of the young wife. "Are you sure he's going to be all right?" she asked the reporter. "He just has to be all right."

In the same newspaper, another guard's wife was also interviewed. WIFE OF PRISON HOSTAGE NERVOUS BUT CONFIDENT capped a story about Mrs. Edward Barrett. Asked how she felt about her husband being held hostage by prisoners, she replied, "He's a good officer and he likes his work. All we can do is pray for the best and I'm hopeful things will work out."

The press also interviewed Dr. William Amodeo, the prison's physician for seventeen years. He said he was concerned that serious health problems could develop in the prison if the inmates dragged out the uprising. "Gastrointestinal disease can occur quickly," he said, "possibly within three or four days."

Just after midnight, the inmates' committee returned to the dome. Knight intended to call for a general assembly to advise the population about what had taken place during their first meeting with the citizens' committee. Instead, the committee members were met with a chaotic scene. While Knight and the others had been in their meeting, Warden Jarvis had initiated a military response. One hundred and thirty troops from Canadian Forces Base Kingston and Camp Petawawa, armed with fixed bayonets, automatic rifles and tear gas canisters, had arrived in military helicopters. They marched in double formation past the main gates and onto the prison grounds.

Convinced that they were about to storm the prison, the inmates panicked. They began smashing anything that hadn't already been destroyed, lighting fires and shattering more windows. Knight was hysterical. "You pull those guys out of here or you've got problems," he shouted over the phone. Jarvis claimed the soldiers were not there to confront the prisoners. They were there for perimeter control and to augment the prison staff, many of whom had been on duty for more than twenty-four hours.[96]

Feeling they had nothing to lose, a mad prison mob decided they were going to kill one of the hostages. Armed with iron bars, they charged up the stairway towards the range where the guards were being held. There, a dozen inmates, including Wayne Ford and Barrie MacKenzie, who were determined to protect the guards at all costs, confronted them. The mob wanted revenge and they wanted blood. Ford and MacKenzie stood their ground until the gang of convicts finally retreated. The guards were safe for now.

MacKenzie knew the situation was becoming more volatile and the lives of their hostages were in danger. If more inmates got onside with the rebels he had just confronted, they could soon be outnumbered and outpowered. He ran back to the phone in the dome area and demanded to speak to the warden, who was waiting in the hospital wing. MacKenzie was irate. He told Jarvis the appearance of the heavily armed troops was endangering the lives of the hostages. Committee member Ron Haggart took over the phone from the warden to try to convince MacKenzie the soldiers were only additional reinforcements and were not going to storm the prison. Haggart told MacKenzie he had spoken with Major Edward Richmond, the commander of the army task force, who confirmed there would be no attempt to quell the rebellion by force unless more violence erupted. MacKenzie listened to Haggart. He believed what Haggart was telling him. This was the first time the two men had spoken directly, but the phone call had established a trust between the inmate and the reporter, a trust that would prove critical in the days ahead.

Later that night, Warden Jarvis received a letter from one of the kidnapped guards that read: "We are being treated alright at the present time, but they have warned us that they will not be responsible for our safety if you come in shooting. They are now forming a committee to negotiate their terms with Ron Haggart of Toronto." It was signed by Ed Barrett.

KNIGHT CALLED THE inmates to the centre of the dome. He needed to restore order. The stress of the situation and lack of sleep were starting to take a physical toll on him, and others were watching for signs of weakness in the self-appointed leader. Surrounded by his lieutenants, Knight pleaded for common sense. Those bothering to listen recalled his desperate words. "The bunch of you who are running around setting off fires are toying with our lives! If the cellblock goes up in flames, we'll all be trapped." Many of the inmates agreed and banged the railing to signal their support.

"What about the undesirables?" an angry Dave Shepley yelled out. "How come these creeps get a share of our grub? We ought to drag them out here and beat their canary brains in. That will convince the doughboys not to try and rush us."

"No, no, no!" shouted Knight as he rushed towards Shepley. He knew an assault on the undesirables would give the army an excuse to attack. The inmates watched as Knight whispered something in Shepley's ear. Shepley listened and then walked away.

AT TWO O'CLOCK on Friday morning, citizens' committee member Arthur Martin called the Commissioner of Penitentiaries in Ottawa. He had agreed to act as the group's chairman. Martin outlined all of the inmates' requests to Paul Faguy, including the inmates' demand for immunity for the leaders of the riot. Faguy responded quickly with a resounding no. At that moment, Arthur Martin later recalled, he knew they were in for a difficult fight. He also knew that with each passing hour the lives of the kidnapped guards were increasingly in peril.

As the five civilian men in crumpled black suits finally walked out of the prison, heading towards local hotels, the well-armed soldiers stationed around the perimeter of the main cellblock were changing shifts. A reporter from the *Whig-Standard* was also camped out. He noticed a weary guard leaving the prison on his way home for a few hours' sleep. On his way past the soldiers, the guard turned to them and calmly said, "Make just one mistake and you'll be bringing six stiffs out of there."[97]

11
RUMOURS AND RUMBLINGS

Friday, April 16, 1971

ON THE MORNING of Friday, April 16, Collins Bay penitentiary inmate Peter Madden woke up in a great mood. He was still reeling from the events of the night before. Madden's stage play about prison life, called *A Criminal Record*, based on a prisoner's view of life behind bars, had opened the previous evening.[98] It was the first production written by an incarcerated inmate and performed in a Canadian federal penitentiary. Staged in the Protestant chapel at Collins Bay, it had received a positive review in the *Kingston Whig-Standard* that morning. The play portrayed the panic of an inmate who has been in and out of institutions since he was sixteen and is sentenced to five more years in the Pen. Madden, who was serving time for a break-in and theft, told a local reporter he had based much of the play on his time served at Kingston Penitentiary. "I grew up in jail, that's the only thing I know about." He was going to begin working on a film version of the story with the National Film Board soon after his parole the following week.

Collins Bay Institution was located only a mile from Kingston Penitentiary. Opened in 1930, inmates from KP worked on its construction. It was built to accommodate the growing number of federal inmates in the Ontario region. Known as "the Bay" by residents and as "Disneyland North" by Kingston locals due to its fanciful, castle-like structure, the prison operated on a graduated tier of punishment: offenders were placed in maximum-, medium- or minimum-security units based on their crime. The same system did not exist at Kingston Pen, where all of the inmates were housed together, regardless of their crime. Murderers were in the same cell-block as car thieves and counterfeiters. First-time offenders, some as young as seventeen, were working alongside hardened lifers. And in that volatile milieu, no one was putting on a stage play.

Ernest Côté, Canada's Deputy Solicitor General, was planning to attend the opening night of the play with his wife. Penitentiaries Commissioner Paul Faguy was also expected. But neither of them showed up. Instead, they were stuck in Ottawa dealing with the ongoing crisis at Kingston Penitentiary.

In fact, Côté and Faguy were meeting with the Solicitor General and acting prime minister Edgar Benson that very morning. Prime Minister Trudeau was still on his honeymoon. An emergency federal cabinet meeting had been convened to brief the ministers on the unfolding drama in Kingston. In a document labelled 'Secret,' their discussions were recorded.[99]

Faguy briefed the ministers on the riot details to date, while the Solicitor General shared the prisoners' six requests that had been outlined to them by the citizens' group. Regarding the current situation within the prison, Faguy stated that the Penitentiary Service felt the environment was deteriorating quickly but there was not any danger to the guards yet. However, he admitted to the gathered politicians that he did not know whether a move to reoccupy the prison would affect the lives of the hostages. While not cheapening the value of the life of a penitentiary officer, Faguy suggested kidnapping and murder were hazards of the occupation.

And in most instances, the longer a hostage was in the hands of his captors, the more dangerous the situation became.

He outlined two possible approaches: the soft one, which was to accept the prisoners' demands, and the hard one, which was to say the government would not give in to threats.

Solicitor General Jean-Pierre Goyer expressed apprehension about the citizens' committee. He was concerned about them keeping the inmates' demands confidential. After all, he knew Ron Haggart was a reporter, and they did not want the list of demands released to the press. He proposed sending a directive to the inmates and giving them until Saturday to decide what they wanted to do. He could then issue a press release on the same day to prepare the public.

He was giving the inmates forty-eight hours. The authorities would then proceed with force before Monday, and preferably during daylight hours on Sunday if an agreement could not be reached. Goyer proposed using guards armed with shotguns to retake the prison while military soldiers would continue to protect the perimeter.

Acting prime minister Benson wanted to know if the inmates would attack the guards if they felt threatened. Goyer assured the cabinet the inmates would not kill the guards and would likely give up on their own once they had time to think the matter through for themselves. Benson said that in talking to the inmates, it was important to assure them they would not be attacked if they surrendered.

AT NINE ON FRIDAY MORNING, Ron Haggart and the other men on the citizens' committee reconvened in a room in the prison's hospital to meet with the committee of inmates. Knight, Saunders, MacKenzie and MacCaud returned, but Lester, the inmates' legal adviser, was a no-show.

The meeting began with Knight arguing for total immunity for those involved in the riot. He agreed immunity from prosecution should only extend to the acts associated with the original assault and kidnapping of the guards but would not include any further potential harm done to the hostages. He said he did not trust the Commissioner of Penitentiaries to give such an assurance of immunity. He wanted a signed agreement from the Solicitor General. Knight then advised the men on the citizens' committee that the hostages would be released on a pro rata basis as the inmate population was evacuated safely from the prison. He proposed one hostage for every one hundred inmates. Knight and the others knew there were angry guards on the other side of the prison walls waiting for them to emerge. They would leave the prison only if their safety was assured.

Arthur Martin was in a precarious situation. As the acting chairman of the committee, he had already spoken to Paul Faguy, the Commissioner of Penitentiaries, and he knew the inmates were not going to be given any immunity. Martin calmly advised Knight and the other inmates sitting in front of him that none of them would be granted any form of immunity from prosecution but the Commissioner was willing to review their other grievances.

Knight exploded. Jumping from his chair, he began pacing back and forth. He knew he had to take some reassurances back to the rest of the prisoners, who were growing more restless and frustrated as the riot wore on.

"Without promise of total immunity, we won't guarantee the safety of the hostages," said Knight.

Martin was taken aback by Knight's outburst. Now he was even more concerned about the immediate well-being of the kidnapped guards. He quickly assured Knight they were doing everything possible to achieve a positive outcome for everyone. He pointed out the citizens' committee were only intermediaries and as such had no real authority to dictate any deals to the government. However, he promised to speak to the Commissioner again about their request for immunity. As Knight continued his diatribe against the politicians, William Donkin, the director of legal aid for York County, spoke up. He promised Knight that if anyone was charged as a result of the insurrection, they would be properly defended, with full resources from the legal aid system.

Knight sat down. He and the other inmates huddled together, whispering back and forth. Donkin hoped his offer hadn't fallen on deaf ears, while Martin worried they were at a dangerous stand-off. As the lawyers sat in awkward silence, Knight leaned across the table and uttered a surprise announcement. "As an act of good faith, we are prepared to release one hostage."

JUST AFTER NOON on Friday, the inmates gathered in the dome area. Witnesses later recounted that a stressed Knight informed the crowd that the inmates' committee had decided to release one of the hostages as an act of diplomacy and to dispel some of the ugly rumours being fed to the media by guards on the outside. Luckily for Knight, the majority agreed. "Who will it be, boys?" Knight asked. "Let's put it to a vote."

As the prisoners assembled inside the prison to vote on which guard would get to go home to his family, more people were gathering outside the prison gates. "We could see hordes of men and women in what appeared to be a carnival atmosphere," wrote former inmate Roger Caron in his book *Bingo!* "The news media were everywhere, even perched in nearby trees, all trying to get an exclusive shot."

Caron also recalled seeing groups of young demonstrators brandishing large banners that read *We support the prisoners' cause.* When the inmates saw those signs, they were hopeful their message was getting out to the world. "It took a lot of guts and conviction for those kids to back us up like that," recounted Caron. "Especially in the midst of the enemy—off-duty guards who were continually feeding the media vicious rumours."

With more media descending on the prison, reporters were desperate for any news about what was going on inside, the more salacious the better. Inmates sitting in their cells listening to transistor radios were hearing reports about gang rapes of young prisoners, mutilations, sodomy and assaults on the guards. "No rapes occurred during the riot," declared Roger Caron. "Any convict caught committing such an act would have been torn apart by the prison population in much the same fashion as an undesirable would have been treated. Of course there was sex during the riot, but only among willing parties. If a blanket was hung over the door of a cell you didn't go in."

With each false story being spread, more anger and resentment was building towards the prison administration, who appeared to be doing nothing to dispel the allegations. The inmates hoped an act of good faith, the release of a guard, would help to dismiss much of the misinformation being circulated.

BIG WAYNE FORD approached the cold, dank cell where the hostages were being kept and removed the heavy padlock and chain. Ford ordered Terry Decker to step forward. Decker, the guard who had originally ordered Billy Knight to tuck in his shirt, providing the spark that ignited the riot, was being taken away. The other guards watched but could do nothing. Decker's knees buckled as other members of the inmate police force surrounded him with their weapons. Two of them grabbed his arms to keep him upright.

Decker was led down the long tier towards the dome. Moving towards the balcony forty feet up from the dome floor, Decker was convinced his death was near. But before he reached the railing, he was led down the winding metal staircase past groups of prisoners. No one said a word to him, but he could feel their eyes watching his every move. He was then blindfolded and led out of the dome area, where he struggled to climb over the many obstacles and barriers that had been erected to keep anyone from entering.

Barrie MacKenzie took Decker's arm and told him he was being set free. "It pays not to be a dog," the inmate told him. Decker thought it was a joke. He was toying with him. They continued down a long corridor as Decker tried to get his bearings. Where was MacKenzie taking him? Then he heard a gate open and an unfamiliar voice. It was Ron Haggart from the citizens' committee.

When his blindfold was removed, Decker saw an eager group of his colleagues waiting for him. He told Haggart he was tired but unharmed.

"Where did you get the black eye?" a fellow guard immediately asked.[100]

"I walked into a door," Decker replied before being rushed away by the warden's staff.

The waiting press were desperate to interview Decker about his ordeal. But within a few hours of being released, reporters were told Decker, his wife and their three-month-old baby girl had left the Kingston area for a paid vacation out of town. The citizens' committee released a statement that quoted Decker saying he and the other hostages had been treated well. "They treated us with respect, calling us sir, boss and even mister," said Decker. "For every sandwich they got we received two and the same thing went for coffee," he added. But despite the press release, rumours continued to swirl around Decker's condition, and local radio stations broadcast stories that claimed Decker had been beaten and was on the verge of a nervous breakdown. Infuriated by these reports, the inmates' committee demanded the administration correct the false accusations. Finally, late in the day an official statement was released from the Solicitor General's department in Ottawa, stating Decker was freed "unharmed and in good health."[101]

A prison official did advise the gathered press that the remaining five hostages would be paid eight dollars an hour, twice their regular rate, because they were considered to be working overtime. "And they'll keep getting that until they are released," he added.

SHORTLY AFTER THE release of Decker, Ron Haggart and Arthur Martin were asked to fly to Ottawa for an emergency meeting with Solicitor General Goyer and his staff. A Canadian Armed Forces helicopter picked them up that afternoon and Deputy Warden Edgar Babcock accompanied them. But just before they left for Ottawa, inmate committee member Norman MacCaud spoke with reporters and described the mood in the cellblock as tense. "The prisoners' biggest concern is keeping open lines of communication with prison officials," he said. "The inmates are calm, but there is a mood of tension because this thing has been going on for two days now."

At four o'clock on Friday afternoon in Ottawa, Haggart, Martin and Babcock met with the Solicitor General and his staff, including Deputy Solicitor General Ernest Côté, Commissioner of Penitentiaries Paul Faguy and the Deputy Commissioner of Penitentiaries, John Braithwaite.[102] Martin presented the list of requests that the committee of inmates had made on Thursday evening. He later testified that he tried to persuade the Solicitor General that, in light of the particular circumstances of the case and because Kingston Penitentiary as a maximum-security institution was scheduled to be closed, the granting of immunity from prosecution would not create a dangerous precedent. The citizens' committee members knew that amnesty (on condition the hostages were released unharmed) was an essential condition to resolving the occupation without bloodshed. But the bureaucrats wouldn't budge. Immunity from prosecution was not going to be granted.

The meeting lasted for seventy minutes. Before leaving the offices of the Solicitor General, Haggart telephoned the other members of the citizens' committee, who had been eagerly standing by in their hotel rooms. He had disappointing news: Ottawa wasn't moving on their position. He suggested a third meeting with the inmates' committee that evening, as soon as he and Martin returned to Kingston.

With the disappointing update from Ottawa, the three lawyers returned to the prison to await the return of Haggart and Martin, but they were soon confronted with a new and troubling situation. As they approached the prison, they could see a dozen camouflaged army vehicles lined up along King Street outside the main gates of the prison. The convoy included a mobile hospital, a radio unit and a field kitchen. Two military helicopters hovered above as battle-dressed soldiers exited the military trucks and marched towards the front gates. Armed with three-foot riot sticks and wire mesh shields, sixty riot-trained troops from the Third Battalion, Royal Canadian Regiment at Camp Petawawa filed onto the prison grounds. More trucks loaded with rolls of barbed wire, wooden poles and barricades were lined up for inspection at the prison's loading dock.[103] One truck carried boxes of gas masks.

Adding to the chaos outside the prison, reporters were scrambling to get a lead on why additional military support had been called in. As one newsman from the *Whig-Standard* recalled, "Gaining information regarding the khaki-clad squads was akin to pulling hens' teeth."[104] It was finally discovered that Warden Jarvis had requested the additional troops, but prison officials weren't saying why. "The troops will augment some of the usual guards at KP, but they are not there for confrontation," said the military press release.

"Are those rifles loaded?" a young reporter asked Major Edward S. Richmond, the commanding officer.

"They may be," replied the husky-voiced veteran soldier. At six foot four, the towering native of Edmonton was an intimidating figure.[105] He then cautioned the newsman to beware of the deadly bayonets the soldiers were carrying. "Not that some of you couldn't use a haircut," he chuckled as he disappeared behind the prison gates.

As the cool spring day faded to dusk, another military truck arrived carrying small green trailers. When the contents of each were released, curious newsmen and spectators quickly stood back. Riot-trained German shepherd dogs—two to each trailer— were now patrolling the penitentiary grounds.[106]

12

UNDER NEW MANAGEMENT

Friday, April 16–Saturday, April 17, 1971

WHEN HAGGART AND MARTIN returned from Ottawa in the early evening, the atmosphere at the penitentiary had changed dramatically. With the increased military presence outside the prison, hundreds of inmates had gathered in the dome. The rhythmic pounding of their defiance, metal against metal, grew louder and louder. They were preparing for an all-out military attack. But what did that mean for the hostages?

"They are in critical danger," a nervous John Maloney told Haggart and Martin. Deputy Warden Chinnery agreed: "I'm certain that the officers' lives are now in jeopardy." They needed to resume negotiations with the prisoners immediately.

The administration had also received word that an inmate in the general population had been viciously attacked. Accused by others of being an informer, several prisoners had beaten him in his cell. Others found him covered in blood, hiding under his bed. He was rushed to the hospital, but word throughout the cellblocks was that some of the hard-core inmates were on the prowl for other stoolies.

AT 1 A.M., THE FIVE-MAN citizens' committee and the four-man inmates' group met in the prison hospital. Arthur Martin wasted little time in telling the inmates that while the Solicitor General would agree to most of their requests, he would not grant them immunity from prosecution. Knight was furious. "It's an act of bad faith!" he yelled.

MacKenzie, who wasn't facing any additional charges arising from the prison takeover, tried to calm Knight down. "Dummy up, just dummy up, we're getting tired of your bullshit," he told Knight.

In contrast to Knight, who was being argumentative and unreasonable, MacKenzie, a 27-year-old from Hamilton, was beginning to show greater control over the current situation. Serving an eight-year prison sentence for assault on a prison guard, MacKenzie was a clean-cut, muscular guy who was known as a con's con—tough as nails and well respected. He adhered to the prisoners' code and wasn't afraid to stick his neck out to help others.

Initially, the citizens' committee members had been concerned by MacKenzie's cool demeanour, but now he was emerging as a more rational leader. Perhaps Knight was not the eloquent spokesman for prison reform that he presented himself to be.[107] Haggart and the others were beginning to realize that Billy Knight had no other reality than his own. His grandiose plans to publicly expose prison conditions were, in the words of another inmate, "Billy's own little ego trip."

Norman MacCaud spoke up and said it was clear no immunity was going to be granted. "We've gone as far as anyone could expect us to go," he said to the group. He was leaning towards the settlement that Martin was proposing, which Ottawa had agreed to in principle. If the prisoners surrendered peacefully, their grievances would be presented to an appropriate board or tribunal, with the participation of the citizens' committee if necessary. In

addition, as Donkin had promised, any inmates charged criminally would receive proper legal representation.

Divisions and personality conflicts in the inmate committee
were becoming obvious. Knight kept saying that amnesty was
still possible. "You're the only one who's saying that," MacKenzie
told him.

The men on the citizens' committee were also reaching the
end of their patience with Knight. Arthur Martin suddenly slapped
the edge of the table with his hand and yelled, "You have a choice
between hanging for capital murder of a prison guard or accepting
charges of kidnapping."

MacKenzie also turned on Knight. He was sick of listening to
his rhetoric about exposing prison conditions. "We don't want
your ping-pong prizes," he said. "Most of your grievances are silly.
The object is to get the guys out of here."

As the meeting dragged on, the inmates still wanted assurances that if they did surrender, there would be no physical reprisals
from the guards. "All we ask is the Solicitor General give us his
word we will not be mistreated," said Knight in a voice hoarse from
fatigue.

"Some of us have reason to fear we might be attacked once the
guards get their chance with us," added the usually quiet Charles
Saunders.

MacKenzie then reintroduced the "pro rata arrangement."
One hostage would be released for every one hundred prisoners
when proof was obtained that none of the inmates had been
harmed. MacKenzie went on to suggest the government announce
the release of the hostages but refrain from publicizing the transfer
of the inmates to other institutions. "That saves the government
the embarrassment of giving in to our demands," he pointed out.
"The public won't know the government made a deal with us."

"That," said Martin, "is a most reasonable request."

Martin and other members of the citizens' committee later testified that they agreed with the pro rata arrangement but thought the prisoners were being overly paranoid about vengeance from the prison guards.

Haggart also wanted the inmates to realize their time at Kingston Penitentiary was over. "You understand that because the main cellblock is totally destroyed, you can all expect to be transferred to other institutions."

"Yeah, like Millhaven," added MacKenzie with a short laugh.

Just before the meeting ended at two thirty in the morning, Knight reluctantly gave in. "So be it, we'll take our chances in criminal court," he said. "But we're going to have to do a lot of convincing to get the diehards to give up and release the hostages."

"Can you put it to a vote?" asked Aubrey Golden.

"It won't be that easy," continued Knight. "Without a majority of the inmates agreeing, a settlement won't be achieved."

"He's right about that," said MacKenzie as he stood up and walked out of the room with Ron Haggart's cigarettes.

The men on the citizens' committee were exhausted. But when the meeting ended, they felt confident they had set in motion a plan for the peaceful termination of the riot. "We began, slowly, to see what our role had to be, although curiously, we never really articulated it to each other," recalled Haggart. "We had to help the prisoners lose in the military sense of arranging their retreat from the territory they occupied, without letting them lose hope." Haggart and the others were optimistic the prison population would vote to accept the terms of the agreement. The committee would then be able to work out a plan for the safe release of the hostages and the transfer of prisoners.

As Knight and his group returned to the dome for a late-night vote, the committee members walked over to the Warden's House across the street to report on their progress to Maloney and Jarvis. Maloney scribbled down notes, which outlined the following:

1) *No immunity from prosecution*
2) *Nobody will go back to the government for a rebuttal*
3) *No bargaining about who is to come out or where they are to go*
4) *Pro rata arrangement for release of guards. One hostage for one hundred inmates*
5) *Right to present grievances with assistance of counsel and right of citizens' committee to observe if required.*

Maloney then called Ottawa. He read his notes over the phone to the Commissioner of Penitentiaries, who agreed that the terms of the arrangement were acceptable to the government. "We have a deal," said a relieved Maloney when he got off the phone. It was the answer everyone in the room was hoping for.

Feeling they had accomplished what they set out to do, the five-man citizens' committee left the prison at four in the morning. Arthur Martin and Aubrey Golden decided to drive back to Toronto, while the three other members of the committee opted to stay and make certain the transfer of hostages went smoothly. As the three men drove to their local hotel, they tuned in to a late-night newscast on the radio and heard the Solicitor General, Goyer, being quoted as saying he was dealing with the riot and he would not be making any concessions for the prisoners. Goyer went on to say everything was under control and the government was in no hurry to make any decisions. He then added that the presence of the armed soldiers was terrifying the inmates.

Ron Haggart, Desmond Morton and William Donkin were shocked by what they had just heard. Why was Goyer lying? He had gone on national radio and said the government was not willing to negotiate with the rioting inmates. He had just destroyed their deal—a deal they had made in good faith with the prisoners' committee, who were sticking their necks out to get the rest of the prison population on board.

But what was more distressing was knowing the inmates at Kingston Pen were likely listening to the same news bulletin on their transistor radios inside the prison. The rioting prisoners were tired, hungry and desperate. Now the whole situation was about to explode. Goyer was bluffing, but he was playing with the lives of the hostages. Had he just signed their death warrants?

Ron Haggart barely got into his hotel room before he threw up in the toilet. The stress of the past thirty-six hours had finally caught up with the seasoned newsman.

WHILE THE INMATES' committee had been in closed-door negotiations for most of the night, the rest of the prison population were trying to survive any way they could. Anticipating a long siege, some of the inmates erected more barriers and booby traps at possible entrance points to the dome area. Loose bricks, steel dinner trays and pails of water were carted up to the top tier of the dome, to be launched at any invading forces. Other prisoners stayed in their cells. They played cards and listened to the news reports. Rumours were flying and distrust was building. Fights were breaking out and inmates were showing up at the prison hospital with injuries inflicted on one another.

Another segment of the population sought relief by getting high. Roger Caron recalled one young prisoner who put on a memorable show while stoned out of his mind on hobby craft glue. Dangling from the top tier of the dome, yelling profanities, the boy threatened to plunge to his death if someone didn't give him drugs. Luckily for him, three members of the prison police force pulled him to safety. Soon after, Barrie MacKenzie confiscated a large pail of glue and poured it down the drain.

At four o'clock on Saturday morning, drowsy inmates were roused from their cells and told there was another meeting and a vote taking place in the dome. Attendance was not optional. Slowly the inmates gathered. They came in groups and in pairs. Fear had pushed everyone into the buddy system.

Using a megaphone to amplify his gravelly voice, Knight called for silence. Standing beside him were inmate committee members MacKenzie and MacCaud. In the front row of the gathering, staring directly at Knight, were Dave Shepley, Brian Beaucage and a few others. Described as a bunch of young punks by other inmates, they were visibly agitated. The group included those who had earlier tormented the undesirables in 1-D.

Knight began his speech by saying the negotiations were proceeding well and they were hopeful for a peaceful resolution.

"You're full of shit!" yelled Beaucage as he grabbed Knight by the throat and swung a metal bar at his head.

MacKenzie lunged at Beaucage. "Take it easy!" shouted MacKenzie.

"He's just so full of shit, gambling our lives away like that," Beaucage yelled.

"Go easy, man," said MacKenzie, trying to defuse the situation.

Beaucage suddenly grabbed the megaphone from Knight. "You've had it, you're through talking," he told a stunned Knight.

The inmates had indeed heard the Solicitor General on the radio saying he was not prepared to negotiate with the rioters. They were fed up with being jerked around. They weren't being told the truth. Beaucage and his angry gang were becoming more aggressive and unpredictable. Words meant nothing to them. They were prepared to fight. As Roger Caron later wrote, "What was building up inside the dome was a mass suicide pact orchestrated by the insane element."

MacKenzie grabbed the megaphone back from Beaucage. A chorus of voices from the circular gallery began yelling, "Let Knight have his say."

"We've lost our civil rights and now we are on the verge of losing our human rights," a visibly shaken Knight declared when he was back in possession of the bullhorn. As much as he tried to reassure the inmates he was working towards an agreeable resolution for all, it was clear to those listening that Knight was no longer in charge. Barrie MacKenzie was, and no vote was going to take place.

ACROSS THE STREET from the main prison gate, the lights were still on in the warden's office. Sydney Roberts, an information officer with the Solicitor General's office, sat in a corner of the office under a picture of Queen Elizabeth. He stared at the newspapers on the table in front of him. convicts wreck prison—hold out for talks, read the headline in the *Kingston Whig-Standard*. FIVE HUNDRED PRISONERS RIOT AT KINGSTON, SIX HOSTAGES HELD, announced the *Toronto Daily Star*. KP DAMAGE SET AT ONE MILLION, stated the *Globe and Mail*. Maloney, Jarvis and Babcock paced the room. There would be no sleep for any of them.

Earlier in the evening, Roberts had spoken with reporters to update the press on the negotiations going on inside.[108] He said the mood of the inmates was one of determination, with no sign of surrendering. He was convinced the prisoners, if necessary, would kill the hostages.[109] He claimed to have spoken with some inmates who told him that certain members of the prison population felt they had nothing to lose. If they failed to gain some concessions or if the troops moved in to break up the rebellion, they would kill the five guards. Roberts said the inmates had homemade weapons, steel bars and pieces of metal, but no guns or knives. "It's a heads-down situation," he reiterated. "No agreement for the release of hostages has been reached." He then advised the press that the Solicitor General's office would not be releasing any further information.

Roberts was not going to tell the reporters what he really knew: the inmates had less than twenty-four hours to surrender peacefully before the prison would be retaken by force. The directive from Ottawa was clear.

In the eerie stillness of early Saturday morning, the steady beat of marching boots on concrete could be heard through the broken windows of the prison. As uniformed soldiers marched double time along the outer wall of the prison, they passed under a ragged Canadian flag suspended from a makeshift flagpole.[110] Underneath the flag, a dirty white bedsheet hung against the grey stone walls. Sprawled in black paint were three words: *Under New Management*.

A REQUEST TO TRANSFER

Kingston Penitentiary, August 2, 1970

ASSISTANT WARDEN ED Babcock loved his job. He'd joined the Penitentiary Service in his early twenties and had worked his way up through the ranks. But some days were harder than others and today was going to be a long one. An inmate had been stabbed in the recreation yard the day before in front of several officers, and it was Babcock's job to investigate the incident. Relations between the custodial staff and administration were already tense because of recent cutbacks and understaffing, but Babcock had a job to do. As was customary in these circumstances, he would conduct a board of inquiry to determine if there were any witnesses to the incident and if any charges would be laid. The Penitentiary Service preferred to deal with these kinds of situations internally. But unfortunately, these incidents seemed to be getting more frequent.

Babcock blamed it on overcrowding. The prison had too many inmates and not enough staff. For the latest attack in the rec yard, Babcock had his work cut out for him.

At approximately 4 p.m. on August 1, inmate #6709, Bertrand Henry Robert, was stabbed in the chest while in the recreation yard. It was Robert's first day out in the general population since his arrival at Kingston Pen two months earlier. He was serving a ten-year prison term for multiple counts of assault on his own children but had never been in prison before.

At the time of the stabbing, there were five prison guards on duty—two in the yard, one in the cage, one in the southeast tower and one outside the yard. When questioned by Assistant Warden Babcock, none of the officers recalled seeing anything unusual in the exercise yard at the time of the incident and none of them saw Robert get stabbed.

Babcock asked the witnesses if they were aware of any plot to attack Robert. Several of them stated they thought there might be, but they hadn't taken it too seriously. Word of his crimes had travelled quickly through the prison population. Everyone despised child abusers.

As his final witness for the inquiry, Babcock called Bertrand Robert. A meek, skinny guy, he remained calm and cooperative during the interview. While describing the events that took place in the exercise yard the day before, Robert said he had been sitting in the bleachers watching the guys play baseball. "I was sitting there for about half an hour when I got hit on the back of the head with a fastball," he told Babcock. Then fellow inmates threw rocks at him, almost hitting him in the head twice. Later, when he was leaving the yard, a group of men cornered him. "I got a real solid blow to the chest. Then I realized I'd been stabbed."

"Could you identify the inmates who stabbed you?" asked Babcock.

"I don't think I could positively identify them," Robert replied.

Babcock knew he was lying. To identify his attackers would be fatal for Robert. Babcock then asked Robert if there was anything else he wished to add that would assist the board of inquiry. "I just wish they would ban newspapers in penitentiaries," Robert replied. He knew the other inmates had read about his trial. "I feel quite safe where I am right now, and that is where I would like to stay." Robert was in 1-D, the dissociation range.

In his investigation into the stabbing, Babcock concluded that the incident had indeed occurred but, like many other similar attacks, no one had seen or witnessed it. Since Robert wasn't willing to identify his attackers, no one would be charged. The official inquiry made three recommendations:

1)   *that Robert be segregated for protection;*
2)   *that Robert be considered for transfer to an institution outside Ontario as soon as possible; and*
3)   *that, wherever possible, inmates with known similar offences be placed under close surveillance.*

Babcock signed his summary and submitted it to Warden Jarvis for review. Jarvis agreed with the first two recommendations but not the third. Jarvis felt a greater degree of surveillance would result in increased segregation for these kinds of inmates. He believed most inmates who were jailed for what he deemed "repugnant crimes" could eventually make the grade within the inmate population.

As institutional protocol demanded, Regional Director John Maloney also received a copy of the board's findings. He concurred with Babcock's conclusions and the remarks by Jarvis. "Cases such as those like inmate Robert are a problem," he wrote. "Most of them do eventually fit into the population and long-term dissociation is undesirable."

Maloney also suggested he wasn't in favour of transferring inmates in need of protection. "I don't have much faith in transfers these days," he said. "However," he added, "I direct Roberts' case to be brought to the attention of the Inmate Training Board and considered for transfer out of the province."

One month later, Robert applied for a transfer to a penitentiary in British Columbia. He stated he feared for his life and did not want to spend the rest of his sentence in permanent lockup.

His transfer was denied.

13
A LONG DAY AHEAD

Saturday, April 17, 1971

RON HAGGART WOKE to the sound of the phone ringing in his Kingston hotel room. He looked over to see the small red light flashing. What time was it? He'd had a hard time unwinding when he got back from the prison at 5 a.m. As a seasoned journalist, he was accustomed to late nights with little sleep, but he had never been in a situation like this. He knew the pressure was building both inside and outside the prison, and something had to give.

Bill Donkin and Desmond Morton were on the phone. The two lawyers sounded panicked and asked Haggart to return to the prison as soon as he could. The government's deadline for an end to the riot was Monday at noon. If the prisoners did not surrender by that time, the well-armed military surrounding KP would retake the prison by force. Donkin and Morton had telephoned Arthur Martin and Aubrey Golden in Toronto to ask them to drive back to Kingston. The two men were already on their way.

The clock radio on the bedside table in Haggart's room read 12:00 p.m. Narrow bars of light peeked through the heavy hotel curtains. Haggart stumbled out of bed and wasted little time in getting out the door. He and the other committee members had to persuade the inmates to surrender. The government had issued its ultimatum and it wasn't going to back down. The riot was an embarrassment to them, and the Solicitor General needed to prove to the public that he wasn't going to negotiate with kidnappers. Haggart knew the next twenty-four hours would prove critical in gaining the trust of the inmates. If the citizens' committee couldn't get the prisoners onside, the 44-year-old newsman feared the more rebellious, hard-core cons would incite a battle they couldn't possibly win.

By Saturday afternoon, Barrie MacKenzie unexpectedly found himself in the role of chief negotiator, and he knew the prisoners' bargaining power with the government was diminishing with each passing hour. He also knew the atmosphere inside Kingston Pen was rapidly deteriorating. Nerves were frayed and tempers were short. Distrust amongst the inmate factions was escalating and more fights were breaking out over scarce necessities such as food and blankets to keep warm. MacKenzie wanted a peaceful resolution and felt most of the prison population was ready to end the riot despite having no assurances against reprisals. But no one was willing to step forward and say they were in favour of giving up. "What about a silent vote?" a few of the inmates proposed. MacKenzie was in agreement, but he knew Brian Beaucage and the smaller, radical group would insist on an open vote, and no one was going to go against them. MacKenzie also had no desire to take on Beaucage and his brooding gang. He knew they were just itching for a reason to turn violent.

OUTSIDE THE PRISON, crowds continued to grow along King Street, with more news cameras and reporters setting up their equipment. A few dozen people, mostly university students, were camped on the grass across the street in front of the Warden's House. Among the crowd was a 24-year-old parolee from Collins Bay Institution.[111] He refused to give his name but, he was happy to talk to reporters about what he perceived to be the main causes of the riot. "What they're looking for is to be treated like human beings," he said. "In prison they herd people around like animals. The government is not getting its money's worth if it expects prisons to rehabilitate inmates."

Another spectator, a pretty young woman, carried a sign that read *Penal Reform Is Necessary!*[112] She told a reporter, "We feel the prisoners' demands are justified."

As spectators continued to gather and chatter amongst themselves, Don Dutton, a well-respected *Toronto Daily Star* reporter and photographer, noticed a burly, well-dressed man standing away from the crowd, chain-smoking. There was something different about the guy. He stood out from the university students and curious gawkers. On a hunch, Dutton approached the man. He turned out to be a former long-term resident of KP. He'd done fifteen years for murder.

"They run in packs in there," he told the reporter. "You have to. No one man can protect himself."

Dutton asked the ex-con if he thought the hostages were in danger. "Holding them just gives the packs time to organize their power play," he said. He predicted they would eventually be freed unharmed. The man explained he'd lived through four days of hell during the 1954 riot, when the place went up in flames. Calling himself a businessman, he said he'd been paroled in 1966 and had no intention of ever stepping foot in any prison again.

Across town, more protesters assembled at the historic City Hall. A group calling themselves Red Morning had driven to Kingston from Toronto the night before.[113]

A spokesman for the group described them as a revolutionary collective. Holding placards that read *All Prisoners Are Political*

Prisoners and *We Support the Struggle of Our Brothers in Kingston,* they were demanding the federal government negotiate with the prisoners.

In response to the support they were receiving, the inmates hung more banners from the broken prison windows. *Justice* was written on one, while another had a peace sign and said *Thanks for Your Support.*

The administrative building across the street from the prison was now operating as a makeshift press centre, but no one was getting any information about what was happening inside. Ottawa had imposed a news blackout when the Solicitor General's office learned that reporters were calling in to the dome area and talking directly to prisoners. This meant no further press conferences or releases, so eager journalists were chasing down any titillating story prison employees were willing to offer. "You won't believe what is going on in there," said one guard as he puffed on a ciga-rette. "Unbelievable atrocities."

It didn't take long for the ugly rumours to spread. Inmates sitting in their cells listening to transistor radios heard the local station reporting on supposed gang rapes, castrations and muti-lations. They were being portrayed as animals.

Angered by the salacious media reports, some of the prison population regretted releasing Terry Decker as an act of "good faith," while others talked of physical retaliation against the kidnapped guards. If the screws wanted something to talk about, they'd give them a story to report on. When word of the allegations reached the prisoners' committee, the members knew they had to prove the lies were untrue. They needed the public to be on their side if they were going to get any concessions from the government.

Billy Knight was irate. He started ranting about getting on TV to make a plea for public sympathy. Others on the prisoners' com-mittee told him he was being unrealistic. He then said he wanted one of the citizens' committee members to tour the cellblocks so they could see what was actually going on. Knight got on the phone and asked to speak with Morton. He wanted to know if the Irishman was willing to go into the prison to prove there wasn't any truth to the horror stories that were being circulated. Morton was still frail from his recent heart attack and Regional Director Maloney was against it, feeling the situation inside was too volatile. But Morton needed the inmates to trust him. "I'm going in," he told Haggart and the other men.

Within the hour, Morton was standing in the centre of the dome amid piles of debris. Hundreds of inmates stared down at him from the circular galleries above. There was an eerie calm, but Morton did not feel in danger. As he mingled with the prisoners, the men told him things were under control and none of them were at risk. They wanted the outside world to know the truth. They weren't brutalizing one another, and the vicious lies being told to the media by off-duty guards on the outside of the prison were only going to escalate the situation. But the prisoners refused Morton's request to visit the kidnapped guards. The inmates protecting the hostages did not want anyone from the outside to know where they were being held. They assured Morton their captives were unharmed.

Morton walked through the darkened cellblocks, including 1-D, where the undesirables were held. He waded through the grimy water that had pooled on the cement floor after the previous hose attack. Most of the men peered out from the backs of their narrow cells, staring as Morton walked past. But a few were desperate to talk to someone from the outside. "We're going to be set on fire and burned to death in our cells," said one inmate. "They are tormenting us," said another. Morton assured them they were safe; the riot leaders would protect them from any further attacks. He would later be haunted by his comforting words to the inmates on 1-D.

When Morton returned from the dome area, he felt more confident that the two committees could reach a peaceful resolution. Sitting around a table in the airless hospital wing, they prepared a carefully worded press release they hoped would dispel any further gossip or hearsay about what was happening inside the prison. The press release stated:

. *The hostages are safe, in good health and are not being threatened. They are being fed regularly. The inmates have organized their own police force that is responsible for safeguarding the hostages.*
. *Complete order is being maintained. There are no sex attacks.*
. *No harm is being caused by or threatened to persons who are locked up in protective custody. Professor Desmond Morton spoke to these men and confirmed this.*
. *Representatives of both committees wish to assure wives, family and friends of those in the institution there is no cause for personal anxiety.*
. *There is no attempt to break out of the institution.*
. *Medical services and sanitary conditions are as good as can be expected under the circumstances. There are no immediate health risks.*
. *Although proper meals are not possible, no one is going hungry.*

The government would not approve the statement and reporters never saw it. Instead, the Solicitor General's office released a shorter version stating the government could not confirm or deny the well-being of any of the hostages or inmates.

As Saturday eventually faded into night, MacKenzie once again found himself addressing the anxious men gathered in the dome. He needed to be careful about what he said for fear of inciting the violent radicals. "I'm not here to tell you guys what to do, but if you decide to pack it all in and let the hostages go, then you have my word that I'll be the last man out, with the last screw."

No one responded. Time was running out. More armed troops had arrived at the prison during the day. Five hundred soldiers now surrounded the prison, waiting for their orders.

MacKenzie was still pushing for the "pro rata arrangement," the exchange of one hostage for a number of inmates until the prison was emptied. But the inmate population was still wavering on a settlement proposal.

Back in the hospital wing, the citizens' committee waited for MacKenzie to return. To add to their stress, they had received a handwritten letter from the kidnapped guards. It read: "Before you storm this place, consider our lives." It pleaded with the government to meet the inmates' demands. All five guards had signed it.

Worn out and frustrated, the committee members agreed to have Warden Jarvis and John Maloney join in the talks. Maloney had been on the phone to Ottawa all day and he told the group that the Solicitor General was still not willing to negotiate with the prisoners. A memo from the Solicitor General's office was read out loud to the committee members. It stated:

1)   *The citizens' committee are not to negotiate in any way, shape or form.*
2)   *The administration wants to know about any proposals from the inmate population.*
3)   *No more information or points of clarification are to be discussed.*
4)   *The minister wants to know first before any answer is given to the inmates.*
5)   *The minister wants to know what they are going to do with the hostages.*

6)   *Once the safety of the hostages has been assured, then the min-*
      ister will review ways and means of working towards a peaceful
      resolution.

DISCUSSIONS WERE AT a dangerous stalemate. The citizens' committee
had no real power to negotiate and MacKenzie and the other prisoners had to figure out a way to get the prison population to agree to
the government's meagre terms. It was going to be another long night.

But just before midnight, MacKenzie received an urgent call
from the inmates in the dome area. He was told he needed to get
over there right away. Without saying a word, MacKenzie slammed
down the receiver and rushed out of the hospital wing. The other
men on the prisoners' committee quickly ran after him.

Judging by the look on MacKenzie's face, Maloney and Jarvis
knew something was terribly wrong. Maloney called the senior
army officer who was on standby. How fast could they initiate an
armed assault if the prisoners turned violent? The seasoned military officer told Maloney the army couldn't launch a full assault
before daylight. It was too dangerous for the soldiers to enter a
darkened prison. There could be booby traps and it would be hard
to tell who the enemy was. It was not the answer Maloney wanted.

Maloney told Jarvis to order the morning guard shift to report
to duty at 6 a.m. instead of 8 a.m. He then called Paul Faguy, the
Commissioner of Penitentiaries, to tell him that all negotiations
had failed and there was some kind of disturbance in the main
cellblock. Faguy said he and the Solicitor General would proceed
to the prison by helicopter.

MACKENZIE, KNIGHT AND MacCaud rushed into the dome. Looking
up, they saw hundreds of inmates leaning over the railings of the
upper tiers brandishing homemade spears and clubs. "What the
hell is going on?" MacKenzie demanded.

Moments earlier, the inmates had panicked when guards on the other side of a barricaded wooden door started chopping at the entrance with an axe. The guards were trying to smash a hole in the wood to put a hose through in case of fire, but the prisoners assumed it was an attack. "The army is coming! The army is coming!" inmates shouted as they heard the wood splintering against the blade of the axe.

For the more militant inmates, it was all they needed to engage in full-out battle. "Get to the top," someone yelled out. They ordered everyone up to the third and fourth ranges. Hundreds of men began racing up the metal stairwells, smashing windows and light bulbs as they ran. Flimsy mattresses were dragged out of the cells and secured to the upper railings to be used as shields if the army started shooting. Metal bars and other heavy objects were stockpiled for the coming assault. Some inmates tore bedsheets into strips and wet them in preparation for a tear gas attack. They had to be prepared for anything.

MacKenzie had little time to react before metal debris started flying down around him. "For fuck's sake," he yelled, "you guys better get with it or a lot of us are going to die." All eyes were on him.

As some of the angry cons reluctantly made their way back down to the dome floor, MacKenzie tried to reassure the population that the army was not attacking but that they needed to surrender.

"Nobody is giving up to the pigs!" came a commanding voice from the top tier. It was a defiant Dave Shepley, straddling the railing and gripping a bullhorn with black leather gloves. "No more talking, it's time to fight." Shepley's voice reverberated through the mouthpiece. Brian Beaucage stood beside him, brandishing an iron pipe. "We're calling the shots from now on," Shepley shouted. "Ain't nobody giving up!"

Inmates began beating their clubs against the railings. Armed soldiers guarding the outside perimeter of the prison could hear

Fire destroys the famous cupola at Kingston Penitentiary.
Toronto Telegram *fonds, York University Libraries, Clara Thomas Archives and Special Collections,* ASC07602

1954 riot destroys the famous
Kingston Penitentiary Cupola.
Queen's University Archives, V25_5-32-1_6

1954 riot destroys the famous
Kingston Penitentiary Cupola.
Queen's University Archives, V25_5-32-1_2F

Military prison on grounds after 1954 riot.
Queen's University Archives, V25_5-32-1_1F

Military prison on grounds after 1954 riot.
Queen's University Archives, V25_5-32-1_4F

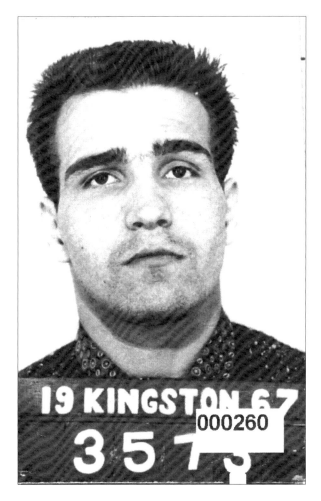

Billy Knight, instigator of the 1971 Kingston Penitentiary riot.
Image retrieved from parole file, Library and Archives Canada

Inmate Wayne Ford.

Cedarhedge—Warden's house.
Queen's University Archives, V23-PuB-ᴋᴘ-Warden-4

Warden Arthur Jarvis.
Courtesy of Canada's Penitentiary Museum

Ron Haggart in his office.
Courtesy of the Haggart family.

Warden Arthur Jarvis listens as Billy Knight speaks to the press. Left to right: Art Jarvis, Billy Knight, Emanuel Lester, Charles Saunders, unidentified reporter.

Fred Ross, Toronto Star *Archives, 1971*

Members of the citizen's committee. Left to right: Ron Haggart, Arthur Martin, William Donkin, Aubrey Golden, Desmond Morton.

Don Dutton, Toronto Star *Archives, 1971*

Soldiers from First Signals Regiment at Barriefield prepare to
enter Kingston Penitentiary.

Fred Ross, Toronto Star *Archives, 1971*

Banners hung by prisoners to thank their supporters.

Fred Ross, Toronto Star *Archives, 1971*

the ominous pounding through the thick limestone walls. It grew louder and louder.

Unable to sway the mob any further, MacKenzie and his crew withdrew and headed back to the hospital wing. They needed something more tangible from the administration that might appease Shepley and the other militants. Time was running out for any chance of a non-violent resolution. They had to act quickly. MacKenzie feared the whole situation had just passed into the hands of madmen.[114]

14

CIRCLE OF TERROR

Saturday, April 17, 1971

"THE FUN IS ABOUT TO BEGIN!" yelled Shepley from the upper tier, moments after MacKenzie left. They needed to find the guard hostages and bring them to the dome. He wanted to put them on display, and if the army invaded, they would be the first ones killed. Shepley and his accomplices ran towards 4-B range, where they knew the guards were being held.

Wayne Ford, inmate #2778, was 285 pounds with a nineteen-inch neck and a fifty-seven-inch chest. He had been put in charge of guarding the hostages after MacKenzie left to take over negotiations on the prisoners' committee. Ford had no intention of letting anyone near the guards. He knew they were the inmates' only potential insurance against a full-out military invasion. Wielding a sledgehammer, he and a dozen other armed inmates were prepared for battle.

"Give us the pigs," demanded Shepley.

"No way, pal," said a determined Ford, gripping his weapon tightly.

The five kidnapped guards locked in a cell farther down the corridor could hear the commotion. What was happening? They looked at each other, terrified, but no one dared to speak. Their jailers had treated them well so far, giving them sandwiches, coffee and cigarettes, but the hostages knew their safety was hanging in the balance. If the army attacked the prison, they would be killed.

The tense standoff over the guards continued as former prison buddies defiantly stared each other down. It was clear that Ford and the other inmates were not going to give up without a ferocious fight. Enraged, Shepley and his gang finally retreated. But if he couldn't get at the guards, he was going to turn all of his fury on another group, a weaker group. He was going hunting for the rats in 1-D.

SHEPLEY AND HIS MEN raced to the cellblock where they knew they would find their targets. With all the commotion in the dome, the undesirables had been left unguarded. They dragged thirteen inmates from 1-D into the centre of the dome. Some grabbed at their captors, whimpering and begging to be released. Others came quietly. All of the men were tied to straight-backed wooden chairs arranged in a circle. A metal chain was bound to their feet. At the centre of the circle were the remains of the brass bell platform, now draped in a white sheet with candles and weapons on top of it.

Acting as a macabre master of ceremonies, Shepley paced around the circle eyeing each of the men. Rock music blasted over the loudspeakers strung around the dome. Gripping the bullhorn in his black-gloved hand, he addressed the spectators hanging over the railings on the upper ranges. "What shall we do, gentlemen?"

"Castrate them."

"Cut their throats."

"Kill them!"

The inmates pounded the metal railings in unison.

"Do we know anyone else who should be here?" Shepley asked the wild-eyed audience. He knew there were more undesirables hiding in the cellblocks. He wanted all of them—the diddlers and the finks, the hated dregs of the prison caste system. No one could hide from his rage.

THE THREE MEN cowering in the back of Harold St. Amour's cell up on the third range could hear the uproar from the dome below. They knew they were in danger. Shepley's men would come for them. Ralph Lake, Melvin Travis and Ron McCorkel scrambled to erect a barricade of overturned bed frames and other furniture. They hung bedsheets and blankets across the doorway, a sign for others to stay out of the cell. But the attackers quickly sniffed them out. Shepley's goons grabbed Travis and McCorkel right away. Lake made a run for it as Brian Beaucage took off after him. Lake raced through the crowded tiers, hoping to lose himself in the mass of grey prison uniforms and the maze of cells. He had to find another place to hide. But some of the other inmates quickly pointed him out to his pursuer. Beaucage finally cornered him and dragged him down to the dome. "I've been waiting four and a half fucking years to get you," Beaucage snarled at him.[115]

SIXTEEN MEN WERE now tied to chairs in the sacrificial circle, surrounded by a dozen fellow inmates brandishing homemade weapons. Satisfied with his catch, Shepley motioned for the hair-raising, rhythmic pounding to cease. The multi-tiered rotunda grew quiet. "The show is about to begin," he announced with an almost giddy lilt.

Carefully setting the bullhorn down on the bell platform, Shepley sauntered over to one of the men chained in the circle. Grabbing a handful of hair, he yanked the inmate's head backwards and rammed his gloved fist into his nose. The silent onlookers heard the sickening crunch. The inmate's body spasmed in pain, but he didn't scream out. Shepley laughed as he watched the bright-red blood pour down the man's mouth and chin.

Inmate Richard Moore was one of those chained in the circle. It didn't take long for one of Shepley's men to single him out.

"I'm going to smash your face in," said Jimmy Oag.

Oag swung his arm back and hit the top of Moore's head with a metal pipe. Then he smashed it across his nose. Moore began oozing blood. It was choking him, but he couldn't move to wipe it away.

Shepley was standing over him with a shiv in his hand. Leaning down, he whispered into his ear, "You're the first one I'm going to kill if those bastards send in tear gas."

Someone threw a sheet over Moore's head. Blood seeped into the dirty white cotton. Then he felt something warm, some kind of liquid falling over his head. Its odour singed his bloodied nose. The mysterious fluid trickled down the sheet, pooling like golden syrup on the floor, mixing with his blood. It was lacquer from the wood shop.

"Should we torch the turkeys?" Shepley shouted through the bullhorn, holding a lit cigarette to the flammable varnish. Many of the hardened criminals watching from above gasped. Sensing their shock, Shepley laughed and took a long drag off the smoke.

Another inmate approached Moore and bent down in front of him. Recognizing the voice, he knew it was Johnny Hance. Moore had always considered him a solid con. "Do you think you'll make it out of here alive?" Hance whispered into his ear.

"No," said Moore.

"You're probably right, son," Hance replied.

Shepley continued to direct the proceedings from the dome floor with his bullhorn, while Brian Beaucage yelled instructions from the third range. All of the men in the circle were covered in bloodied bedsheets and the beatings seemed to grow more intense now that their captors didn't have to look at their faces. The attackers struck the men with their fists, hammers, metal bars, anything that would inflict pain. The inmates being tortured tried not to cry out, as any sound brought on more taunting and cruelty. When one of the prisoners complained that he was choking on his own blood, one of the militants carrying a wooden tool studded with spikes drove the pointed ends into the man's shoulders and the back of his head.

Richard Moore could do nothing but listen to the sickening thuds as weapons struck each inmate again and again. Then, from behind his chair, someone pulled at his hands to tie them tighter and a voice said, "Now I'm going to have a little fun with you."

When the guy squatted down in front of him, Moore could see his face. It was Robbie Robidoux. He had a *Fuck the World* tattoo on his wrist. He looked stoned.

"How many ribs are in a man's body?" Robidoux asked.

"I don't know," said Moore.

"Take a guess?" the eighteen-year-old said.

"I don't know," repeated Moore.

"Then I guess we'll find out." Robidoux jumped up and began pounding Moore in the ribs with a metal bar. Moore's body slammed against the back of the chair with each blow. He felt woozy. It was getting hard to breathe. Robidoux laughed. "I think I broke this guy's ribs," he said.

"Leave him alone," Moore heard someone say. "He's almost gone."

15
THE EXECUTION LIST

Saturday, April 17, 1971

By all the tests that can be applied, it is perfectly clear that the greatest threat to prison order always lies in the small group of violently unstable men, usually at least mildly paranoid, which every prison holds.

—H.W. Hollister, former inmate

BARRIE MACKENZIE and the other committee members rushed back to the hospital wing to try to get some kind of last-ditch concession that would end the standoff. But he was told the bureaucrats weren't going to budge. Ron Haggart and the other members of the citizens' committee sat in an unused doctor's office unable to negotiate any further. The government had put them in a no-win situation and now everything was going haywire. Five guards remained captive and all they could do was sit and wait.

MacKenzie paced up and down the hospital corridor. He kept calling the dome to find out what was happening, but no one would tell him anything. He demanded to speak to Dave Shepley, but Shepley was far too busy to take a phone call.

THE ROCK MUSIC continued to pulsate throughout the cellblocks. The deafening beat helped drown out some of the chilling sounds coming from the centre of the rotunda. Some inmates hid in their cells when the beatings began. Others stood frozen on the catwalks above, watching in terror. Reluctant to shout out or intervene for fear they would be next, the spectators pretended to go along with what was happening to the ghostlike figures strapped to the chairs. When one of the undesirables begged his torturers to ask the prison population to take a vote on whether to continue the beatings, Shepley laughed and butted out his cigarette on the man's battered face. He and the rest of his gang had no intention of stopping until all of the men in the circle were dead, and two of them in particular were high on the execution list.

Robbie Robidoux hated Brian Ensor, the convicted child molester from Hamilton. Ensor had been attacked two days earlier when the militants broke into range 1-D, but Robidoux and the others believed Ensor still needed to pay for his crimes.

Now Ensor was tied to a chair in the sacrificial circle, his head and face covered by a sheet stained crimson red from his broken nose. His captors took turns hitting him with their fists and homemade weapons. They taunted him. Finally someone struck him so hard his chair fell backwards and his head hit the concrete with a sickening thud. Fresh blood seeped onto the floor as he lay motionless. Then, while hundreds of inmates watched from above, another attacker brandishing a crude knife bent over Ensor and dragged the jagged blade down his right thigh. His skin instantly split open, revealing flesh and bone. Screams from beneath the white sheet pierced the stale air and his body began convulsing. As Ensor's blood flowed from the open gash on his leg, one of his other tormentors bent over him and placed a cup under his leg to collect the red liquid. It was a chalice stolen from one of the chapels.

"Here's to you, sucker," the grinning inmate said as he brought the goblet to his mouth. Wiping away the excess from his lips, he whispered to Ensor, "Time for you to die."

Bertrand Robert was next. Everyone despised him for what he had done. Word of his crimes had arrived at the Pen before he had. Local newspapers had covered the bizarre story of the man from Chatham, Ontario, who was accused of burning his five children by placing them on a hot stove burner.[116] The man, in turn, blamed his housekeeper, saying she was evil. According to him, he hired the woman, who claimed she was a nurse, to take care of his children after his wife left. He soon realized she was beating the children to keep them under control, but he felt powerless to stop the abuse. Court documents revealed the children, aged five to eleven, had been starved and burned and had multiple injuries.

Despite his protestations of innocence, Robert was convicted of five counts of assault, one for each child. He was sentenced to ten years in a federal prison and sent to Kingston Penitentiary. As soon as he arrived, he was a marked man. His fellow inmates didn't feel his penalty fit the crime. They had already tried to kill him once, stabbing him in the exercise yard, but since that incident a year earlier he had been housed in the protective unit, 1-D. This time he wasn't going to get away.

"That's for boiling your kids," said one con as he whacked him over the head. Another torturer placed a burning candle on top of his head and told Robert he'd beat his brains in if it fell off. When it did, Robert was struck over and over with a metal pipe. Two other attackers simultaneously swung their pipes, hitting him on each side of his head and knocking him to the floor. Robert's body twitched uncontrollably until he passed out. When he came to, the beatings resumed.

MACKENZIE RETURNED to the dome around three thirty in the morning. He was alone. Charles Saunders and Norman MacCaud had refused to return, fearing they would be attacked. As MacKenzie entered the rotunda, he saw the circle of bound bodies covered in sheets. He felt sick. There was no movement, no sounds. Blood everywhere. Metal bars, knives and wooden clubs littered the crimson floor. Who were they? He couldn't see any of their faces. The guards?

He couldn't tell Haggart and the others. If anyone found out, the army would storm the prison. They'd all be dead. Shepley and the others had all but sealed their fate. MacKenzie had little left to bargain with.

"God help us," he said.

RICHARD MOORE had passed out from the beating. He wasn't sure how long he'd been out, but he was on the floor still tied to a chair. He heard someone say, "This one's gone." Did they mean him? He tried not to move. The pain in his chest was unbearable. Then someone untied his hands and feet. The sheet covering his face had fallen off, but he dared not open his eyes. He heard more movement, chairs being dragged across the cement, and moaning. Suddenly he was being dragged too. Where were they taking them?

Moore lay motionless while others shuffled around him. He swallowed the blood trickling down his throat. When he thought his attackers had finally left, he opened his swollen eyes. He strained to make out his surroundings. He was back in 1-D. There was a guy lying beside him. He was still tied to a chair and his face was so swollen he was barely recognizable. It was Brian Ensor. Was he alive?

Moore heard someone coming. The guy stood over Ensor and kicked him. "You're not dead yet, you cocksucker," he said. "I'm going to finish you off."

Moore recognized the voice. It was Robbie Robidoux, the inmate who had broken his ribs. Robidoux began hitting Ensor over the head with a steel locking bar three to four feet long. Ensor's battered body convulsed with each blow. Then it stopped.

Robidoux was finally satisfied. He turned to walk out of the range, but not before spitting on Ensor's body. Moore knew he had just witnessed a murder.

MACKENZIE RETURNED to the dome just before five o'clock on Sunday morning. The bodies were gone. Broken chairs and bloodied bedsheets were piled in a corner. Someone had tried to mop up the floor, leaving murky red streaks. Shepley and his gang had disappeared into the darkened bowels of the prison, but MacKenzie knew they'd be back. Some of the other prisoners had made their way back down to the dome floor armed with crude weapons. After what they had witnessed, most of the prisoners were ready to surrender. More men were going to die if they didn't end the standoff. MacKenzie was their only hope.

MacKenzie picked up the phone in the dome area and called the hospital wing. Gripping the telephone receiver in one hand and brandishing a pair of tailor's shears in the other, he asked to speak to Haggart.

"How much time do we have to make a decision?" he asked, his voice cracking.

"Until 5:15 a.m.," Haggart replied without thinking through his answer. At the same time he looked across the room and saw Arthur Martin anxiously motioning to his watch.

"Earlier," Martin mouthed.

"You have to make a decision by 5 a.m.," Haggart said, his voice starting to stutter. "You've got to be ready to release the hostages immediately and come out when ordered."

"We need more time," yelled MacKenzie into the phone, his voice so hoarse he could barely speak. "We're not all on the same wavelength in here."

Haggart heard others yelling in the background. MacKenzie said he couldn't get a unanimous decision from the men. Some were still holding out for amnesty. Haggart asked him what was going on in the dome. Rumours of torture had already made their way to the hospital wing. But before Haggart could get an answer, MacKenzie hung up.

At 5:07 a.m., MacKenzie called Haggart again. "How much longer do we have?" he asked.

Haggart looked out the dust-stained window of the hospital wing. He could see a narrow band of sky cresting the prison wall. "It's dawn," he said, "and the army always attacks at dawn."

MacKenzie hung up.

Haggart didn't actually know if the army was about to storm the penitentiary, but he did know three things: there was an official plan in place to attack; there was a military general on the prison grounds; invasions were always led by generals.

MacKenzie called back. "Can you give me another half-hour?" he asked. "We need more time."

"I can't guarantee what will happen in the next half-hour," said Haggart. "I suggest in the next two minutes you get a decision."

He could hear MacKenzie speaking to someone and then a voice in the background bellowed, "You have two minutes to make up your fucking minds." MacKenzie came on the phone again. Haggart listened to his demands and then repeated everything he was hearing to Deputy Warden Chinnery, who in turn was managing another phone line to Maloney. Maloney was waiting across the street with the Solicitor General and his staff, who had arrived from Ottawa.

"They want to go out sixty men at a time," MacKenzie finally told Haggart.

"Can you assure me this is a unanimous decision?" Haggart asked. But before MacKenzie had a chance to answer, the prison erupted.

"Get back, get back!" Haggart heard soldiers yelling outside the door to the hospital wing.

Without warning, hundreds of inmates were running down a narrow corridor from A-block towards the hospital wing entrance. Word had quickly spread that the army was about to attack. Running, pushing and shouting, the prisoners were trying to get out. The charging men suddenly confronted Professor Morton, who had been standing with armed guards at the steel barrier between A-block and the hospital wing. "Come forward one at a time, one at a time," Professor Morton shouted. He knew the soldiers would fire at the stampeding prisoners.

But Morton was too late. Before the inmates reached the hospital door, three shots rang out. The soldiers fired into the ceiling of the corridor. "Get back, get back," yelled the soldiers. The convicts stopped in their tracks, but now they were trapped in the passageway between the dome and the hospital wing.

"Don't go into the corridor," Haggart yelled to MacKenzie, who was still on the phone.

"Tell the fucking screws to back off."

"They're holding their fire," Haggart said.

He heard MacKenzie shouting to the inmates in the corridor to stay put. Trying to calm the situation, Haggart suggested if MacKenzie brought a hostage down, they could release sixty of the men waiting in the corridor. MacKenzie wanted a guarantee that he wouldn't get shot if he brought out a hostage. Haggart assured him he would be safe.

Finally, MacKenzie said he was willing to bring out one of the hostages, but he wanted all of the prisoners stuck in the corridor between the dome and the hospital wing to be freed. The administration quickly agreed and released all of the inmates into the exercise yard. "Tell them we want to see our first hostage now," said the Solicitor General.

Haggart asked MacKenzie to bring out one of the hostages. But MacKenzie said he didn't believe the prisoners had been released into the exercise yard. "They are in the yard," Haggart said. "No one has been harmed."

MacKenzie still refused to bring out a hostage.

Finally, Professor Morton agreed to go into the yard himself to count the inmates. They needed MacKenzie to co-operate. Morton counted 206 prisoners and relayed the information to MacKenzie, but he still refused. MacKenzie wanted one of his men to count the prisoners. MacKenzie sent Johnny Hance to count the inmates in the exercise yard. Hance reported back to MacKenzie that there were 206 inmates in the yard.

Haggart asked MacKenzie to come out with one of the hostages. MacKenzie still refused. What if guards were beating the inmates in the yard? Haggart assured him no one was being harmed. MacKenzie also wanted a guarantee the men would be moved to other prisons unharmed. He wanted Hance to supervise the loading and departure of each of the buses. He told Haggart he didn't trust anyone.

Catching his breath, Haggart was trying to keep calm. He wanted to appease MacKenzie and get the hostages out alive, but he knew the Solicitor General was quickly losing patience.

"Is everything under control now?" he asked.

The phone went dead.

Just before six o'clock on Sunday morning, MacKenzie walked the first hostage over to the hospital entrance. The prisoners had voted on who would be released first. It was young Kerry Bushell, dressed in a baggy prisoner's uniform. MacKenzie, still holding the pair of shears, quickly disappeared back into the prison.

16

THE BEST SHOW IN TOWN

Sunday, April 18, 1971

ON SUNDAY AFTERNOON, Joseph Wilfred Kealy, or Wilf as everyone liked to call him, was enjoying a much-deserved day off. It was a clear spring day, sunny with a slight chill in the air, but the daytime temperature was expected to go up to fifty-five degrees. As the detective inspector of the Kingston Police, the past few months had been particularly hectic for Kealy. Crime in the Kingston area was on the rise as the city continued to grow, and with only ninety-two active officers the police force was severely understaffed. But Kealy loved his job. He had joined the Kingston Police in 1946 after his service with the Provost Corps during the Second World War.[117] Policing was in his blood, and he was very good at what he did.

Kealy and his wife, Betty, didn't live far from police headquarters on North Bartlett Street. With five kids, their house was always buzzing with activity. Betty was a great cook and Kealy was looking forward to a relaxing Sunday lunch. But when the phone rang, he had a feeling his day off wasn't going to turn out as he had hoped. He was right. It was John Maloney. He was calling from the warden's office at Kingston Penitentiary.

Three days earlier, just after midnight, the Kingston Police had received a call from Assistant Warden Babcock. He'd told the sergeant on duty there was a major disturbance inside Kingston Penitentiary. Babcock said they didn't need the police yet but would keep them posted on developments. Despite Babcock's assurances that the riot was contained within the prison, Sergeant Flewelling and Detective Breen decided to drive over to the prison to personally assess the situation. When they arrived, they met with Babcock in the administration building. Babcock informed them the prisoners had complete control over the recreation hall, two of the ranges and the chapels. The inmates had destroyed the interior of those areas and were holding six guards hostage. The local military had been put on alert and Warden Jarvis had called in forty off-duty guards. Before they left the prison, Babcock assured the officers the riot would likely be resolved within the next twenty-four hours. But as a precautionary measure, Flewelling assigned two cruisers to the area.

Over the next three days, the Kingston Police heard little from Babcock or any other prison official.

Now, seventy-two hours later, Kealy was on the phone with John Maloney. The Regional Director told him the riot was over but there had been a violent attack inside the dome area. There were unconfirmed reports of multiple murders of inmates by fellow prisoners. Maloney didn't know how many were dead.

The call had lasted only a few minutes, but it had changed the course of the police detective's day. He wasn't going to enjoy the wonderful lunch his wife had prepared. Kealy grabbed his keys and headed towards the door. He likely wasn't going to be home for dinner either.

BACK AT THE PRISON HOSPITAL, Haggart was still on the phone with MacKenzie. After releasing Kerry Bushell, MacKenzie had returned

to the dome area to try to convince the rest of the prisoners to surrender. MacKenzie told Haggart he would release one hostage for
every sixty prisoners. Solicitor General Goyer would not agree to
the deal. Since over two hundred inmates were already out, he was
demanding all of the remaining hostages be released. Once they
knew all of the guards were safe, the inmates would be transported
to other institutions. MacKenzie refused Goyer's demands.

While tense negotiations continued with MacKenzie, most of
the freed inmates were relieved the riot was over. Many had witnessed the savagery in the dome and knew it was only a matter of
time before the military stormed the compound. What had begun
as a peaceful protest against poor living conditions and the
impending transfer to Millhaven had turned into kidnapping, total
destruction of the prison and savage brutality. Now they would be
sent to other institutions, where conditions might be even worse.

While they waited for their names to be called to board a bus,
many of the prisoners hung out on the bleachers in the rec yard,
smoking and enjoying the warm afternoon sun. Others had been
moved into the gymnasium, where they sat watching the hockey
game between the Montreal Canadiens and the Boston Bruins. It
was a big game—the seventh of the quarter-final series. The Habs,
with a rookie goaltender named Ken Dryden, were defending their
lead against Bobby Orr and the Stanley Cup champion team.

AS THE DAY WORE ON, more dishevelled inmates, sixty at a time,
emerged from the bowels of the century-old prison. They had been
ordered to come out with their hands on top of their heads. This was
a security measure in case any of them were hiding concealed weapons, but it was also to prevent any excited inmates from making rude
gestures with their hands that might incite the guards or soldiers.

After more back and forth, the government had eventually
agreed to the pro rata arrangement. They wanted this event to be

over. Once all the guards were safe, they needed to get into the prison to find any injured prisoners. What carnage would they discover?

As each group of inmates walked into the fresh air, squinting at the sunlight, MacKenzie released one of the hostages. Guard Douglas Dale was brought out next, followed by Joseph Vallier and Donald Flynn. Senior keeper Ed Barrett was last. He had refused to leave until all of his men were safe. A doctor examined all of the officers and reported that they were in good physical condition, but all of them were "excited and emotional."

Finally, a worn-out-looking MacKenzie emerged from the empty prison. He had kept his word—all of the guards had been freed unharmed and he was the last man out. Solicitor General Goyer greeted MacKenzie and guided him over to where Haggart was standing. The two men who had stayed on the phone together for more than twelve hours were finally meeting face to face.

Haggart put his hand on MacKenzie's sleeve. "Thank you, Barrie," he said. "You are a great man."

MacKenzie stared blankly at the dishevelled news reporter. "Fuck off," he said. "I didn't do it for you. I did it for the guys in there."[118]

WITHIN MINUTES OF a local radio station announcing the riot was over, curious onlookers started arriving at the prison. Some carried transistor radios so they wouldn't miss the hockey game. Traffic was backed up all along King Street, and soon over two hundred people were standing around gawking and gossiping while vendors set up carts to sell soft drinks and hot dogs. Rino Pizzinato brought his whole family, including the dog. "There's not much doing in Kingston on a Sunday," he told a *Whig-Standard* reporter. "This is something special."

"This is the best show to hit town since the winter carnival," said another excited spectator.

With no official announcement and a news blackout, the bystanders and reporters milling around had little information about what had happened inside the prison.[119] Rumours were rife. "I hear there are fourteen dead," said Dave Smith, a local research lab technician. "Sixteen," another claimed. "Those prisoners should all be put in the army and sent to Vietnam," argued an elderly bystander. "Too many nice boys are getting killed over there."

While the spectacle continued outside, the prison was eerily quiet inside. The main cellblock was empty except for a group of middle-aged men in suits standing in the dome area. Maloney and Jarvis stood with Goyer and Faguy. Edgar Benson, finance minister and Member of Parliament for Kingston, was also there. He was the acting prime minister as Trudeau was still on his Barbados honeymoon; he was due back that evening. The men stood amongst the rubble and destruction of the central rotunda. They knew the 136-year-old fortress was finished.

INSPECTOR KEALY ARRIVED at KP on Sunday afternoon as requested. After receiving the phone call from Maloney, he had contacted two of his top men, Sergeant William Hackett and Detective M. Finn. When they arrived at the prison, they were directed to the Warden's House across the street. From there, they watched as the circus-like setting in front of the prison continued to grow. Kealy was hopeful the crowds outside the prison would quickly disperse. He and his men needed to get inside to investigate the scene. A hastily written telegram to the assistant field commissioner of the OPP noted unconfirmed reports of multiple murders and of guards claiming to have seen torsos and other body parts through windows inside the penitentiary. Kealy had noticed a white station wagon with blacked-out windows driving through the main gates of the prison earlier. He recognized the car. It belonged to Dr. Stuart Patterson, the Frontenac County coroner. No one knew how many bodies were inside the prison, but the Coroner's Office in Toronto had been put on alert in case extra staff were needed.

By late Sunday afternoon, over a dozen military ambulances had transported all of the seriously injured inmates to the Canadian Forces Hospital in Barriefield. Bertrand Robert was in serious condition at Kingston General Hospital. The rest of the prisoners, who had waited most of the day, were loaded onto school buses, twenty to forty inmates per bus. As each bus emerged from the prison gates, cheers rang out amongst the crowds. The inmates smiled and yelled back. Many of them waved, while others gave the peace sign.

ONTARIO PROVINCIAL POLICE cruisers armed with shotguns accompanied each of the buses headed towards other correctional facilities. Warkworth Institution, Collins Bay Institution and Joyceville Institution, all medium-security prisons, had been put on notice. However, most of the buses were headed straight for Millhaven. Only fourteen miles west of Kingston, it was a short ride.

As the inmates departed from the prison, local reporters stood outside the Warden's House, hoping to interview one of the guard hostages. They had all been released, but there was no sign of them. Kerry Bushell, the first guard freed, had been quickly ferried away from the prison grounds by corrections staff, to be reunited with his new bride. He had been told not to talk to anyone. Donald Flynn's wife had arrived at the prison but refused to speak to the press on the advice of the Solicitor General's office. The other guards and their wives had not been seen. However, a prison spokesman announced to the waiting press that each of the guards would receive six hundred dollars in overtime pay for the extra hours they had been held hostage during the riot.[120]

For Assistant Warden Edgar Babcock, the four-day ordeal had been the toughest in his long career with the Penitentiary Service.

He was the main contact for the hordes of press who had descended upon the prison. He had only slept four hours in four days. And while he was totally done in by the ordeal, there had been one unexpected windfall from the uprising. Babcock had collected all of the film canisters discarded by television crews on the prison grounds.[121] As a local Boy Scout leader, he knew they could be put to good use. "They're watertight and they float," he told a local reporter. "Just what we need for our survival kits." When asked what his plans were now that the riot was over, Babcock said, "I know where there's a cold beer and it's not far from here."

AS THE FINAL buses departed, Ron Haggart and the other men on the citizens' committee were anxious to put the Kingston ordeal behind them and get back to their lives. The past four days had left everyone emotionally and physically drained. Desmond Morton, still recovering from his heart attack, said he was thinking of checking himself into a hospital to recover. "I'm not tired," he told a *Toronto Daily Star* reporter before he left the prison. "I'm finished."

Four of the men from the committee drove back to Toronto, while an exhausted Haggart returned to his hotel room to sit down at his typewriter. He was on a deadline. His editor at the *Toronto Telegram* was holding tomorrow's front page for his story.

Haggart and the others were relieved at how the riot had ended. They had managed to resolve the prison uprising without the army retaking the prison by force, an outcome that would have resulted in multiple casualties. And they had kept their word to Barrie MacKenzie. The inmates had not been mistreated and they were safely on their way to other institutions.

But Haggart and the others had no idea what was awaiting the new arrivals at Millhaven. For the rest of his life, Haggart would regret not getting on one of those buses to accompany the prisoners.

BACK INSIDE THE PRISON, Kealy and the other detectives worked their way through the destruction of the main cellblock. They were looking for victims but getting through the wreckage was dangerous. The corridors were littered with smashed furniture, torn mattresses, bedsprings and plumbing fixtures.[122] In some sections the debris was piled five or six feet high. Murky water seeped into the hallways from broken pipes. Inmates' private letters and cherished photographs lay soaked and ruined in the rubble. The odours of five hundred imprisoned men, the archaic sewage system and stale cigarette smoke permeated the air. In some areas, long sections of the iron locking bars that normally ran on a track above the cell doors hung down from the ranges like pretzels. On the fourth tier, forty feet above the floor of the main dome, the police found an arsenal of stockpiled objects. Plastic pails full of iron knobs smashed from the locking systems, coils of heavy chain and stacks of steel dinner trays had all been strategically placed along the railings, ready to be hurled at an invading army.

All the furniture from the guards' room was destroyed. Chairs, tables and benches were broken and stacked as barricades against the doors leading into the ranges. The altars and pews from the prisons' religious chapels were all smashed, and an organ from one of the sanctuaries lay in pieces on the dome floor.

Moving farther inside the rotunda, the police discovered more destruction. The cinder-block walls surrounding the dome were covered in blue painted peace symbols and four-letter words. Threadbare bedsheets hung down from the catwalks, displaying crudely painted slogans:

Pigs eat little children!
White is beautiful!
The devil made me do it!

In the centre of the dome, the detectives found the cast iron base of the hated brass bell, minus the bell. A white cloth and chalice stood in its place. Surrounding the makeshift altar they found remnants of the previous night's violence. A dozen wooden chairs were scattered around the dome floor. Ripped, stained bed-sheets lay in crumpled piles. Metal bars, chains, hammers and other handmade weapons littered the floor. Pools of blood were streaked across the floor. A dirty, pink-hued mop was leaning against one of the chairs. It was clear to the seasoned detectives that something sinister had taken place where they stood.

The police continued onto the ranges. They worked through the night, using portable lights to search for victims. The power to the main cellblock had been shut off in case any electrical booby traps had been set along the wire railings.[123] When the detectives moved down the darkened passageway towards cellblock 1-D, they saw it was in complete ruins. Water-soaked mattresses, furniture and other debris had been thrown into the corridor. All of the cell-locking mechanisms had been smashed, leaving the doors wide open.

Walking down the passageway, the detectives spotted some-thing sticking out of an air duct. They moved closer. It was a leg. The leg was attached to a mangled body. It looked as though some-one had attempted to hide it. They gently pulled the body out. Could he still be alive?

The man's hands were tied behind his back with strips of blood-soaked cloth. His battered face was unrecognizable and the side of his head was caved in. The body was covered in slash marks and there was a deep cut along the full length of his upper right thigh, exposing the bone.

Kealy stood over the inmate, looking into his frozen, dead eyes. The Kingston Penitentiary riot had just turned into a murder investigation.

17

HEROES AND VILLAINS

Monday, April 19, 1971

ON MONDAY MORNING, the Kingston coroner held a press conference. Dr. Patterson identified the dead prisoner as Brian Ensor, inmate #9370, of Hamilton, Ontario.[124] According to his prison file, Ensor had been an inmate at Kingston Penitentiary since November 27, 1962.

Kingston pathologist Dr. McEllicotte had conducted a post-mortem earlier that morning at Hotel Dieu Hospital. Patterson announced that the official cause of death was blunt force trauma with a hammer or iron bar. Ensor's skull had been crushed, and he had suffered numerous other injuries. His hands were tied behind his back and his feet bound together with strips torn from a bedsheet.[125] He had been dead for at least twelve hours before he was found. Brian Ensor was twenty-six years old.

Dr. Patterson told the press that a second victim was unconscious and in critical condition at Kingston General Hospital. He was also suffering from severe head wounds and was not expected to survive. His name was Bertrand Henry Robert.

Dr. Patterson also informed the press that reports of some of the prisoners being raped and castrated by fellow prisoners had been wildly exaggerated.[126] He confirmed that none of the inmates beaten in the final hours of the riot had been sexually assaulted. But, he added, it was a wonder that more of them hadn't been killed.

"NO DEAL, AND NO CONDITIONS," said a buoyant Jean-Pierre Goyer in the House of Commons on Monday afternoon.[127] The Solicitor General, who had flown back from Kingston to Ottawa on Sunday evening, was briefing the House about the end of the riot. Goyer told the politicians the rioting prisoners had been holding out for a guarantee of immunity. They did not want any criminal charges brought against them for the insurrection. "We did not agree to any conditions," he insisted. "There will be no immunity."

Goyer claimed he was uncertain why the prisoners had rioted in the first place.[128] According to him, their initial demands had seemed ill-conceived. He believed the inmates wanted to destroy the dank, overcrowded penitentiary before their transfer to the new $18-million institution at Millhaven. When NDP Member of Parliament Perry Ryan stood up in the House and asked if the cells at the newly constructed penitentiary were bugged, Goyer denied there were any such devices in the prison. Not satisfied with Goyer's answer, Ryan asked again.

"Will the Solicitor General say categorically that there are no bugging devices in the cells of these prisoners?"

"I say, Mr. Speaker, that there are no spying devices," replied Goyer. "That is the question I was asked."[129] Goyer chose not to mention the new closed-circuit television that would monitor inmates' every move, and how each cell could be filled with tear gas at the push of a button.

Goyer then announced that an independent board of inquiry would be convened to look into the causes of the Kingston riot and identify all those involved.[130] He denied reports that penitentiary officials in Ottawa had received warnings that there would be a rebellion in Kingston Penitentiary. But this was a lie. Warden Jarvis had written to his superiors three months before the riot saying, "This place is about to explode." No one had bothered to respond.

"THE HERO OF THE Kingston Penitentiary riot is a prisoner named Barrie MacKenzie," said a defiant Aubrey Golden during a press conference on Monday afternoon in Toronto.[131] Golden told reporters that when fighting broke out amongst the prisoners on Saturday night, MacKenzie was the only one from the prisoners' committee who went back into the dome area. "MacKenzie went back in alone and negotiated all night long. He risked his life going back in there and he prevented a bloodbath." Golden praised MacKenzie for the safe release of the guards and prisoners on Sunday. "He walked every one of the guards to safety and he was the last man out of that prison," said Golden.

On the same day, Desmond Morton invited a group of reporters into his home on Oriole Road in Toronto to talk about his experience in Kingston.[132] "The group of convicts I dealt with were brave men," said Morton, referring to his visit to the dome area on Saturday night. He reiterated that all the prisoners he had encountered treated him respectfully. He also talked about visiting the range where the so-called "undesirables" were housed. "At that time they were safe," said a visibly upset Morton. "Unfortunately that changed for reasons unknown to me."

He wanted the public to know that many of the inmates he spoke with did not want anyone killed or injured. He believed most of them were confused, panicked and anxious for the riot to be over quickly, without bloodshed. "The prisoners who negotiated with the citizens' committee were only concerned with saving lives," Morton said. "Mercy should be shown to them."

Morton also praised Barrie MacKenzie for his role in the drama. He said MacKenzie going back into the dome alone on the last night of the riot was like something from a Wild West movie.[133] "He just said, 'I'm off,'" Morton recalled. "I thought he would get the last hostage out but we would never see him again. I thought he was going to his death."

Then Morton went on to criticize the Solicitor General for mishandling his role in the prison riot.[134] Goyer had blocked the release of a conciliatory statement that had been drafted by Morton and the other committee members early Saturday evening, after Morton had toured the prison. The document stated the hostages were safe and the inmates intended no harm to anyone. Instead, the Solicitor General issued his own release saying he wasn't willing to give any concessions to the prisoners and the penitentiary would be retaken by force if necessary. "The inmates had radios in their cells," said Morton. "After hearing Goyer's statement, they felt we had let them down." Morton claimed Goyer's ultimatum pushed the more violent radicals over the edge. They felt they had nothing to lose. They knew they would be murdered or beaten if they surrendered. They had heard wild stories of prisoners being shot to death in their beds after a riot at Saint-Vincent-de-Paul Penitentiary near Montreal, and some of the Kingston inmates believed it.

Morton suggested Goyer could have personally spoken to the inmates and reassured them.[135] He could have used a bullhorn to tell the inmates no one would be beaten if they abandoned the main cellblock and walked out of the prison. "In short," said Morton, "Goyer blew it!"[136]

Morton also expressed a few opinions related to penal reform. Although he had been to Kingston Penitentiary many times, he said he had not realized the brutality of the place until his four days as a citizen negotiator. "Everything is demeaning and degrading in there and the prisoners are constantly reminded not to think of themselves as human beings. The convicted person is considered a non-person. Inmates, he claimed, spend most of each long day in their cells with no significant work or freedom. "Hell, you can't even lock a dog up in the yard all day by itself and expect it to be amiable," said Morton.

Friday, April 23, 1971

AS THE KINGSTON POLICE began the difficult work of interviewing inmates, the brutal events of the final few hours of the riot were coming to light. Sex offenders and suspected stool pigeons had been rounded up and viciously tortured. The beatings had occurred late Saturday night, just hours before the prisoners had finally surrendered. One inmate was dead, another was in a coma, and fourteen were in the hospital. It was going to take months of investigation to figure out exactly what had happened in the dome that night. Hundreds of inmates watched the macabre show from the railings above the dome, but few were willing to talk to the detectives. They were scared to go against the inmates' code: never snitch to the cops. But five days after the riot, Detective Kealy finally got the break he was hoping for. One of the undesirables, a prisoner who had been herded into the central dome and tortured, was finally conscious. His name was Richard Moore and he was willing to talk.

Moore told the detectives he thought he wasn't going to make it out of the dome alive. He had suffered a serious concussion, a broken nose, several cracked ribs and other painful injuries. He told the cops that soon after the riot began, some inmates ran into 1-D and began taunting the guys on the range. They grabbed a few of them out of their cells and beat them. Then more attackers returned with a fire hose and sprayed all of the inmates on the range with water. Their mattresses were ruined, as were most of their belongings. The tormenting continued on and off for the first couple of days and then it suddenly stopped.

But on Saturday night, some of the same dangerous inmates returned to 1-D and ordered everyone out of their cells. They dragged the men into the dome area and tied them to chairs. Moore described how Dave Shepley and others had repeatedly ridiculed them and struck them with their fists, metal pipes and other weapons to inflict maximum pain and suffering. The more the men bound in the circle begged for their lives, the more vicious the attackers became. For even the veteran detectives, the graphic details of the assaults on the undesirables were hard to stomach. Then Moore went on to describe the brutal murder of Brian Ensor.

By the time he was finished talking, Moore had named at least eight men responsible for the attacks on the men in 1-D. When asked if he would testify against them, he hesitated. He knew what happened to inmates branded as stool pigeons.

AS THE INVESTIGATION progressed, six detectives worked in teams of two, interviewing all of the inmates.[137] There were approximately five hundred prisoners in the main cellblock at the time of the riot. They had to get more of them talking in order to find all of the inmates responsible. What the detectives didn't realize at the time was that another investigation, involving multiple assaults, would soon demand even more police manpower.

18

RETRIBUTION

Late April 1971

"**SOMETHING IS WRONG** if our work at Kingston Penitentiary—the proudest achievement of my life—has all been destroyed by making us flunkies of the Solicitor General," said Desmond Morton. The blunt-spoken law professor was addressing the annual lawyers' club meeting at Osgoode Hall, and he was not in a good mood.

Two days after the riot ended, Morton had received an urgent message from a former Kingston prisoner saying he and others had been severely beaten when they arrived at Millhaven. Norman MacCaud, a member of the prisoners' committee during the riot, told Morton the prisoners were forced to run a gauntlet of guards once they stepped off the buses. The guards, armed with clubs and riot sticks, beat the prisoners mercilessly. MacCaud said the series of blows across his head had left him with a gash that required six stitches and his legs were black and blue.

After Morton received MacCaud's desperate call, he left Toronto and drove to Millhaven right away. But when he got to the prison, he was initially refused entry. Morton insisted on seeing his client and was eventually allowed in. MacCaud's injuries were enough to make Morton contact OPP Commissioner Eric Silk to demand the beatings be investigated. The prison administrators would not allow him to see any of the other inmates MacCaud said had been attacked by the guards.

A few days later, Morton received another "cry for help" from a second Millhaven inmate, who was contacting him on behalf of Billy Knight. Apparently Knight also had been beaten by the guards and had been treated for a fractured skull at Kingston General Hospital. Morton demanded to know how many other Kingston inmates had been attacked when they arrived at Millhaven.

As he had made clear in the press days earlier, Morton blamed the Solicitor General for the way the riot had unfolded. He believed it would have ended two days earlier if Goyer had agreed to give the convicts guarantees against beatings and reprisals. "Goyer should have guaranteed no retaliations of any sort." Morton angrily suggested the Solicitor General had used the citizens' committee to lure the convicts out of the main cellblock. "We were conned into getting them onto those buses."

PROFESSOR MORTON was also astonished by the lack of urgency shown by the Swackhammer commission, which was appointed by Goyer to investigate the causes of the Kingston Pen riot. Why weren't members of the commission going to Millhaven to look into the brutal beatings of the Kingston inmates at the hands of the guards?

The three-man commission headed by Toronto lawyer William Swackhammer was scheduled to begin its inquiries on June 7 at Royal Military College in Kingston.[138] Also on the committee were W.T. McGrath, executive director of the Canadian Criminology and Corrections Association, and H.E. Popp, director of security for the Penitentiary Service. Toronto lawyer Ian Scott would be acting as counsel for the board.

The Swackhammer inquiry was the first independent investigation into a penitentiary riot in Canada. Usually such incidents were handled internally by the warden of the institution and the regional administrators, but the intense press coverage had put pressure on the Solicitor General. The three-man commission had the task of determining the immediate cause or causes of the riot and whether the revolt was spontaneous or planned. The inquiry was expected to take several months and would be closed to the press and to the public.

On the same day Morton was speaking at Osgoode Hall, Arthur Martin sent a request to the Solicitor General's office requesting the citizens' committee be allowed to visit Millhaven Institution to investigate reports of prisoner beatings. In a heated phone call with Deputy Solicitor General Ernest Côté, Martin said he and the other committee members had made a personal commitment to the inmates that they would not be harmed if they surrendered. They had been outraged to learn that some of the inmates had been assaulted. They demanded to go to Millhaven to speak with the inmates directly.

Their request was denied.

Not willing to give up, Arthur Martin sent a letter directly to Goyer outlining his concerns: "On behalf of the citizens' committee and myself, I wish to take issue with the policy of your department in refusing the request of the committee to visit Millhaven Institute and speak with prisoners transferred from Kingston Penitentiary." He urged the Solicitor General to fully investigate the alleged beatings and file appropriate criminal charges against any guards involved.

He received a reply stating Goyer was unavailable for comment.

ON THE MORNING of Wednesday, April 28, 1971, Warden Don Clark and Deputy Warden Bell were in their regular policy meeting at Millhaven Institution. Just after 11 a.m., Clark received a phone call from the front administration building. Four Members of Parliament had arrived unexpectedly and were requesting to tour the facility and meet with inmates. The federal MPs were John Gilbert (Toronto–Broadview), Arnold Peters (Timiskaming), John Skoberg (Moose Jaw) and Frank Howard (Skeena).

Howard was no stranger to the inside of a federal prison. He had been convicted of armed robbery in 1943, when he was eighteen. After a troubled childhood in and out of foster homes, he and an accomplice had robbed two jewellery stores and a hotel at gunpoint. Sentenced to six years, he served twenty months behind bars and was paroled in 1945. After he left prison, Howard became a labour union organizer for the International Woodworkers of America and entered provincial politics in 1952. In 1957 he won a seat in the House of Commons. He had a strong passion for prison reform.

With no protocol in place for unannounced visits, Clark was unprepared. He proceeded to the administration building to meet the uninvited guests. He knew why the politicians were there, and he knew their presence was going to cause trouble, but he didn't know how he was going to stop them from entering a federal institution. He needed to get in touch with John Maloney right away.

The following day, Howard stood up in the House of Commons to complain that he and three fellow New Democratic Party members had been thrown out of Millhaven.[139] While they were interviewing a prisoner who claimed he'd been beaten by guards following his transfer from Kingston Pen, word came from the warden that they were to leave the prison immediately. Howard protested that as Honourable Members of Parliament they had the traditional privilege of visiting federally supported institutions, including penitentiaries. In fact, a year earlier Howard and two other MPs had visited Saskatchewan's Prince Albert Penitentiary after inmates staged two hunger strikes to protest their living conditions. After their unannounced visit the MPs had called for an immediate formal inquiry into the conditions at Prince Albert. They said the Saskatchewan penitentiary was lacking adequate rehabilitation programs, recreational activities and facilities, proper meals, and humanitarian communication between staff and inmates.[140]

Goyer defended ordering Howard and the other MPs from Millhaven on the basis that they had no statutory right to be there. Although the Penitentiaries Act of 1886 had listed MPs as "privileged visitors," the Act of 1961 had abolished the entire category. Goyer, who had been appointed to his position only four months earlier, had decided to exercise his right to disallow their visit. "Millhaven is currently overcrowded," he said. "The psychological climate there is tenuous and we have to be careful. My first responsibility is to see there are no more riots and to see to the protection of the prisoners."

"What have you got to hide?" Howard shouted from the other side of the House. "Evasiveness is no substitute for intelligence."

"Mr. Speaker," Goyer responded. "I did not appeal to the intelligence of the honourable member but to his courtesy and I see he lacks both."

Members on both sides of the House began cheering and yelling.

"May we have order, please?" asked the Speaker. The debate was getting heated and Goyer was definitely in the hot seat.

The three NDP members also attacked the Solicitor General on the upcoming Swackhammer inquiry. Peters argued the investigation should be transparent. "The public should know exactly what happened at Kingston Penitentiary immediately before, during and after the prisoners' uprising. We should know why the riot happened and what can be done to prevent similar disturbances." But Goyer had insisted the hearings remain closed to the media and public to ensure neither inmates nor correctional staff suffered from any misinformation or gossip that might unfold during the hearings. "I'm not interested in front pages of newspapers," Goyer said in defending his decision. "I'm interested in justice being done and I don't believe in a trial by press."[141]

The three politicians went on to say that one of the main causes of the riot was prisoners' fears they would be electronically spied on in their cells at Millhaven and would have no privacy. Howard, Peters and Skoberg said they too had apprehensions about Millhaven. While touring the institution, the MPs grew concerned about its suitability and readiness for prisoners. Although the new cells were painted in pastel colours and the floors were made of rubber tiles, the cell doors had look-in panels instead of bars, making them more claustrophobic. They also found beds and prisoners' clothing piled in heaps, the recreation area was a mud field, and the technical and machine shops were still under construction. In addition, the prison was dangerously understaffed. Skoberg warned that if the prisoners were cooped up all day with nothing to do, there could be a buildup of resentment and tension. There could be another riot.

The Members of Parliament weren't the only people concerned about Millhaven. Queen's University criminologist Stuart Ryan denounced Millhaven as a "glorified hole" of bulletproof glass and stainless steel that we should all be afraid of. He said the new maximum-security prison had been designed so that men could be controlled like cattle in a slaughterhouse.[142] He believed the very structure of the place would create a more repressive regime. "If conditions at the new institution are not considerably better than those at Kingston, the lid's going to blow off that place too," said Peters.

The MPs and the professor were right: resentment was building at Millhaven, but it wasn't due to the lack of recreational activities. Something else was brewing, and it was causing great unrest amongst the prison population.

IN THE SPRING 1971 edition of the *Advance*, a newsletter published by inmates at the Joyceville correctional facility, there was an informative article about new penal programs and preventing future riots.[143] Paul Faguy, the Commissioner of the federal Penitentiary Service, had been a guest speaker at the annual meeting of the Kingston branch of the Elizabeth Fry Society the previous month.

Speaking to the group over sandwiches and tea, Faguy said prison riots, such as the recent one at Kingston Penitentiary, could be prevented in future by better communication between inmates and staff. As a result, the government was conducting a working group to establish regular interaction between guards and prisoners. And this was only one of several programs the government was considering to combat the growing tension within federal prisons. "We as prison officials have learned a great deal from the recent Kingston riots," he said. "And we intend to train many of the present custodial staff to become effective correctional officers who will be ready to assist inmates in guidance, counselling and management of inmate programs." Questioned about the high recidivism rate in Canada, Mr. Faguy said it was obvious that current programs were not working. "Improvements within the service will not be the final solution," he said. "We've got to fix the problem at the source—to provide ways to prevent rather than to cure."

Faguy also told his captive audience that additional working groups were studying the design, size and possible location of new penitentiaries. While he defended the government's ten-year construction plan for new maximum-security facilities like Millhaven that had begun in 1963, he advised the group that the Canadian Penitentiary Service had halted all work on the other proposed maximum-security prisons until a complete reassessment of their design had taken place. "We must take a longer and harder look at our present designs," he said.

In closing, Faguy further impressed the ladies by announcing the creation of work study groups for other programs, such as better psychiatric services, better reception services, improved ratio of staff to inmates and a review of prison uniforms. "Ultimately we want to help resocialize and rehabilitate inmates," Faguy said.

It all sounded promising, but Faguy failed to mention that the working groups would be limited to members of the Canadian Corrections Association and the Canadian Penitentiary Service. There would be no external input.

19

RUNNING THE GAUNTLET

Friday, April 30, 1971

TWO DAYS AFTER the Members of Parliament attempted to meet with inmates at Millhaven, ten detectives from the Ontario Provincial Police arrived at the institution to begin their criminal investigation into the alleged assaults on the Kingston prisoners.[144] Inspector A.W. Goard of the OPP criminal division in Toronto was heading up the team. They knew it wasn't going to be an easy investigation, but word had come directly from the Ontario Attorney General, Allan Lawrence, that the assault complaint from the prisoners was to be dealt with in the same manner as would be extended to any citizen of the province. Writing to the Commissioner of the Ontario Provincial Police, Lawrence said: "I know that you share my desire to make absolutely certain that if any offence has been committed in the handling of these prisoners then the necessary evidence will be brought forward." Due to the fact that the accused were all public officials, Lawrence wanted the investigation to be thorough. "I want as full if not fuller investigation as possible," said the minister. "Therefore, full steam ahead."[145]

Warden Clark and his staff at Millhaven were willing to co-operate with the police investigation into alleged assaults, but they had other problems to contend with at the prison. Tensions were high, and the unrest between the prisoners and the guards was palpable. There had even been talk of a possible hunger strike amongst the inmates. Staffing levels were at a minimum to allow guards who had worked overtime after the riot a much-needed break, and those still working were trying to maintain stability in an institution that was still under construction.

In order to expedite their investigation, the police detectives divided into five teams of two. They would interview inmates, guards, medical staff and anyone else who came into contact with the transferred prisoners. They worked long hours throughout the weekend, as many of the prisoners were reluctant to talk to the investigators. Inmates didn't know whom to trust anymore. What if there were more reprisals, more beatings by the guards?

The team interviewed forty-six inmates who had arrived from Kingston Penitentiary on Monday, April 19, the same day that Norman MacCaud and Billy Knight claimed to have been assaulted. During the course of the interviews, many of the inmates stated they had been viciously assaulted by club-wielding guards upon their arrival. They told the investigators they had been loaded shackled onto the buses at Kingston Penitentiary and driven with a police escort to Millhaven. When the buses arrived at the back of the new prison, the prisoners were ordered to run down the steps of the bus, up the stairs to a loading platform, through a door and then down a series of corridors to the cell areas. As each inmate approached the first door, he was struck on the back of the head with a blackjack baton swung by one of the guards. But that wasn't the end of their ordeal. Then each man was forced to run the gauntlet.

The gauntlet was a long, narrow corridor lined with guards. Each guard was armed with a thirty-inch riot stick, which they used to strike the inmates as they ran by. At the junction of the next corridor, the inmates were forced to strip naked and submit to a body search. Many of the inmates were punched and kicked in the groin. Then they were sent down another corridor towards their cells, where more guards were waiting for them. The guards continued to strike them across the backs and legs.

According to many of the inmates interviewed, the guards had singled out certain inmates who they knew had instigated the Kingston riot. Those prisoners were repeatedly beaten after running the gauntlet.

THE INVESTIGATION into the assault by the guards at Millhaven was proving more complicated than even the seasoned detectives anticipated. Concerned about jeopardizing the Kingston Pen murder case, they couldn't interview some inmates they had been told about until the Kingston Police got the chance to interview them about the murder of Brian Ensor. Their investigation into the alleged assaults on Billy Knight and Norman MacCaud now included dozens of potential victims and numerous potential perpetrators. Bloodied clothing and riot sticks with dried blood on them were confiscated.[146] The prison's medical staff examined each victim and charts were created to show who was claiming injuries. Many of the men had deep bruising on their backs and legs. Knight had a six-inch gash on his head.

By the end of the first week, the ten-man investigation team were convinced that several Millhaven prison guards had indeed committed multiple criminal offences. But they needed to do more work to prove it. If that meant having to interview all 130 members of staff and 350 inmates, they were willing to put in the hours. No guard had ever been charged with assaulting an inmate in Canada, so if they planned to follow through with this, they needed to make sure their case was airtight.

WHILE THE INVESTIGATION into the guards at Millhaven was front-page news, little was being said about the six guards who had been kidnapped during the riot. Only one of them had spoken to reporters after the rebellion. Joseph Vallier allowed a local reporter to interview him at his home.[147] He told the *Kingston Whig-Standard* that he and the other guards were protected by a roster of inmates who would rotate every eight hours. He said the inmates kept assuring them they would protect the guards. They said, "Those donkeys downstairs are not coming up." While they were confined, the guards tried to put up a good front despite their fears they might not survive. They asked for magazines and cards and passed much of the time playing euchre. The inmates broke into the canteen and brought them toothbrushes, tooth-paste and tobacco. They had coffee, biscuits and sandwiches. On a few occasions the guards were asked to write notes saying they were safe.

On the last night of the riot Vallier said the situation got very intense. "The inmates went berserk when they saw the army troops and machine guns. We thought it was the end." Glancing over at his wife, he continued, "If it hadn't been for those prisoners pro-tecting us..." He didn't finish the sentence.

Kerry Bushell and his wife Elaine had left their apartment in Kingston soon after the riot to avoid reporters who kept showing up at their home. They didn't know where to go, so they jumped in their car and just kept driving. Terry Decker and the other guards were on sick leave and weren't talking to the press. Each of the guards had received a personal letter of gratitude for his bravery from Solicitor General Goyer and each received the six hundred dollars in overtime pay they had been promised. They were also expected to testify at the board of inquiry convened to investigate "the Disturbance at KP," as the Canadian Penitentiary Service referred to it.

A WEEK AFTER THE RIOT, the papers ran a small story related to the guards. The union representing federal penitentiary officers was seeking compensation for each of the men. In a letter to Solicitor General Goyer, Paul Gascon, the secretary-treasurer of the Public Service Alliance of Canada, was asking the government to grant five thousand dollars in compensation to each of the officers who were held hostage. The union was also suggesting each of the guards get one month's leave with pay to facilitate their physical and mental recovery. In his letter, Gascon reminded the Solicitor General of the dangerous working conditions that corrections officers faced every day. "The guards who were held hostage have paid the price of their dedication by facing the threat of death during the period when they were held hostage by the rioting prisoners," wrote Gascon. He went on to say the guards had suffered mental and physical hardship and it was the duty of the Government of Canada to compensate them.

In his prompt response to Mr. Gascon, Solicitor General Goyer acknowledged the difficult environment and inherent hazards encountered in a correctional officer's day-to-day role. Goyer also acknowledged the mental anguish the men must have suffered during the riot, but he did not agree that they should be compensated for their unfortunate ordeal. "As you are aware, the officers concerned have been treated as if they were performing their normal duties and have been paid at the appropriate overtime rates. They are also entitled to sick leave if necessary," he wrote. "While we all deplore this recent incident and recognize that the officers concerned appear to have stood up very well under it, it is nevertheless recognized that the risk of assault is a continuing condition of employment and therefore I can see no justification for your request for special compensation."

Several weeks after the riot, all six of the kidnapped guards returned to work at Kingston Penitentiary. Terry Decker had

received $807.76 in workmen's compensation benefits for his inju-
ries.[148] Decker and the other guards resumed their normal duties
at the prison, but their lives had been changed forever.

Toronto, May 13, 1971

THE AD FOR THE COMMISSION of inquiry into the Kingston Penitentiary riot appeared in all the major daily newspapers almost a
month after the uprising. Its appearance released another firestorm
of criticism about how the inquiry was being handled. The Canadian Bar Association urged the federal government to hold the
inquiry in public and to provide counsel to anyone appearing
before it.[149] John M. Hodgson, the vice-president of the association, stated that he and other members were deeply concerned
about the integrity of the proceedings. "I consider it essential the
commission conduct its hearings in public," said Hodgson.

COMMISSION OF INQUIRY

INTO

CERTAIN DISTURBANCES

AT KINGSTON PENITENTIARY

*Take Notice that the Commission of Inquiry will conduct
its initial hearing at the Massey Library,
Royal Military College, Kingston, Ontario on Monday
May 17, 1971 at two o'clock in the afternoon.*

*The Commission of Inquiry is authorized to examine
and determine the immediate cause or causes of certain
disturbances at Kingston Penitentiary commencing
on April 14th, 1971 and thereafter, their nature and
extent, the security measures in force at Kingston*

Penitentiary and other related matters. A copy
of the Terms of Reference of the Commission of Inquiry
is available from the undersigned on request.

Dated at Toronto this 13th day of May 1971
Ian Scott
121 Richmond Street West
Toronto, 110, Ontario
Counsel to the Commission of Inquiry

In a letter to Jean-Pierre Goyer, the John Howard Society was requesting the commission make its findings available to assist the public in becoming aware of the long-term problems that existed in corrections.[150] The newspapers were also reporting that a committee from the United Church of Canada had written to Solicitor General Goyer asking that the proceedings of the commission of inquiry be open to the public. Reverend Gordon K. Stewart said they had been prompted to write to the Solicitor General after the allegations of inmate beatings at Millhaven penitentiary.[151]

Responding to critics of the government's decision regarding the commission of inquiry, Norman Riddiough, the director of information for the Solicitor General, stated that the general public was the last group that should be told what went on in Canadian prisons.[152]

On the same day the ad for the commission of inquiry appeared in newspapers, inmates at Millhaven went on a hunger strike.[153] Member of Parliament Arnold Peters (NDP, Temiskaming) told the press that he had heard about the hunger strike from an inside source at the prison. Prisoners were complaining they had been segregated and isolated since the Kingston riot and were not being allowed to see their lawyers. Others were upset about the conditions at the new facility and the lack of exercise. "It seems to be just a manifestation of a critical problem brought over from Kingston," said Peters. He was demanding that the government investigate conditions at Millhaven before even more serious problems developed.[154] Justice Minister John Turner told the House of Commons he would ask Solicitor General Goyer to look into the matter.

Conservative and NDP members of the Commons justice committee were still pressing the government for an immediate visit to Millhaven, but Solicitor General Goyer was refusing their request, claiming their visit could interfere with official police inquiries that were being conducted. Goyer told the committee members it would be better for them to wait until prison conditions returned to normal. "It wouldn't be good to cause any more excitement than necessary in the present climate," said Goyer. "We open the doors and run the risk of another riot or we close the doors and run the risk of criticism."

Arnold Peters argued the committee could possibly prevent another riot by looking into some of the current complaints.[155] But how were members supposed to know the facts if they couldn't visit the prison? "If you don't know the truth, keep quiet," snapped Mr. Goyer.

A motion by Conservative MP Eldon Wood from Calgary North requesting the committee be allowed to visit Millhaven to interview guards and prisoners about the Kingston–Millhaven events was defeated by a vote of five to three.

Goyer had successfully prevented Members of Parliament from visiting Millhaven, but there were still more questions to be answered. MP Harold Stafford from Elgin wanted to know why Bertrand Robert's request to be transferred out of Kingston Penitentiary had not been granted.[156] Information had come forth that Robert had requested a transfer months earlier because he feared he would be slain by other prisoners. Now he was in a coma and not expected to live. Goyer refused to comment, saying the assault on Robert was now a police investigation, but he stated Robert had received special protection while in Kingston, as did others like him.

Member of Parliament Terrance Murphy from Sault Ste. Marie was not satisfied with Goyer's response. He told the House that when the justice committee had toured some prisons the previous year, they found that men like Robert were protected by segregating them from the rest of the prison population. "They live in conditions we would not expect a dog to live under," Murphy said. "They spend twenty-three and a half hours a day in cramped cells and looked like hungry chickens begging for food." Everyone knew child molesters, sexual deviants and squealers were at the bottom of the social hierarchy in prisons and were subject to brutal treatment. He went on to suggest the government consider building special institutions for these kinds of prisoners.

WHILE NEWS OF a hunger strike at Millhaven was attracting public interest, Professor Morton was also in the press again with more allegations against the Penitentiary Service. Morton had received word that nineteen prisoners had been transferred out of Millhaven and were in solitary confinement at Collins Bay. Twelve of those, according to his sources, were considered "ringleaders" of the Kingston riot. Morton was demanding to know why the inmates had been moved. "To be placed in solitary confinement is to suffer punishment of an extreme nature," said Morton. "And to date, none of these men have been charged with any crime."

Morton was questioning the rights of prisoners under the Canadian Bill of Rights. "Can it be that section two of the Bill of Rights, the fundamental freedoms of all Canadian citizens, does not apply to prisoners in Canadian penitentiaries? That they may be lawfully, although arbitrarily, punished without the right to counsel, to a fair hearing and to the presumption of innocence?"[157] If so, Morton argued, the Canadian Penitentiary Service had placed the prisoner beyond the pale of Canadian law. "If a prisoner is a non-person under our law, then the Swackhammer Commission is redundant," stated Morton.

A young Toronto lawyer by the name of Clayton Ruby was also appealing to the courts to have his client removed from solitary confinement. Ruby claimed his client, Brian Dodge, was being kept in a cell measuring nine feet by six and was only allowed out for thirty minutes a day. "The cells aren't fit to hold any human being," argued Ruby. "And for eating and drinking, my client is given a bowl which resembles the bowl I feed my dog with."[158]

Glen Morris, one of the other inmates being held in solitary, had apparently set fire to himself and had suffered third-degree burns on his left foot.[159] "I won't be responsible for what happens to me," he told his lawyer. "We are being kept in isolation and the pressure is too much for us." He also told his lawyer that five other inmates had cut themselves, including Robbie Robidoux, who needed thirteen stitches to close a self-inflicted wound on his leg. Another inmate had swallowed pieces of broken glass and had to be taken to Kingston General Hospital.[160]

Billy Knight was also languishing in solitary confinement at Collins Bay penitentiary. His lawyer, Barry Swadron, had taken his complaint to the Ontario Supreme Court. Swadron stated to Justice Eric Moorehouse that Knight's confinement was a violation of his rights under the Canadian Bill of Rights. Swadron declared the Bill gave Canadians protection against arbitrary detention and cruel and unusual punishment.[161] "He elected not to live within the rights of society," Judge Moorehouse replied to the lawyer. "I don't listen very sympathetically to civil rights under those conditions." The judge added that Knight's detention in solitary confinement was possibly for his own protection. "The men who

run these institutions have a difficult and important job to do."
Billy Knight and the other Kingston ringleaders would remain in
solitary confinement.

ON SUNDAY, MAY 16, Detective Kealy received a call from Kingston
General Hospital. It was a call he had been expecting. Bertrand
Henry Robert had died from multiple fractures to the head. Surgery was performed to stem the bleeding in his brain, but the
damage was too severe and he never regained consciousness. He
was thirty-four years old. The Kingston riot was now a double
murder investigation.

DORCHESTER PENITENTIARY, NEW BRUNSWICK
May 20, 1971

IT WAS A SMALL news report on the front page of the *Toronto Daily
Star*. Two prisoners had been shot at Dorchester Penitentiary in
New Brunswick after 232 inmates had barricaded themselves in
the prison's recreation hall the previous night. Guards had shot the
prisoners while they were trying to escape, but a prison official
said the wounds were not serious. The revolt had lasted fourteen
hours and all of the inmates were back in their cells by ten o'clock
the following morning. Little else was said about the event, but it
prompted a swift reaction from the Solicitor General.

Speaking to reporters a few days later, Goyer said he was not
going to carry out reform of Canada's penal system if prisoners
didn't act responsibly. Goyer said prisoners weren't helping their
cause by creating disturbances. "I'm not going to take the risk of
moving into reform if the inmates are not able to behave." Goyer
added that prisoners would gain nothing from violence and dis-
order; instead, these would only delay a restructuring program.

This reflected a marked difference in attitude towards prisoners from the one Goyer had expressed just a few days earlier, when he spoke to the John Howard Society in Vancouver. Goyer told the gathered crowd that the riot at Kingston Penitentiary had been stirred by frustrated human dignity. "Inmates want to be considered citizens," Goyer said. "This is perhaps why it was so difficult for them to formulate their grievances." He said the problems in prisons were related to human values and social isolation. Outbreaks such as the one at Kingston could be expected if prisoners were cut off from the world.

He told the Society the federal plans for the $18-million prison in Mission, BC, had been cancelled and would be replaced with a system emphasizing rehabilitation.[162] The penitentiary was part of the ten-year construction program announced in 1963 and was to have housed four hundred inmates. One million dollars had already been spent to purchase the land. Goyer went on to say the designs of the two new maximum-security prisons already built—Millhaven and Archambault, north of Montreal—were oppressive. His department was now thinking in terms of smaller prisons and situating them closer to major cities in order to provide greater access to psychiatric help, families and parole services.

With respect to the Dorchester incident, Goyer said he would order a federal inquiry, but added that its findings would not be made public.

20

INNOCENT UNTIL PROVEN GUILTY

May 27, 1971

THE MEMO ARRIVED first thing Thursday morning.[163] Allan Lawrence, the Attorney General of Ontario, had been expecting it.

Re: Assault Charges—Millhaven Guards

This morning I was advised that eleven guards employed at Millhaven Penitentiary will be charged with assault. There will be a total of 24 counts of assault causing bodily harm with respect to a number of guards and common assault with respect to other guards.

The charges are being laid this morning under the direction of Mr. C.M. Powell. The guards will be summonsed to appear in Provincial Judges Court, Napanee.

In the event that you may wish to make an announcement in the House, there will be a news blackout until

2pm today. May I please have your direction regarding publicity?

H.H. Graham
Deputy Commissioner, Operation
Ontario Provincial Police

The following day, Lawrence announced the charges against the guards to the press but refused to reveal their names. In Ottawa, Solicitor General Goyer advised the press that disciplinary action would not be taken against any of the guards by the Penitentiary Service itself.[164] "They are innocent until proven guilty," stated Goyer. His department would provide legal counsel for the eleven, as was customary. Commissioner of Penitentiaries Paul Faguy said the guards would not be suspended. "We cannot presume guilt," said Faguy. The guards would be working as usual at Millhaven Institution.[165]

Having read Ron Haggart's column in the Toronto Telegraph *I feel I must register my protest to the cruel treatment of the inmates from Kingston Penitentiary by the guards at Millhaven. It really makes me wonder what the world is coming to that this cruelty can be happening in our province of Ontario. We wouldn't treat our animals such as this. To live in fear, regardless of the severity of their crime, it would seem to me that it would be impossible to rehabilitate these persons to any degree. As human beings there must be some element of dignity.*
—letter to Mr. Robert Stanbury, MP for Scarborough, from Mrs. Norma Agnew, Agincourt, Ontario[166]

Napanee, June 3, 1971

ON AN UNSEASONABLY warm Thursday morning in June, a large crowd began to gather early at the Lennox and Addington County Memorial Building on Dundas Street in Napanee, twenty miles west of Kingston. It was going to be a busy day at the courthouse and some of the locals wanted to make sure they got a seat inside for the proceedings. Reporters from Kingston and Toronto were also anxious to get into the tiny courthouse.

Eleven prison guards employed at Millhaven penitentiary were scheduled to appear in provincial court, criminal division, in front of Judge P.E.D. Baker. Stuart Willoughby, a Kingston lawyer, was representing all of the accused. He had been hired by the Solicitor General's office. Until now, the names of the accused had not been released to the media. The Solicitor General's office had stated safety concerns as the reason it would not release the identities of the guards. After all, they were still working at Millhaven and were in close contact with inmates.

Judge Baker was swift in his proceedings as he read out the criminal charges against the penitentiary employees standing in front of him. Only ten of the accused had shown up, as one was ill in hospital. The guards were charged with twenty-four counts of assault against eight inmates.[167] With little emotion, all of them pleaded not guilty.[168] And now their names were out:

1) *Grant Snyder*
2) *Bernard Evans*
3) *Peter Hinch*
4) *Albert Sweet*
5) *Robert Earl Goodwin*
6) *Paul Joseph Cote*

7)   *Lester Lindstra*
8)   *George Huffman*
9)   *George Perrault*
10) *Earl Northmore*
11) *Daniel Cahill*

The guards were charged with assaulting convicts Allan Gauld, Norman MacCaud, Chico Santana, William Knight, Robert Walters, William Crosby, Brian Beaucage and Johnny Hance. They would go to trial on July 19. Reporters rushed from the courthouse to meet their afternoon deadlines.

Later that day, speaking to reporters outside the Ontario Legislature, Attorney General Allan Lawrence described the charges as "pretty unique," because they were based on the credibility of prisoners' statements about alleged beatings.

Whig reporter Sheldon MacNeil, who had covered the Kingston riot from the beginning, was in the Napanee courthouse when the guards were charged. Now he was hearing rumblings of a planned protest at all federal penitentiaries across the country. According to his sources, correctional officers were gearing up for a national strike in response to the charges laid against the officers accused of beating the inmates at Millhaven. The Penitentiary Service usually dealt with such situations internally. That had been the case earlier in the year, when guards at Saskatchewan Penitentiary were suspended after prisoners said they had been beaten with chains.

"This is a trial of the citizens," said Paul Gascon of the Public Service Alliance of Canada, which represented the guards' union. "If citizens allow such things to go on, inmates will have the right to riot and no force can be used against them to quell it." He bragged that the union was powerful and would be working with its own lawyers to fight the charges against the guards. "There are people who are trying to destroy authority," he said of the prisoners. "If the government wants to free the inmates, then it should change the laws." Mr. Gascon added that as long as there are riots and outbreaks of violence in prisons, force would have to be used by guards. "Prison staff morale is running low and could become a very serious problem if the guys at Millhaven are convicted," said another representative of the Public Service Alliance.[169]

Sheldon MacNeil knew that a national protest by federal guards could create a huge ripple effect across the country and would be dangerous. MacNeil contacted the Solicitor General's office for more information but was told they had no comment.[170]

On June 16, a twelfth guard at Millhaven was charged with assault causing bodily harm.[171] William Orser would appear in court on July 19 with his co-workers.

WHILE WORKING ON the story about the prison guards, Sheldon Mac-Neil received word about an upcoming gathering in Ottawa. The wardens of Canada's penitentiaries would be meeting on June 21 to discuss new guidelines on dealing with the press.[172] Since the news blackout during the April riot at Kingston, there had been a clampdown and administrators at many of the federal institutions would not discuss any matters with the press, nor were press allowed into any of the prisons. As a result, the Solicitor General's office was being bombarded with questions and inquiries about prisons across Canada. "At the conference we will be laying down guidelines to return local autonomy to wardens when dealing with the press," announced Norman Riddiough, information director for the Solicitor General's office.

In an interview with the *Kingston Whig-Standard*, Riddiough also said his department was conducting a survey in Kingston and six other cities to ascertain the public's attitude towards corrections. Four Queen's University students were canvassing Kingston residents and asking their views on establishing halfway houses for inmates in their neighbourhoods. Other survey questions would ask their opinions on sentencing and parole. "Most people so far have been very interested," said Riddiough.

June 4, 1971

A SMALL ARMY of police were standing outside the Frontenac County Courthouse on Friday when two yellow school buses pulled up along the west side of the building at 11 a.m. Fifteen uniformed Kingston city police officers stood side by side along with ten provincial police. They were prepared for trouble in case the crowds already gathered on the other side of the street got rowdy. The press were there too, hovering at every vantage point, cameras ready, waiting for the bus doors to open. Senior inspector Wilf Kealy had arrived early and was standing patiently with the other detectives.

Wearing dishevelled prison greys and handcuffs, eighteen straight-faced inmates slowly descended from the buses, moving single file towards the limestone building. The foot-long chains on their leg irons scraped against the cement as they walked with their heads down.[173] They were escorted upstairs to the large courtroom, already packed with over eighty spectators. Sitting in the prisoners' dock, most of them appeared indifferent to their surroundings, chewing gum, joking and talking amongst themselves as they waited for the judge to arrive. Two of the convicts were wearing newer prison garb with no identifying prisoner number. Solicitor General Goyer had removed the numbers shortly after the riot in a step towards humanizing prisons. Inmates were now referred to by their given names. Two policemen and four prison guards stood behind the prisoners.

The cocky group of former KP inmates were there to face multiple charges of murder and kidnapping. The inmates would be brought before Judge Baker, the same judge who had arraigned eleven prison guards on charges of assault the day before. Only some of the inmates had legal counsel.

Crown attorney John E. Sampson represented the province. The hearing was conducted in two parts. First, Judge Baker read out the charges in connection with the violent deaths of Brian Ensor and Bertrand Robert. Each inmate stood as his name was called out:

> *William David Shepley (24), Windsor*
> *Brian Lester Beaucage (23), London*
> *Robert Francis Robidoux (18), Toronto*
> *David Sylvester Birt (24), Charlottetown*
> *James Robert Oag (24), London*
> *Donald Oag (20), London*
> *Glen Archer Morris (24), Townsriver, New Jersey*
> *Edward Maxwell Fowler (18), Toronto*
> *Harold Kenneth St. Amour (39), Pembroke*
> *Ernest James Bugler, St. Thomas*
> *Edward Fulton Johnston (22), Clarkson*
> *Wayne Herbert McGurgin (28), Toronto*
> *Brian William Dodge (27), Petrolia*

In all, thirteen inmates were charged with non-capital murder. The judge accepted no pleas.

"My client is being subjected to a type of pretrial punishment by being confined to a dissociation cell at KP," said lawyer George C. Conn when his client's name was read out by the judge.[174] Conn was representing 24-year-old David Birt. Conn told the court his client was "in the hole" without shower facilities and was forced to sleep in the same clothes he was wearing in court.

Conn also demanded more information about the alleged offences from Crown attorney Sampson. What was the manner of death for the two victims, the exact time of death, and what was his client's alleged participation in the deaths? Conn then asked for a list of names of potential witnesses.

Sampson was clearly frustrated by Conn's demands. He reminded the court he had already advised the lawyer that more information would be released at the preliminary hearing, "which as far as I'm concerned can begin today," said Sampson.

Not willing to back down, Conn agreed with the Crown attorney.

Judge Baker overruled them both.

After announcing the murder charges, Judge Baker then charged seven inmates with kidnapping the guards during the riot:

William James (Billy) Knight (27), Dresden
Charles Wayne Saunders (22), Wallaceburg
James Robert Adams (31), Mount Clemens, Michigan
Allan Lafreniere (25), Toronto
Leo Joseph (no information)
Paul Barrieault (24), McAdam, New Brunswick
Brian William Dodge (27), Petrolia

Dodge was the only inmate charged with both murder and kidnapping.

Billy Knight, who had instigated the riot and who had led the prisoners' committee in negotiations for better living conditions, sat expressionless in the courtroom when he and his co-conspirators were charged. Knight's lawyer, Barry Swadron of Toronto, stood up and advised the judge he would be requesting a change of venue for his client at the preliminary hearing scheduled for the following week.

Before Judge Baker could adjourn the court, one of the inmates asked to speak. "I would like to ask the court to investigate the conditions under which we have been living at Millhaven since the trouble," said Glen Morris, who was charged with two counts of non-capital murder. "I don't mean an investigation by some government agency," he added. "Send in the health department." He described sleeping on concrete beds and receiving no medical treatment.[175] "We haven't been convicted yet," said the tall, bespectacled Morris. "Don't we have any rights?"

Brian Dodge then addressed the court to complain he had been attacked by the guards supervising him. He was being held at Kingston Pen since the troubles had begun brewing in Millhaven.

"Speak up," said Sampson.

"I can't," complained Dodge. "They smashed my teeth and I haven't eaten in seven days."

Judge Baker did know that a police investigation had been launched into a recent incident at Collins Bay penitentiary, but it wasn't inmates who had been harmed. Five former prisoners from KP who were being held in dissociation cells since their transfer had allegedly assaulted two correctional officers. One guard was punched in the face while the other had injured his shoulder.

Judge Baker turned to the Crown attorney and said: "Take note that the accused are claiming mistreatment before their trail. Will you look into this?"

"Okay," replied Sampson.

Inmate Charles Saunders then stood to ask the judge why the names of the eleven Millhaven guards charged with assaulting prisoners following the riot had not been released to the public prior to their court appearance the day before. The names of all of the convicts had been released to the press days before their court appearance.

"Once all information is filed with the court, it becomes a public document," replied the judge. Saunders was not going to get an answer.

"Do we have to come to court in leg irons?" shouted Allan La Freniere, who had been charged with kidnapping.

The judge looked down at the prisoners and replied that he wasn't aware they were in leg irons. "I'll look into it," Judge Baker said.

Surprisingly, the reported ringleader of the attack on the undesirables remained silent throughout the hearing. Dave Shepley had said very little to anyone since April. He had undergone surgery to repair his jaw, which had been broken during the riot, and he had actually requested solitary confinement since arriving at Millhaven, stating that he felt he had an unhealthy control over the other inmates. The prison psychologist, Paul Henry, interviewed Shepley and observed he was extremely tense and anxious. "Shepley is a manipulative, sociopathic individual, who is usually concerned with his own image and keeping face with others: a highly dangerous individual on account of his inner drives for attention." Henry also noted that Shepley suffered from a major psychiatric disability, which could be called both psychotic and neurotic.[176] Regardless, Shepley was determined to be mentally capable under section 14 of the Criminal Code and was fit to stand trial.

AT THE END OF THE HEARING, the inmates were locked back into their handcuffs and escorted down the rear staircase of the courthouse building to the buses waiting in the back lane. The case was adjourned until June 8, 1971.

For Kealy and the other Kingston detectives, the events at the courthouse had been rewarding. This was the culmination of one of the largest investigations their department had ever undertaken.

For three weeks they had worked from morning till late at night. They had interviewed more than five hundred prisoners, many of whom were too afraid to say anything. But finally a few inmates had gone against the inmates' code of never squealing to the cops and had revealed the horrors they had witnessed on the last night of the riot.

One inmate told the detectives he was afraid to testify but that he had something to offer: he could do a drawing of the attack on the undesirables. He knew his life would be in jeopardy if it was ever discovered. Detective Sergeant Bill Hackett was hesitant to believe a sketch would help their investigation, but they needed any evidence they could get. Hackett had the inmate secretly moved to the local Holiday Inn.[177] For two days the prisoner worked on a detailed pencil drawing of what he had witnessed in the dome, while a guard sat outside his hotel room door. When the drawing was done, it revealed more than the police could ever have imagined. The haunting sketch depicted a circle of helpless men bound to chairs, while others stood over them brandishing weapons, ready to strike. It was exactly the sadistic scene other witnesses had described to the detectives. But the drawing revealed one additional key detail: the prison numbers on the attackers' uniforms. Now Hackett and the other detectives just had to make sure all of their witnesses stayed alive in order to testify.

July 13, 1971

THE PRELIMINARY HEARING for the thirteen inmates charged with the murders of Brian Ensor and Bertrand Robert began on July 13, 1971. Chief Judge Arthur Otto Klein was presiding. The 61-year old, originally from Walkerton, Ontario, was the head of the provincial criminal courts.

Thirty Kingston Police officers and prison guards accompanied the accused into the Frontenac County Courthouse, where their lawyers were waiting for them. Most of them appeared unshaven and all of them were wearing prison uniforms. Two air-conditioning units and a new sound system with microphones had been installed in the courthouse in anticipation of a long, difficult session.[178] A special prisoners' dock had also been built to allow the large group of defendants to see and hear the witnesses. A solid row of guards sat behind the prisoners, while police officers blocked the windows and doors leading from the courtroom.

It was now up to Crown attorney John Sampson to present sufficient evidence to have the convicts committed for trial on the murder charges. Sampson confirmed to the court that a number of prisoners who would be called as witnesses during the hearing had been transferred to Quinte Regional Jail in Napanee for their own protection.

Before the proceeding began, Judge Klein issued a ban on the publication of any evidence and the names of the witnesses.[179] No press would be allowed into the courtroom. Klein also had the prisoners' handcuffs removed, but their leg irons would remain on throughout their court appearance.

On the first day of the preliminary hearing, Crown attorney Sampson called a total of six witnesses, five of whom had been prisoners at Kingston Penitentiary during the riot. The thirteen accused sat quietly, listening to their fellow inmates do the unthinkable. They were going against the inmates' code to never rat on another con. There would be a heavy price to pay.

By the third day of the hearing, ten inmate witnesses had given damning testimony against the accused, and the shackled inmates sitting in the prisoners' dock were becoming more agitated. After the lunch hour recess, inmate Brian Dodge refused to

board the bus at Kingston Pen to be transported back to the Frontenac County Courthouse. He was eventually carried onto the bus.
When the prisoners arrived at the courthouse, another brawl
broke out when the convicts refused to enter the courtroom.[180]
Ernest Bugler and Glen Morris struggled with police officers while
the other inmates yelled insults and threats. The afternoon session
was delayed for over an hour while the police and prison guards
attempted to restore order.

On the fourth day of the preliminary hearing, the thirteen KP
convicts were committed to stand trial for the murders of Brian
Ensor and Bertrand Robert. After eleven eyewitnesses had been
called to testify by the Crown, the defence lawyers had reluctantly
conceded there was sufficient evidence to proceed to trial.

Before the inmates were removed from the courtroom, lawyer
Clayton Ruby, representing Brian Dodge, made a plea to have his
client removed from solitary confinement at Kingston Pen, where
he had been since June 8, when the murder charges were laid.[181]
"My client lives in a cement cell not fit for any human being and
is only allowed out for half an hour of exercise each day," Ruby told
the judge. "When the trial begins, I want my client sane," he added.
The twelve other defence lawyers made similar requests.

Judge Klein advised the lawyers he did not have the authority
to grant requests from prisoners to be removed from solitary confinement, where all of the accused were being held. The Penitentiary
Service had the sole authority to determine how and where prisoners were kept.

Upset by the judge's remarks, one of the inmates jumped from
the prisoners' dock and attempted to attack a police officer standing nearby. He was quickly apprehended and dragged out of the
courtroom. The other prisoners began yelling obscenities at the
judge and Glen Morris threatened to kill every uniformed person

present in the court if he was ever released from custody.[182] He then refused to leave the courtroom and had to be carried out.

Toronto lawyer Henry Rosenthal, representing Wayne McGurgin, told Judge Klein that the medieval conditions at Kingston Pen were the cause of the verbal and physical outbursts from the convicts. The inmates were being punished before being convicted and were showing signs of deterioration, he insisted. "We should avoid in any way having these men arrive for trial as mental and emotional cripples," said Rosenthal.

No date was set for the murder trial, but Crown attorney Sampson said he was prepared to proceed at the opening of the Ontario Supreme Court assizes on September 7.

At the conclusion of the preliminary hearing, defence counsel requested the Crown Attorney's Office supply a summary of evidence of witnesses not called at the hearing but who might be called at the trial. John Sampson reluctantly agreed to supply the statements as long as defence counsel did not disclose the names of any of the witnesses to their clients or anyone else who would divulge the information.

On July 26, 1971, Crown attorney Sampson sent a synopsis of the evidence given by the witnesses to all thirteen defence lawyers. Two weeks later, Sampson was informed that a copy of the sensitive document had been leaked. Someone posing as a lawyer for one of the defendants had obtained a copy from the courthouse. The man said his name was George Rose.

It didn't take long for the document to show up in all of the local penitentiaries, including Millhaven, Kingston Pen and Collins Bay, where most of the murder suspects were being held. It was quickly dubbed "the Rat List,"[183] and the men on that list were in serious danger.

A PLEA FOR HELP

Mr. Harold E. Stafford
Member of Parliament
House of Commons
Ottawa, Ont.

June 17, 1971

Dear Sir,

What happened at Kingston to those poor humans called (unde-sirables) during the riot was pure horror. These poor humans didn't deserve to be murdered and beaten. It was only a miracle that saved the others from being put to a senseless, savage death. Not only was it the beatings they received at the end, but their own terror and fear they went through for four days. The very first night of the riot they had the water hoses turned on them and even a few were roughed up. Can you imagine sir, what hell they went through? And yet these men were supposed to be under protection for their lives. What I saw made me sick.

The reason I'm writing you is that I'll be soon in fear of my own life. You see sir; the reason is that I gave a written statement to the city police. I suspect to be called to testify at the trial of the inmates charged over the Kingston riot. Once I testify sir, my life isn't worth a damn for I'll be known in jail slang as a (informer, a stool pigeon).

My fear is so deep and real, that almost every night I think of cutting my wrists with my razorblade or hanging myself. I just pray and hope with other inmates as well as myself who do testify we will be given protection. It wasn't easy for me to give the police a state-ment, but then I saw poor humans savagely beaten and murdered, by so-called solid cons. It made me sick to my stomach and I shall never forget, and it really made me see myself for what I really was and I didn't like it.

May I say this for myself, before this happened I was considered a solid convict, but now I'm sick of jails, convicts, and life. Still I want to live, and against one or two I have a chance, but not against the prison population. Sir, it's not that I don't trust you, but I can't bring myself to sign, not knowing if this letter will get to you. Please sir, look into the matter of protection for those inmates that will need it. In a month or so I myself will be asking for protective custody.

Thank you, Involved Inmate

Member of Parliament Harold Stafford forwarded the letter he received from the inmate at Collins Bay penitentiary to Solicitor General Goyer and Paul Faguy, Commissioner of Penitentiaries. Stafford was certain that steps were being taken to afford special protection to the witnesses in the Kingston Pen riot but wanted to confirm his assumptions directly with the Solicitor General.

Mr. Harold E. Stafford
Member of Parliament
House of Commons
Ottawa, Ontario

July 13, 1971

Dear Mr. Stafford:

Your letter of June 16, 1971 from an inmate who was involved in the Kingston riot has been considered very carefully in my Department.

The man who wrote to you is, of course, only one of the many who have raised issue of protection. There is every possibility of course, that their safety may be endangered. This could be true even though they may not have given statements to the police or if they have given statements, they subsequently refused to testify in an open court.

As you know, mere suspicion that an inmate has given information to the police could be enough to endanger his safety, and there is no doubt that the danger is very real. The letter written to you is only one of the symptoms of fear amongst inmates who may be called to testify.

At the present time, there is no absolute guarantee of safety to the inmates themselves and even their relatives on the outside. We have no facilities in Ontario to completely isolate inmates who have already given information to the police agencies, or who may testify in court later. The possibility of threat exists whether they are in maximum, medium or minimum-security institutions. Perhaps Millhaven Institute affords greater safety because of the control and direct observation available there. I can only state that our institutional staff are well informed on the situation and we will do everything we can to protect those who cooperate with law enforcement agencies.

At the moment, therefore the situation is a static one. There will be no laxity in vigilance and while it may appear that we are taking a negative view, this is very much the opposite of our thinking. We shall have to await the outcome of deliberations and act as situations dictate.

Thank you for writing.

Yours sincerely,

Hon. Jean-Pierre Goyer, P.C. M.P.
Solicitor General of Canada

21
BOUND IN DARKNESS

I have no crystal ball to predict what will happen in Canadian penitentiaries.

—Hon. Jean-Pierre Goyer, Solicitor General,
Commons Debates, May 20, 1971

SOLICITOR GENERAL GOYER had a problem. He had inmate eyewitnesses who were prepared to give evidence at the trial of the thirteen prisoners accused of murder in the Kingston Pen riot, but he had no place to put them where the government could guarantee their safety. They couldn't stay in any of the federal penitentiaries. If word got out, they would be killed. And the provincial institutions were ill-prepared to accommodate potentially dangerous criminals. Approximately forty inmates needed to be rehoused and protected. Some of the prisoners who had already given evidence had been taken to the Quinte Regional Detention Centre in Napanee, but the inmates there were already complaining about their treatment.

In a handwritten letter to the *Toronto Daily Star*, a group of six inmates confined to the Quinte jail wrote about their plight. In their plea for help, they complained they were being unfairly imprisoned and lacked all privileges such as recreation, radio, television and

204 MURDER ON THE INSIDE

canteen. They were risking their lives to testify for the prosecution in the Kingston riot murder trial, and now they were stuck in a worse place than Kingston Pen. Didn't the government owe them some consideration and respect? "Please come to our aid," asked the writer. "We are human beings bound in darkness. Come to Napanee, converse with us. Let some light in. Please HELP!" The letter was signed, "On behalf of the six in darkness."[184]

Three days after the letter was written, one of the six inmates was indeed moved out of the Quinte jail. D. Robertson, inmate #6646, was admitted to the Kingston Psychiatric Hospital and put on suicide watch. The Solicitor General's office sent a letter to him at the hospital expressing their sincere appreciation for the co-operation he had extended to law enforcement in relation to the murder trial.

Because the inmates' letter had reached the press, Solicitor General Goyer finally reached out to Syl Apps, the Minister of Correctional Services for the province of Ontario, to request additional accommodations in several provincial institutions. The federal government was willing to pay each jail a rental fee and a per diem rate for each inmate they accepted. In reply, L.R. Hackl, the Ontario Deputy Minister of Correctional Services, agreed to a $1.00 per day rental fee and $19.90 per diem cost for each inmate. In addition, the provincial department wanted reimbursement for any costs associated with transporting inmates from one jail to another and for bringing on extra staff as needed.

Ottawa, July 20, 1971

IN ANOTHER ATTEMPT to appease public concerns, Solicitor General Goyer announced that prisoners in federal penitentiaries would now have the right to elect committees to make recommendations on conditions and work programs within each prison.[185] The new system, effective August 1, 1971 would involve thirty-two federal penal institutions. "We recognize committees of prisoners elected by the inmate population can provide vital communication between the inmates and the prison administration," said Goyer. No decision-making authority or administrative powers would be delegated to the committees, but "they will work to encourage support and recommend projects for the general welfare of the inmates," added the Solicitor General.

Members of prisoners' committees would be elected twice a year by secret ballot and would meet once a month. They would forward any suggestions or recommendations to the prison warden.

Following the Kingston riot, several members of the Opposition in the House of Commons had felt that it was a lack of communication between inmates and the prison administration that had caused tensions to boil over. A spokesman for Goyer said the department had already been studying the question of prisoners' committees for some time, but the decision to implement them had been accelerated by the events at Kingston.

According to the Deputy Commissioner of Penitentiaries, "What happened at Kingston points to the need for better communication between inmates and the prison administration."

"The spirit of this reform has already begun here," said Millhaven warden Donald Clark. He told the *Kingston Whig-Standard* that committee elections were expected to be established at the penitentiary without any serious difficulties. The prison already had a radio and television committee and a recreation committee. "Communication leads to better understanding," he added.

While Goyer's implementation of prisoner committees gave the illusion of better communication within the penitentiaries, it still fell short of providing any form of public oversight. The 1938 Archambault Royal Commission to Investigate the Penal System had recommended a revolutionary idea in which boards of ordinary

citizens would be given the authority to visit and inspect penitentiaries regularly and without warning. This would mean, in effect,
that prison administrations would become answerable to a group
of citizens who had no professional connection to the administration of justice. Goyer and the Liberal government were just the
latest in a long line of successive governments that chose to ignore
Joseph Archambault's recommendation.

Napanee, July 20, 1971

JOHN HANCE STOOD in the witness box in the Napanee courthouse.
The federal prisoner was making history. He was the first Canadian
inmate ever to testify against a prison guard. The trial of eleven
Millhaven Institution guards charged with assaulting the Kingston
Penitentiary prisoners was a landmark case. Reporters from
Kingston, Ottawa and Toronto were crammed into the old court-
house. Refused a press table, the journalists sat in shabby wooden
chairs trying to take notes.

Provincial court judge Donald Graham of Toronto was presiding. He had already denied a request from Kingston lawyer
L.H. Tepper that the trial of the guards be stayed until the murder
trial of the thirteen Kingston convicts was completed. Mr. Tepper
argued that some of the prisoners being called in the guards' assault
case were also charged with murder. "These proceedings will receive
a great deal of publicity and it could be prejudicial to the accused
at the murder trials," said Mr. Tepper. Judge Graham disagreed.

John Hance began his testimony by identifying the ten guards
present in the courtroom.[186] The eleventh guard, George Huffman,
was absent because of illness. Hance told prosecutor Clayton Powell of the Attorney General's department that four guards—Edgar
Sweet, Robert Goodwin, Peter Hinch and Lester Lindstra—beat
him on the neck and back with blackjacks as he was being taken

off the bus at Millhaven on April 19. The four other guards then beat him with riot sticks as he entered the prison. He said he was forced to run down a corridor lined with guards before his leg irons were removed. At the end of the corridor, Hance claimed he was stripped naked and beaten again. When asked about his injuries, Hance testified he was not allowed to see a doctor for his injuries until May 3, sixteen days after the assault, when Warden Donald Clark ordered the entire prison population to be examined by the staff doctor.

Dr. Donald Workman confirmed Hance's claim.[187] He had examined the inmate on May 3 but found only abrasions on his knees. According to the doctor, Hance had no other visible injuries.

The next witness also confirmed what John Hance had told the court. Cyril Roussey, a 51-year-old inmate serving twenty years for robbery, testified that he and eleven other prisoners had been forced to run a gauntlet of club-wielding guards when they arrived at Millhaven. He saw two of the accused guards, Hinch and Sweet, strike John Hance.[188]

The third witness was William David Shepley. Spectators in the courtroom took special notice of him as many had heard he was the leader in the Kingston Pen murders. Shepley appeared calm and composed as he took the stand. He told the court he saw guard Peter Hinch strike John Hance and a number of the other prisoners during their transfer.[189] He testified that the inmates were beaten as they left the bus and crossed the platform into a corridor of the prison. "They were hitting us and beating us so fast that with the leg irons on, we just couldn't keep up with it."

Constable Carl Hansen of the Ontario Provincial Police detachment in Kingston told the court he watched the unloading of prisoners after escorting the bus to Millhaven with three other officers. He testified that he saw inmates pushed but not struck by guards. However, under cross-examination he admitted, "I didn't keep a constant watch on their movements."

On day two of the trial, Judge Graham abruptly changed the court proceedings to a preliminary hearing after defence lawyer Stewart Willoughby suggested the *Kingston Whig-Standard* newspaper had intentionally interfered with a fair trial. Willoughby, who was representing all of the charged guards, told the judge the paper had reported Canadian Armed Forces troops were on standby for possible duty at Millhaven should trouble erupt because of the trial. The defence lawyer wanted the writer and the paper cited for contempt.

Judge Graham told Willoughby he did not have the power to order any of the newspaper's employees arrested. "I have not read the article," the judge said. "But if I had, it certainly wouldn't influence me."

Whig-Standard staff writer Bruce Dawson was surprised his story had garnered such a heated response from the lawyer at the trial of the guards. He had indeed reported that Canadian Forces troops were on alert in case of a possible strike by guards at Millhaven. Dawson was following a tip he had received from an unidentified military spokesman who said troops from Petawawa had been on standby for ten days. The military man described the operation as hush-hush and declined to give any further information. Wanting to verify the story, Dawson contacted K. Robinson, the information officer for the Public Service Alliance of Canada, who said he could not comment on the possibility of a walkout by prison guards. "Any action in this regard would be illegal," he said, "but you can't rule out the possibility of a walkout." He told the *Whig* reporter that morale among the prison staff was running low and could become very serious if the Millhaven guards were convicted of assaulting prisoners.

Millhaven warden Donald Clark confirmed troops were on standby. "It is a precautionary measure in the event of general security problems," he said.

On the third day of the preliminary hearing, prosecutor Clayton Powell called more inmate witnesses, who testified they too had been methodically and systematically beaten by the guards at Millhaven.

Finally, Patrick McKegney, the assistant deputy warden at Millhaven, testified he had supervised the unloading of the prisoners from Kingston Pen on April 19 but did not witness any convicts being struck by guards.[190] McKegney told the court he instructed the guards to only "tap" the convicts on the backside if they hesitated or refused to move along.

By the end of the third day, after twenty witnesses had been called, eight Millhaven guards were committed to stand trial on seventeen of the twenty-five charges of assault. The judge said no evidence had connected guards George Perrault, Earl Northmore and Daniel Cahill to the allegations made against them.[191] The remaining eight guards elected to stand trial by judge and jury and were released without bail.

August 17, 1971

FOUR MONTHS AFTER the riot, five of the six Kingston Penitentiary prisoners charged with kidnapping six guards pleaded guilty to a lesser charge of forcible seizure.[192] The charges against them had been amended after four hours of negotiations between their defence lawyers and officials from the Attorney General's department. The maximum sentence for kidnapping was life imprisonment, while forcible seizure was only five years.

One of the lawyers representing the accused said his client, Charles Saunders, joined in the plot to seize the guards as a last resort to bring public attention to the atrocious conditions and intolerable rules the inmates were living under at Kingston Penitentiary.

Clayton Ruby, who was representing Brian Dodge, argued his client acted as a result of long-standing grievances about their treatment and living conditions. "The motive was different from the ordinary run-of the-mill event," Ruby said to the judge. "It was not for profit or escape but to try to better the prison system they live in."

The five inmates who accepted the plea deal were: Leo J. Barrieault, Allan La Freniere, Charles Saunders, Brian W. Dodge and Robert J. Adams. As the five men stood in front of provincial court judge Donald Graham, there was one person visibly absent. William (Billy) Knight, considered the ringleader of the April prison riot, was not in the courtroom with his friends. He had no plans to plead guilty to anything and would take his chances with a judge and jury.

22
HIDING IN PLAIN SIGHT

BILLY KNIGHT'S PRELIMINARY hearing began shortly after the other inmates had entered their guilty pleas and were led out of the courtroom. As soon as the hearing began, Barry Swadron, Knight's Toronto lawyer, stood up to ask Judge Graham if his client could move from the bench in the prisoners' dock to sit closer to him at the barristers' table. It was an unusual request, but the judge allowed it.

Now sitting directly behind his lawyer, Knight took on an air of professionalism, casually chatting with a law student and writing down notes. Dressed in a stylish grey suit, white dress shirt and blue striped tie, Knight's appearance had changed dramatically since his last court appearance. His hair was longer and brushed low across his forehead, a much different style from his usual 1940s high pompadour. He appeared well tanned and was now sporting a moustache and black-rimmed glasses. Earlier in the day, inmate Allan Lafreniere was overheard asking, "Where are my glasses? I can't see anything without my glasses." It looked like Knight had decided to borrow them.

The first witness called was guard Terry Decker. He told the court how, on the night of April 14, 1971, at approximately 10:30 p.m., he was attacked by inmates William (Billy) Knight and Charles Saunders. Decker testified that he was following normal prison procedures that night, moving seventy-eight inmates from the prison recreation hall down a corridor, through the dome and up to the second-floor range of cells in the four-storey cellblock. Six guards were waiting in the main dome ready to receive the inmates. As the prisoners filed past Decker in the hallway, he noticed Knight's shirt hanging out, which was a violation of the penitentiary dress rules. He looked directly at Knight and told him to tuck in his shirt. Without warning, Knight swung around and punched Decker in the stomach, knocking him to the floor. Before he could catch his breath, he said another inmate was on top of him, punching him in the face and dragging him backwards towards the recreation hall so the other officers farther down the corridor could not see what was happening. Decker was hit hard in the eye, which caused it to hemorrhage. Knight grabbed the range keys out of Decker's hand, tearing the ligaments in the guard's fingers.

As Knight took off down the range with the keys, another inmate, Charles Saunders, stood over Decker with his knee jammed into the guard's throat. Trying to contain his emotions as he recounted the attack, Decker said he couldn't yell out to warn the other guards and felt helpless in preventing Knight and the others from instigating the riot.

Reading from a typed synopsis of the investigation completed by the Kingston Police, Crown attorney John Sampson proceeded to tell the court that while Decker lay wounded on the floor outside the recreation hall, Knight rushed into the dome area, where he grabbed a wooden box filled with keys and a flashlight. He then yelled at guards Dale, Bushell and Vallier to come down to the dome floor from where they were standing on range two. Knight and fellow inmate Allan Lafreniere attacked Dale to try to take the keys he was holding for range two. Knowing the keys were critical for releasing more inmates, Dale reached through the locked barrier gate leading to the keeper's hall and dropped the keys out of the inmates' reach. Furious, Knight hit Dale across the mouth with the flashlight, splitting his lip open. At the same time, inmates Robert Adams and Leo Barrieault charged into the dome and overpowered guards Donald Flynn and senior keeper Edward Barrett, who was the officer in charge that night.

Meanwhile, two officers back in the recreation hall noticed a guard's cap lying in the corridor leading to the cellblock and instantly knew something was wrong. A prison officer was never seen without his cap. Guard Raymond Pattison ordered all of the remaining inmates still gathered in the corridor to move back into the recreation hall while he went to investigate. As he reached the barrier where Decker was supposed to be stationed, two inmates rushed towards him. It was Billy Knight and Brian Dodge. Knight shone a flashlight in Pattison's face and kicked at his hands while Pattison attempted to hold the barrier shut. The guard managed to lock the gate and ran back to the rec hall.

The Crown told the court that once Knight and his gang had overpowered the officers on duty, the six guards were herded together into one of the cell wings. Then inmates Brian Dodge and Allan Lafreniere took any personal effects and money from the guards before moving them to an air duct between two cell ranges. Later that same night they were moved again, to a cell on the fourth level of the prison, where another inmate told them to change into prisoners' clothing for their own protection.

Sampson said that the police investigation into the kidnapping of the guards confirmed at least four of the six guards held captive by the inmates had been physically attacked during their abduction.

This was a much different record of events from the statements made during the riot by officials of the Solicitor General's department. When Terry Decker was released on the second day of the riot, Goyer's office issued a press release stating Decker had been treated well and his eye injury had been caused accidentally.

Turning back to the witness, Crown attorney Sampson asked Mr. Decker if he could identify William Knight, the ringleader of the attack on the guards and ensuing riot. Decker looked carefully around the courtroom. Knight, sitting behind his lawyer, gently pushed up the eyeglasses perched on the bridge of his nose and continued to doodle on the legal pad in front of him. An awkward silence fell over the courtroom as those in attendance waited for the guard to point out the prisoner who had attacked him. Finally, Decker said he could not see the inmate, William Knight, in the courtroom.

"Are you sure you do not see the accused in the courtroom today?" asked Sampson.

"No, I don't see him."

Knight did not look up. Judge Graham asked Decker to try again. "Take your time, do it carefully." But Decker still couldn't point out Knight.

After Terry Decker left the courtroom, Crown attorney Sampson complained to the judge that the accused was hiding in plain sight behind his lawyer. The judge agreed, and Knight was moved to the counsel table beside his lawyer, Mr. Swadron, and two others.

The next witness called was guard William Babcock. Although he had not been taken hostage by the inmates, Babcock recounted how he had witnessed the attack on Decker and the other guards. When asked to point out inmate William Knight, Babcock said he did not see him. Crown attorney Sampson stood up and began pacing in front of the witness box. He asked the witness to carefully look at all of the occupants in the courtroom. Babcock looked again. Finally, he pointed a finger at one of the men sitting at the counsel table taking copious notes. "The moustache nearly fooled me, but I think that is Knight."[193] Babcock had pointed to one of the lawyers sitting at the table, not William Knight. Sampson abruptly turned and walked back to his seat.

The next two witnesses were guards Douglas Dale and Joseph Vallier. Both men recounted the terrifying events on the night of April 14, 1971, when they were assaulted and kidnapped by Knight and his gang. However, at the end of their testimony neither of them was able to identify Knight in the courtroom. Frustrated, the judge asked Vallier to step down from the witness box and look around the courtroom. Vallier walked past the row of lawyers sitting at the front table and finally pointed to one of them while saying something about the man's moustache. Knight's lawyer, Barry Swadron, bowed his head, thinking his client had finally been identified. The man with the well-trimmed facial hair whom Vallier had pointed to slowly stood up to address the court. "I think I should identify myself," he said. "My name is Clayton Ruby."

Without positive identification from four of the Crown's key witnesses, Judge Donald Graham felt he had no choice but to dismiss the charges against William Knight. For some unknown reason, senior keeper Ed Barrett and guard Kerry Bushell were never called to testify.

Hearing the news, a group of young people sitting in the courtroom began cheering and clapping. Crown attorney Sampson reportedly threw his pencil across the desk in frustration. Barry Swadron patted his client on the back. Knight finally looked up from his doodling and removed his glasses. He didn't need them anymore.

ON AUGUST 27, 1971, the five inmates who had helped Billy Knight overpower the prison staff and take control of Kingston Penitentiary accepted a plea deal for forcible seizure of the six guards. Judge Graham sentenced them each to a three-year jail term. The sentences would run consecutively, which meant they would finish serving out their original sentences before beginning their new prison terms.

At the sentencing hearing, Crown attorney John Sampson requested the Attorney General's department reconsider charges against William Knight. Referring to Knight's altered appearance, Sampson told the court: "The figure of justice may be pictured as blindfolded, but it is not aided by a disguise." Judge Graham agreed with Sampson and said he believed that Knight was more culpable than the five men he had just sentenced. "There may be other events which direct the force of justice against that individual," said the judge before adjourning the court.

Sampson wasn't the only person frustrated by Knight's trickery. His acquittal infuriated the guards he had attacked. Knight had skilfully planned out his disguise and it had worked. The inmate who had planned and instigated the Kingston Penitentiary riot would not serve a single extra day in prison for what he had done.

When Knight returned to Collins Bay penitentiary after his final court appearance and exoneration, guards at the prison seized his razor and made plans to photograph him before he could change his appearance again. But a day later, when Knight sat down in front of the camera, his hair was combed straight back and he was no longer sporting a moustache. Guards later discovered Knight had broken a piece of glass from his cell window to give himself a fresh shave.

23

THE KINGSTON THIRTEEN

They weren't murdered, they were killed.
I don't think of them as people, they are animals.

—Edward Johnston, accused in the deaths
of Brian Ensor and Bertrand Robert[194]

October 28, 1971

ON A COOL AUTUMN MORNING, the trial of the thirteen prisoners accused of murdering Brian Ensor and Bertrand Robert during the Kingston Penitentiary riot began in Kingston before Mr. Justice William Henderson. Representing the Crown were lawyers W.A. Newell of Bracebridge and Peter B. Tobias from Huntsville.

Three of the defence lawyers had requested separate trials for their clients, arguing that evidence given at a joint trial could prejudice the case against their clients. Another defence lawyer had requested a change of venue. The judge dismissed all of their motions. The thirteen accused would be tried together, something that had never occurred before in an Ontario court.

Each of the inmates had pleaded not guilty to both counts of non-capital murder, even though Brian Dodge had already given a written statement admitting to the murder of Brian Ensor. Glen

Archer Morris had also confessed to his part in the beatings of the undesirables.

The trial attracted a great deal of attention and hundreds lined up outside the courthouse hoping for a seat inside. Some of the spectators were anxious to get a glimpse of the "Kingston Thirteen," as the newspapers were calling them. Other onlookers, young, free-spirited students, were there to support the prisoners and their right to a fair trial. But before the trial commenced, Justice Henderson, dressed in a blue robe and scarlet sash, addressed members of the public. He said he would not allow his courtroom to become "a haven for bums."[195] The judge expected a professional atmosphere in his courtroom. "If people haven't got decent clothes to put on, there are social agencies they can go to for assistance." Although he didn't specify what attire he considered suitable, the judge instructed the police to ensure people were dressed properly when they came into the courthouse.

Jury selection proceeded for the next few days, with over four hundred people being called. When the jury was finally chosen, Judge Henderson looked down at the twelve white men from his high-backed, dark-maroon chair and told them the trial of the Kingston Penitentiary inmates would be one of the most complicated criminal trials ever held in Canada. The judge also advised the press not to print the names of any of the witnesses to protect them from reprisals.

On Monday, November 1, 1971, the thirteen accused prisoners shuffled into the dark-panelled courtroom. Wearing freshly pressed suits and shiny black shoes, the men smiled and winked at spectators as they were seated side by side on the courtroom's front bench. Their handcuffs were removed, but their feet remained shackled together.[196] A row of prison guards stood behind them and twenty Kingston Police officers were stationed around the courtroom.

Inmate Brian Beaucage scanned the packed courtroom for his mother. He knew she would be there. Isobel Beaucage had travelled from London, Ontario, during the preliminary hearing and hadn't missed a day. Brian was her first-born son and his mom was very protective of him. She would often write letters to prison authorities if she thought he was not being treated well. Both of his parents, who were hard-working, churchgoing people, had always supported Brian despite his extensive criminal past dating back to 1964. Now they were sparing no expense for his legal counsel.

The first witness took the stand. It was Corporal Lawrence Smith of Belleville District Headquarters Identification Branch. He presented architectural drawings of the prison and photographs he had taken of the penitentiary showing the debris and destruction of the cellblock. He also presented photos of other articles that had been collected after the riot. One image showed a flag with a skull and crossbones and the word *justice* printed underneath.

The second witness was Bernard Fleming, the assistant deputy warden of Kingston Penitentiary. Mr. Fleming, a short, stocky man with horn-rimmed glasses and thinning blond hair, testified he was not working on April 14, the night the riot began, but was called back to the prison later that night. When he got there, he entered a small building known as the keeper's hall, which was connected by a corridor to the dome. The steel barrier across the corridor was locked. He looked through the barrier and saw five of the accused men running around with steel bars in their hands. He said he continued to watch through the bars of the barrier until the inmates on the other side blocked it with tables and mattresses.

He went on to tell the court he was one of the first prison officials to enter the cellblock after the riot ended on April 18. He described finding the body of Brian Ensor with the Kingston detectives. "His head was smashed in. We had to turn him over to make identification. I knew he was dead." He said Ensor had a big bulge in the middle of his forehead, his trousers were torn, and he had a large gash in his leg three to four inches deep. "It was wide open."[197]

Fleming also described another inmate who was carried out on a stretcher from the prison. "His face was covered in blood. It was just a mess. I couldn't recognize him." He later found out it was Bertrand Robert.

Fleming talked about the cell wing known as 1-D containing the dissociation cells. This was where men were kept apart from the rest of the prison population for their own protection. He explained the class system in the penitentiary, with child molesters, sex offenders and informers at the bottom of the scale. "They do not fit in," said Fleming. "They do not associate. They need protection particularly in a maximum-security institution."

Fleming also told the court about the predictable daily routine of the penitentiary and how the brass bell in the centre of the dome controlled every activity of every day. Sixteen hours a day was spent in cells and the prisoners were under constant surveillance. "The prisoners had no privacy, but on the night of April 14, when the inmates took control of the prison, all routine and rules were gone." He heard stories of inmates drinking homebrew, sniffing glue, taking tranquilizers and other illicit drugs. According to what he was told, homosexual inmates put on a "girlie" show and other inmates "opened house" for sex.

Strangely, none of the lawyers present challenged Fleming's version of the salacious events that had taken place during the riot. Instead, several of the defence lawyers sought to establish his opinion of their clients before the rebellion. Fleming told the court that some of the accused murderers were model inmates. Glen Morris worked in the library and on occasion in Mr. Fleming's office, while Brian Beaucage was considered to be one of the more stable prisoners. Harold St. Amour repaired electrical equipment in the penitentiary and David Birt had never caused the deputy warden any concerns.

Fleming was then questioned about the lighting in the dome. Would the normal lighting, four five-hundred-watt bulbs on the ceiling, be sufficient illumination to identify anyone on the floor of the dome, even from the fourth storey? Fleming said the lighting was ample for correct identification.

On the third day of the murder trial, the first eyewitness, a former KP inmate named James Brawley, was escorted into the packed courtroom. The 26-year-old man, dressed in an ill-fitting suit, kept his head down and only glanced at the judge and the Crown attorney when spoken to. All of the prisoners he was testifying against were sitting a few feet from him in the courtroom and he knew, in their eyes, he was a rat. They would kill him if they got the chance. He was now an inmate at Millhaven, and he feared for his life. But as soon as he was paroled, he was leaving Canada and heading straight back home to Florida.

The American told the court he had been arrested in Toronto in 1970 for attempted robbery and was later convicted of possession of burglary tools and carrying a loaded thirty-eight-calibre revolver.[198] He was serving his time in Kingston Penitentiary when the inmates took over the prison on April 14, 1971.

On the final night of the riot, the witness said he was standing on the second tier of the dome when he saw a group of inmates, including an old man who he knew was crippled with arthritis, being dragged into the centre of the rotunda kicking and screaming. They were forcibly tied to chairs that were arranged in a large inward-facing circle in the middle of the rotunda. He told the court he did not know most of the men but recognized Brian Ensor. "They started beating them, breaking their noses and tormenting them," he said. "There was so much blood."

He described how bedsheets and blankets were thrown over their heads. Apparently this was done to confuse the army. If the soldiers attacked, they would not know if the ghostlike, bloodied figures tied in the circle were inmates or guards.

The witness then outlined the role played by each of the accused. He told the court Dave Shepley acted as master of ceremonies. "He had the bullhorn and he was telling people what to do." Then Brian Beaucage went around the circle and broke men's noses with a karate chop while Robbie Robidoux beat the inmates with iron spokes from the cell-locking devices. The witness said he also saw one of the other accused, Glen Morris, pour hot lacquer over an inmate's head and then smash a glass into it. "It was running down his face," he said.

But it was Edward Fowler, the witness claimed, who attacked two of the men with a knife. Fowler was the one who cut open Brian Ensor's leg, leaving a gash about two and a half inches deep along the full length of his right thigh. "And then he cut old man Malone." After Fowler inflicted the wounds on the two defenceless men, a few of the other torturers urinated into the fresh open cuts.

Asked if he recalled any incident involving a black prisoner in the circle, the witness said he did. "Someone went down to the circle and pulled the coloured guy out because he had an affidavit that proved he wasn't a child molester. He was put against the wall, still tied to the chair, but his nose was already broken and blood was streaming down his face."

"Who was it that took the black man out of the circle?" asked one of the defence attorneys.

"Harold St. Amour was there along with Jimmy Oag, and Jimmy's brother was around too," the inmate replied.

"His brother was around? What do you mean 'around'?"

"Well, he was around the circle and he put a knife to the man's throat."

The defence lawyer seemed surprised by this information. "He put a knife where?" he asked the witness.

"To his throat. He told the man, 'If you don't tell me the truth, I will cut your throat.'"

"Did the fellow tell him the truth?"

"Yes, sir."

"Was the black named Travis? Do you recognize the name?"

"The Negro could have been Travis, yes, sir."

"I don't think they like to be called Negroes," snapped the lawyer. "They call them black."

"Black, sir?" asked the witness. "You know, it don't make no difference. I have a lot of Negro friends."

The witness went on to tell the court that another man, a white man, was also taken out of the circle. He was a small, wiry guy named Ralph Lake. Harold St. Amour argued for his release and convinced Shepley and the others to let him go.

After the two men were removed from the circle, the beatings continued. The torture only stopped when everyone in the circle stopped moving. Then, as the witness recalled, Shepley and a few others dragged the undesirables back to 1-D and threw them on top of one another like garbage. Back in the dome, other inmates tried to clean up the remnants of the attack using bedsheets to soak up the blood on the cement floor. "Someone even tried to use a mop," said the witness, "but there was just too much blood."

Under cross-examination, the witness was asked about the atmosphere in the cellblock at the time of the beatings. The young man said the tension in the prison was high. The inmates were told that the armed troops outside the prison were preparing to attack at any moment. "The guys doing the beating felt they had nothing to lose because we'd all be dead once the army forced their way in."

The witness told the court that most of the prison population gathered to watch the beatings. Shepley and his gang had ordered them to. There was a fear that anyone who objected would be taken downstairs and put in the circle. "You did not know who was standing next to you. Would they rat you out?" Most of the men watched in an awkward silence broken only by the screams of the victims and the laughter of their attackers. No one tried to interfere. "Would you?" he said. "There was nothing we could do."

When the witness finished his testimony, Justice Henderson instructed the reporters present that they were not to publish the man's name in the press.

Next to testify was a 31-year-old convicted thief named John Zelinsky, with a criminal record dating back to 1957. He described how he watched the beatings from a second-storey catwalk. David Shepley had a bullhorn and yelled, "We'll get all the diddlers, stool pigeons and sex offenders out in the ring, and then we'll get the guards and kill them." There was talk of throwing the guards off the top-floor railings if the army attacked. He described the inmates who inflicted the beatings as "the big wheels, the tough guys, and they were set on having a party."

The inmate witness identified Shepley, Fowler, Bulger and Beaucage as the men who dragged the undesirables out to the dome floor. He then identified Morris, Fowler, Robidoux and Johnston as the ones who tied them to chairs. He described how 22-year-old Edward Johnston picked up one of the men in a chair, turned him upside down and dropped him headfirst onto the cement floor. The man's head gushed blood. "I walked away after that," said the witness. "I just got sick and walked away."

Defence lawyer Arthur Maloney asked the witness if he too had taken part in the riot. The man said he was not involved. "What did you do?" asked Maloney.

"Just walked around and tried to keep out of trouble, out of everybody's way."

"I suppose you armed yourself like everybody else did?"

"Yes."

"Did you do any damage to the prison?"

"No."

Zelinsky told the defence lawyer that he had been involved in a previous riot in 1962 at the British Columbia Penitentiary. He threw a pop bottle out an open window and ended up getting fifteen paddles and ninety days' remission and put in segregation.

"So you decided not to cause violence this time because of your prior experience?"

"Yes, sir."

Zelinsky went on to say he had two jobs during the riot.[199] He was to look after the distribution of sandwiches, soup and coffee—a task he shared with two of the accused, David Shepley and Glen Morris. The witness said his second job was to make periodic checks on the undesirables locked in 1-D. He was to make sure they were not being attacked and report back to Billy Knight, whom he identified as one of the leaders of the riot. He said he did not realize the undesirables had been taken from 1-D until it was too late.

Before he was finished his testimony, Zelinsky was questioned by another defence lawyer. "Let me ask you this," said Mr. Humphrey. "Other than being a disinterested spectator, do you have any motive for giving evidence against the accused today?"

"Yes, sir," replied Zelinsky. "What they did was sickening, utterly sickening. This wasn't a riot. I've been in a riot. This was a torture chamber. People were beating people up for no reason at all. I say all these people are guilty and they should pay for it."

THE FOLLOWING DAY, the accused were once again escorted into the courtroom in leg irons. The first witness of the day was a 24-year-old convicted bank robber currently on parole. He told the court he saw one of the accused, James Oag, walk up to several of the inmates bound in the circle and test them to see if they were still conscious.

"How did he do this?" asked Mr. Sampson. "How did he test them?"

"With a cigarette."

"What? What did he do with a cigarette?"

"Burn them."

"How?"

"On the legs and I think he burned a few of them on the face."

The witness said all of the inmates moved or shouted out when the lit cigarette touched their skin, except for Brian Ensor. The witness then recalled how James Oag bragged about breaking eight noses and his brother Donald Oag was also revelling in terrorizing men in the circle. "He came over and cut one of the inmates' legs with a knife and then told someone to grab a rag and tie it around the inmate's leg to stem the bleeding."

The witness then told Crown prosecutor Tobias he saw Robert Robidoux put a fire hose up to the mouths of three or four of the inmates and spray them.

"A fire what?" asked Sampson.

"A fire extinguisher with a pump."

When cross-examined by defence lawyer Elmer Sopha, who was representing Harold St. Amour, the former inmate admitted smashing the religious chapels during the riot. "But I don't think wrecking property can be compared," he said. "I'm not an animal. These are human beings." The inmate was then asked if he had given a thumbs-up signal, indicating he approved of the beatings, while he watched from above. He admitted he had. "I had no love for those sick people from the dissociation cells, but I did not want them tortured and killed."

The witness told the court William Knight had made an impassioned speech two days earlier against violence in the dome after Brian Ensor had been beaten in his cell on the second day of the riot. Knight told the entire population that any violence would not help their cause. The witness said Knight and one of the accused, Brian Dodge, moved Ensor into 1-D for his own protection. Dodge then pocketed the keys to that wing.

The witness identified David Shepley as the ringleader, the main wheel stirring up the action. He said Shepley's principal function was to make sure the guys in the circle got a good "working over."

"Shepley was running around the dome floor encouraging everyone, smoking a big fat cigar like he was in the war days of Churchill."

"You're lying!" yelled David Shepley from the prisoners' box. "He knows he's lying, your Honour. He's lying for his own benefit."

"I am telling the truth," he insisted.

As the trial continued, more witnesses testified about the brutal events of the final night of the riot. Edward Francis Patricks, a 44-year-old convicted armed robber, had originally told the Kingston detectives he was reluctant to testify at the trial, but he didn't want the accused to get away with what they had done. Now he was following through on his word. Patricks spoke about the last night of the riot, when all of the inmates were called to the dome. He identified most of the accused sitting in the courtroom and suggested there had been others involved as well. He saw Robbie Robidoux drag Ralph Lake into the circle. "Robidoux had his arm around Lake's throat, there was a commotion, I saw a knife flash, and then I saw Lake fall to the floor." Patricks also told the court he witnessed Robidoux dragging another inmate, old man Malone, towards 1-D face down. He heard Robidoux say: "You're supposed to be dead, you old bastard." Robidoux had something in his hand. Patricks saw him stab Thomas Malone at least twice and heard Malone scream out. At that point, Patricks said, he couldn't watch anymore and went back to his cell.

If anyone could confirm what Patricks had just told the court, it was the next witness. Thomas Malone was sworn in and took his place in the witness box. Malone stated he had been an inmate at

Kingston Penitentiary since February 29, 1970. He suffered from bad arthritis in his ankles and was hard of hearing. Under questioning by Crown attorney Sampson, Malone described the assault he endured on the last night of the riot. In the early morning of April 18, he was dragged out of his cell and forcibly tied with chains to a metal chair in a circle. The men in the circle were beaten with bare fists and steel rods that had been broken off from the wheels of the prison locking mechanism. Every man in the circle had his nose broken before being blindfolded. "I saw them coming around to my turn and then bang! One blow broke my nose."

"What happened after the blindfold went on?" asked Crown attorney Sampson.

"Well, sir, I was told I was going to be cut."

"Were you cut?"

"Yes, sir, I was."

"What cut you?"

"Well, I was blindfolded. I didn't see it, but I imagine it was a razor blade. Dr. Neuman put in eleven stitches to close the four gashes."

Mr. Sampson then asked Malone if anything else had happened to him. Malone paused before answering. Reliving the events of that night was clearly upsetting the man.

"Yes," he replied, "they were not satisfied with cutting me. They dumped and rubbed salt into the gashes and then, believe it or not, sir, they urinated on us, on the salted, bleeding wounds. I could not walk for a week after, and I was two weeks in the hospital."

Thomas Malone went on to describe what happened after the beatings. He said the men were dragged out of the circle with their hands still tied behind their backs and were thrown onto the cold, wet floor in D-block. The floor had two inches of water on it from the broken radiators. The pipes had been taken from the radiators to break open the cells. "I lay there for two hours, along with the others, until they released us and gave us a smoke."

"Can you tell us who else was lying there in D-block with you?" asked Sampson.

"Well, Mr. Ensor was lying right beside me, but I could see his brains coming through his forehead. They told me he was dead."

ON THE NEXT DAY of the trial, a 25-year-old inmate named Dennis Robertson took the stand. The shy man, who was repeatedly asked to speak up, described what he saw as "a nightmare too horrible to remember." He stated there were thirteen or fourteen convicts doing most of the beatings. "Some were carrying bars, pipes, others had knives." He said Dave Shepley had a knife about fourteen inches long. He described how the armed inmates were criss-crossing through the circle smashing the poor inmates across their heads and faces. The witness said he saw accused inmate Glen Morris, who had the nickname Yankee, beat one of the undesirables mercilessly about the head with an iron bar.

"What was he doing?" asked Mr. Sampson.

"He was just going back and forth across the guy's scalp. He looked like a man cutting grass with a scythe," he said. "If you're going to kill a guy, just kill him."

The witness also identified Ernie Bugler, Dave Birt, Jimmy Oag, Brian Dodge and Robert Robidoux as some of the other inmates who were hitting the men in the circle with iron bars.

"Have you told us everything that you observed?" Sampson asked.

"Not everything, no. I seen guys get their legs cut open."

After watching the beatings, Dennis Robertson told the court, he believed none of the prisoners in the circle would make it out alive.

THE NEXT WITNESS was certain he was going to be killed. He was one of the prisoners tied in the circle on the last night of the riot. Richard George Moore had given the police a detailed account of the vicious attack he endured on the last night of the riot. Now he was sitting in the courtroom facing his tormentors. The chubby-faced 21-year-old originally from Coquitlam, British Columbia, was convicted of car theft in 1968 and sentenced to eighteen months in jail. But he had earned an additional six years in prison for trying to escape from Burwash Correctional Centre. Transferred to Kingston Penitentiary, he ran into problems with some of the older wolves— aggressive guys looking for a kid. After refusing to have sex with two inmates, his life was threatened. Fourteen months prior to the riot, he asked to be put in 1-D block for his own protection.

Moore described how he and the other inmates in the dissociation cells were led out to the dome floor, tied to chairs and beaten. He could name only a few of the other inmates in the circle when he was asked. "There was Bob Sheahan, myself, Brian Ensor, Bob Roberts, Les Demer, Julius Martisz and a guy by the name of Legere."

Moore then told the jury that it was an inmate by the name of Harold St. Amour who had tied him to the chair with rags. But he added that St. Amour looked scared. "He looked like he hated what he was doing. I thought he might be in some danger." Moore knew St. Amour and considered him a friend. St. Amour had helped him learn how to operate a sewing machine in the prison shop. "I bear him no malice."

Moore went on to detail the beatings he and the other men endured. He described how David Shepley came over to the men in the circle and hit several in the face with his gloved hand. "Then the guys really started going haywire," he said. At that point another inmate approached him and tried to break his nose.

"Who was the person that came to break your nose?" asked defence lawyer Sopha, who was representing Harold St. Amour.

"It was Mr. Oag."

"Which one? There is James Oag number seven and Donald Oag number nine," said the lawyer, pointing towards the row of defendants.

"Jimmy Oag," replied Moore. "James Oag."

"Was your nose broken?"

"No, sir."

After the initial attack, Moore said that Shepley hollered up to the fourth range and had the inmates toss down bedsheets, which were then put over their heads. "After the bedsheets were thrown over us, they started beating us even worse," said Moore. "What they were beating me with I couldn't tell you, but it was pretty heavy."

Moore described what happened next. Robert Robidoux walked up to him and asked him how many ribs he had in his body. Moore said he didn't know. "Then let's find out," said Robidoux. He started hitting Moore and then Robidoux yelled out, "Hey, I think I've broken his ribs." A voice called back, "Hey, man, that's cool." By that time, Moore said, he was close to passing out, but Robidoux wasn't finished with him. "He asked me another silly question, and then smashed me in the kneecap."

Questioned by Arthur Maloney, Robidoux's lawyer, Moore was asked if he was certain it was Robert Robidoux who had attacked him. Moore told the lawyer he could identify his attacker because Robidoux was in 1-D earlier in the riot to harass the inmates. Moore also said that Robidoux was dressed differently. "He was wearing some kind of costume."

"Costume?"

"I don't know what he was wearing. He had a bandana around his forehead. He was decked out like a Mexican bandito."

"Mexican bandito?"

"I don't know what he was wearing, but it wasn't no jail clothes."

After the beatings, Moore said the other men in the circle were dragged back to 1-D still tied to chairs and dumped in a pool of water. "I laid there thinking I'm the only one alive in a whole pile of bodies."[200]

He then told the court he could see Brian Ensor lying a few inches away. "I was lying six inches from him." He heard someone breathing and when he looked up, the accused Robert Robidoux was standing over Ensor. "He was smiling, a big smile...a sick smile." He heard Robidoux say: "You're still alive...I'm going to finish you off, you cocksucker." Robidoux then began smashing Ensor's head in with an iron bar. "He hit him about fourteen or fifteen times and then he took off."

Robidoux's lawyer, Arthur Maloney, was anxious to cross-examine Moore about the identity of the man he saw strike Ensor. Moore said he was adamant the man he saw was Robidoux. But how could he be sure if his eyes were closed? Moore told Arthur Maloney he kept his eyes down, trying to go unnoticed, but when he looked up, he saw Robidoux.

Moore told the court he also saw Bertrand Robert lying in a cell in 1-D. His head and face were so badly beaten he was unrecognizable. "You couldn't even tell if it was a face, it was all puffed up and out of proportion."

THE NEXT WITNESS told the court he had not been housed in 1-D at the time of the riot but was still victimized by Shepley and his gang. The convict had been sent to prison five years earlier for several charges of indecent assault and was considered a dangerous sex offender. Other inmates had shown a lot of animosity towards him because of the nature of his crimes. "Sex offenders are strong-armed and muscled by the other prisoners," he said. But one of the accused, Harold St. Amour, had befriended him and protected him in the prison. "I had no trouble because of St. Amour," he said. He spent the first night of the riot in St. Amour's cell with two others while rampaging inmates smashed and destroyed everything they could throughout the cellblocks.[201] After the riot began, Amour chased away several inmates who

John Maloney inspects damage to the rotunda after the riot.
Fred Ross, Toronto Star *Archives, 1971*

Inmates leaving KP for
Millhaven after the riot.
Fred Ross, Toronto Star *Archives, 1971*

Ambulance leaving Kingston
Penitentiary after the riot.
Fred Ross, Toronto Star *Archives, 1971*

The rotunda after the riot.
Toronto Telegram *fonds, York
University Libraries, Clara Thomas
Archives and Special Collections,*
ASC07621

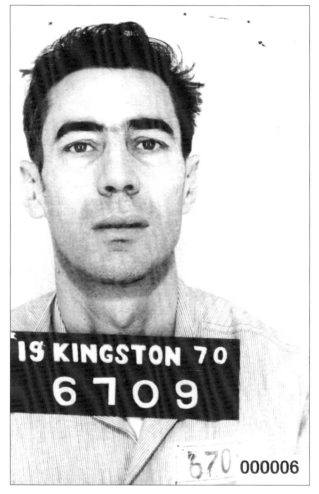

Inmate Bertrand Robert.
Image retrieved from parole file, Library and Archives Canada

Guard Joseph Vallier
and family.
Don Dutton, Toronto Star
Archives, 1971

Guard Kerry Bushell
and wife Elaine leaving
the prison grounds.
Fred Ross, Toronto Star *Archives, 1971*

Kingston prisoners arrive at Frontenac County Courthouse.
Ted Dinsmore, Toronto Star *Archives, 1971*

Justice flag found in the prison after the riot, Kingston Police, 1971.
Courtesy Canada's Penitentiary Museum

Destruction of the cell block.
Toronto Telegram *fonds, York University Libraries, Clara Thomas Archives and Special Collections,* ASC07620

Kingston Penitentiary inmates leaving Frontenac County Courthouse, June 4, 1971.
Queen's University Archives, Kingston Whig Standard, *V142-8-232*

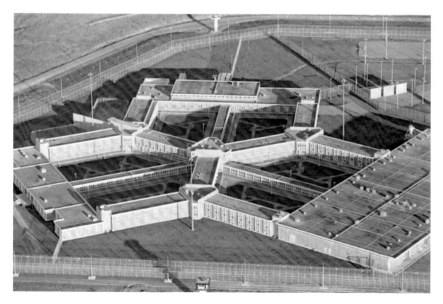

Aerial photo of Millhaven Institution, 1977.
Queen's University Archives, Kingston Whig Standard, *V142-14-129*

were bothering him. "He showed me, as far as he was concerned, I was just another human being and he would protect me."

In the early hours of April 18, the inmate heard a commotion on the floor of the dome and was ordered to come out of his cell to watch. He saw inmates dragged into the centre of the dome from the dissociation cells in 1-D. Then Brian Beaucage came up behind him and said, "You don't belong in the general population." Beaucage clubbed him over the head with a ten-inch-long iron spoke from the cellblock's locking mechanism. He fell to the ground, but Beaucage pulled him to his feet and dragged him into the circle. Then his hands and legs were tied to the chair with strips of bedsheets. He watched in terror as the attackers walked around the circle beating their victims with their hands. He identified the Oag brothers as two of his assailants. "Donald Oag was following behind his brother James, smacking people with his hands and busting their noses."

After the beatings went on for about twenty minutes, some of the prisoners watching from the upper tiers started to leave. The witness heard David Shepley announce over the bullhorn, "Don't go away, the show is just beginning."

Then a sheet was thrown over his head and he was repeatedly kicked and hit. Feeling that he was going to pass out, he heard another voice say, "Don't touch this man anymore, we're saving him for something else." It was Harold St. Amour. St. Amour bent down and asked him if he had any kind of document that would prove he was not in prison for rape or attacking children. He told St. Amour there was a submission from his trial in his cell that would prove his crimes. St. Amour ran to the inmate's cell, found the document and brought it back to the dome. St. Armour showed it to the ringleaders hoping to get the man released. Finally, three of the accused—Harold St. Amour and the Oag brothers—untied the inmate from the chair and carried him to a cell.

ON THE LAST DAY OF THE TRIAL, another nervous inmate took the stand to testify against the accused. After two weeks of graphic testimony about the torture inflicted upon the undesirables on the last night of the riot, the jury thought they had heard the worst of what had happened, but what the next witness had to say would haunt them long after the trial was over.

To the shock of the gathered crowd, the former prisoner sitting in the witness box told the court he saw one of the accused drink the blood of Brian Ensor as Ensor lay wounded on the floor of the dome. The witness identified the inmate as 25-year-old Glen Morris. He saw Morris catch the blood in a cup as it oozed from Ensor's leg wound. A smiling Morris than raised the cup and said, "Here's a toast," and drank it. One of the jurors let out a gasp as the rest of the courtroom fell eerily quiet. The clean-cut, bespectacled Morris, sitting in the prisoners' dock, showed no reaction.

Defence lawyer William Murphy, who was representing Morris, jumped up to say he had no prior knowledge of the alleged incident.[202] Under cross-examination, Murphy asked the witness why he had not reported this incident to the police when he was originally interviewed. Why hadn't he mentioned anything about blood drinking at the preliminary hearing in July? "I had too many things on my mind," said the witness. "I was all shook up." He agreed with Mr. Murphy that it was an unusual incident to forget.

"I'm suggesting you made all this up," said Murphy.

"No, sir, I'm not."

Asked why he and the others didn't go into the dome to stop the beatings, the witness said it would have been impossible to interfere. "You've got all those sadistic people down there doing all those things. Man, you would have been a fool to try to stop them."

24

THE COST OF KILLING

November–December 1971

ON THE MORNING OF THURSDAY, November 11, forty-five minutes after the trial of the Kingston Thirteen was scheduled to resume, Judge Henderson called the jury into the courtroom. He advised them the trial would be adjourned until Monday.

The judge had received an early morning visitor to the courthouse. Millhaven warden Donald Clark had shown up unannounced to tell Judge Henderson the trial was creating problems at his institution, where several of the accused were being kept in solitary confinement. Warden Clark had already put in a call to the Canadian Forces Base in Kingston and asked them to be on alert. Another riot was brewing.

AS THE TRIAL ENTERED its fourth week, the Crown had called only eight of its forty listed witnesses. With each of the thirteen defence lawyers taking turns questioning every witness, the days were dragging on. Plus, the defence lawyers had their own witnesses to be heard after the Crown rested its case. One lawyer, W.R. Poole of London, who was defending Brian Beaucage, told the judge he had fifty witnesses to call. Convinced his client was innocent of the charges, Poole had closed his law office in London and moved to Kingston for the preliminary hearing and trial. An unofficial estimate of the legal aid costs for the defendants was sitting at $175,000 and the trial looked as though it wasn't going to end any time soon.

On Monday, November 22, twelve of the accused prisoners in the beating deaths of Brian Ensor and Bertrand Robert pleaded guilty to one count of manslaughter.[203] The thirteenth, Brian Beaucage, pleaded guilty to assault causing bodily harm. Justice Henderson instructed the jury to consider the pleas and said the jury should treat the accused as a whole, not separately. He then went on to describe what the evidence suggested took place in the Kingston Penitentiary dome in the early hours of April 18. The judge told the jury they must consider the charged emotional atmosphere that existed in Kingston Pen at the time when Brian Ensor, a convicted child rapist, and Bertrand Robert, convicted of burning his children, were tied in a circle with other so-called undesirables. When word spread that the army was preparing to attack, the tension built to a fever pitch, according to the judge. Then, when they were convinced the army was coming in, "things just got out of hand," said the judge.

"Given the conditions," he continued, "I doubt if an ordinary man would have had his stability and control."[204] He went on to say that the very sight of the undesirables—sex offenders, child molesters and informers—had generated an emotional and irrational response from other inmates, but he saw no indication from the evidence they had informed the intent to kill. He asked the jury not to consider how the accused had acted, but how a reasonable man might have reacted. He told the jury that murder might be reduced to manslaughter if the accused did the killing in the heat of passion or provocation. He said the conditions in the prison were such that they took away the intent of the accused to commit murder or even presume that their actions would lead to death. Justice Henderson concluded: "Combined with the acceptance of the Crown, I have no hesitation in putting these pleas before you ... I feel that the ends of justice will be met by accepting these pleas."

The jury deliberated for less than two hours before coming back with their decision. They would accept the pleas.

ELEVEN OF THE ACCUSED prisoners were sentenced immediately. They showed no emotion.

William David Shepley (25)
Manslaughter re: Ensor
15 years concurrent
(Serving a twelve-year sentence for armed robbery
since 1970)

Glen Archer Morris (25)
Manslaughter re: Robert
11 years concurrent
(Serving an eight-year sentence for robbery since 1970)

Wayne Herbert McGurgin (24)
Manslaughter re: Robert
2 years consecutive
(Had three more years to serve on various charges)

Edward Maxwell Fowler (19)
Manslaughter re: Ensor
7 years concurrent
(Serving a five-year sentence for robbery since 1969)

Harold Kenneth St. Amour (39)
Manslaughter re: Robert
2 years concurrent
(Serving a life sentence for rape since 1964)

James Robert Oag (25)
Manslaughter re: Robert
8 years concurrent
(Serving a life sentence for non-capital murder since 1968)

Ernest James Bugler (25)
Manslaughter re: Robert
3 years concurrent
(Serving a life sentence for murder since 1968)

Donald Oag (20)
Manslaughter re: Robert
3 years consecutive
(Serving a six-year sentence for robbery since 1969)

David Silvester Birt (25)
Manslaughter re: Robert
3 years consecutive
(Serving a three-year sentence for break and enter and
theft since 1969)

Edward Fulton Johnston (22)
Manslaughter re: Ensor
3 years consecutive
(Serving a three-year sentence for break and enter and
theft since 1970)

Brian William Dodge (28)
Manslaughter re: Robert
3 years consecutive
(Serving a four-year sentence for break and
enter since 1970)
(Also convicted of forcible seizure during riot and
sentenced to three years consecutive)

Robbie Robidoux and Brian Beaucage were sentenced ten days later.

Brian Lester Beaucage (23)
Assault causing bodily harm re: Ensor
21 months concurrent
(Serving an eight-year sentence for manslaughter)

Robert James Robidoux (17)
Manslaughter re: Ensor
6 years concurrent
(Serving a three-year sentence for armed robbery)

When asked if they had anything to say, a few replied they were sorry for what they had done. Edward Johnston said: "I was sick at the time and didn't realize what I was doing."

Justice Henderson then turned to one of the inmates, Glen Morris, who had been accused of drinking Brian Ensor's blood. The judge looked at him and asked, "You'll be a good boy from now on?" A surprised Morris nodded yes. Spectators in the courthouse listened in disbelief. The judge then asked him what he wanted to do with his life. Morris told the judge he wanted to be a printer more than anything else and write poetry. "It's the only thing I can do in life is write," said the convicted murderer.

"I hope you'll never have trouble with the law again," the judge said.

Then the thirteen inmates hobbled out of the prisoners' dock one by one in their leg irons. They were handcuffed and escorted out of the courthouse. The remaining charges against the accused were adjourned *nolle prosequi*, "we shall no longer prosecute." The Kingston Thirteen murder trial was over.

THE NEWS OF THE VERDICTS and the judge's controversial comments prompted an immediate outcry. Many thought the Kingston murder trial had resulted in a complete miscarriage of justice. For such serious offences, including torture and murder, a group of dangerous criminals had been given what appeared to be very light sentences. The sentences imposed ranged from two to fifteen years, and seven of them were concurrent, meaning the defendants would serve from two to five years' time beyond the expiration of their original sentences. This was the judgment despite the maximum penalty for manslaughter being life imprisonment. The convicted men had shown themselves to be vicious, sadistic and capable of losing control. Would any of them be capable of rehabilitation and a safe reintegration into society? It was also noted that among the guilty men who had taken it upon themselves to punish the undesirables, two were in prison for non-capital murder and one was serving a life sentence for rape.

The cost of killing in a Canadian penitentiary had just been declared cheap—two to five years extra. The dead and injured inmates were considered the lowest of the low in prison culture, and the judge himself had said that the sight of these men had generated an emotional and irrational response from the thirteen accused. Justice Henderson also suggested the accused were reacting in the heat of passion and provocation and did not know their actions would lead to death. Yet according to witnesses the vicious beatings went on for over two hours and one of the accused who repeatedly hit Brian Ensor with an iron bar said, "You're still alive...I'm going to finish you off." What did these verdicts imply for other sex offenders or those labelled "undesirable" in federal prisons across the country?

That was the question asked by Solicitor General Jean-Pierre Goyer in a letter addressed to Ontario Attorney General Allan Lawrence. Goyer said he had grave concerns about the sentences imposed.[205] He felt they were markedly inadequate. He admitted to Lawrence that providing proper protection for inmates convicted of sexual crimes or crimes against children was one of the biggest problems they had in prisons. But deterrence was one of the only weapons they had against such attacks. If the current sentences were allowed to stand, Goyer feared other inmates would believe that similar attacks could be committed with relative impunity. Goyer urged Lawrence to appeal the sentences.

A FEW DAYS AFTER the Kingston riot murder trial concluded, a confidential report submitted to the Solicitor General's office recommended Canada's federal penitentiaries be replaced by mini-prisons.[206] The Mohr Committee appointed by Solicitor General Goyer soon after the April riot was suggesting all of the country's maximum-security prisons be closed and replaced by a network of radically redesigned smaller institutions. Members of the committee suggested the mini-prisons be close to major cities instead of situated in isolated rural locations, in order to attract more professional staff. They also recommended that prisoners be allowed to enrol in school or university outside the prison, to attend theatre and sporting events in the community, and to go home on weekends to be with their families. The smaller facilities would accommodate a maximum of 130 inmates, who would live in dormitory-like units of twelve men each. This was a much different approach from cellblocks of hundreds of inmates stacked on top of each other.

Two or three guards would be assigned permanently to each unit so they could get to know each prisoner. The objective of the mini-prison was to give each inmate a sense of individuality and a feeling of home.

The committee suggested that Ottawa build an experimental prototype facility in Mission, British Columbia, the site of what was to have been a new maximum-security facility modelled after Millhaven. Goyer had cancelled the new prison after the Kingston riot.

The Mohr Report was part of a larger review and potential overhaul of the entire Canadian federal prison system. The hundred-page document echoed many of the findings and recommendations of the 1970 Ouimet Report on Criminal Justice and Corrections. Solicitor General Goyer said he was looking forward to reviewing the report.

The Globe and Mail, Letter to the Editor, December 3, 1971

I agree wholeheartedly that the convictions handed out (concurrent sentences) in the case of the thirteen prisoners who took "justice" into their own hands during the riot at Kingston Penitentiary were woefully inadequate for the nature and circumstances of the crimes committed. My incredulity was not abated when the shallow explanation for the light sentences given by an Ontario Supreme Court Justice, which in itself was almost a blanket exoneration for the vicious beatings.

But it appears the real tragedy of the whole affair has been entirely overlooked. It is a frightening thought that more than five hundred men could stand helplessly by and watch while a handful of fellow prisoners systematically pulverized defenceless fellow human beings. (Cam P. Copeland, Cornwall, Ontario)

Letter to Allan Lawrence, Ontario Attorney General, December 6, 1971

At the risk of seeming trite, I am going to remind you that not only must justice be done, but it must be seen to be done. The disgrace of the "wheeler-dealer" case at Kingston must be expunged and surely it is open to you to appeal the verdicts on behalf of the Crown. No slippery talk of time and tax savings can be accepted. One can be appalled at the crimes of Ensor and Robert, and one is, but it seems to me we are in danger of more or less condoning an even greater attack on society. (Name redacted)[207]

The Globe and Mail, Letter to the Editor, December 20, 1971

The conclusion of the trial of the Kingston Thirteen must have left many Canadians both bewildered and angry at what is one of the most distasteful deals in recent jurisprudence. We have for a long time prided ourselves on our compassionate judicial system, however it is clear that this compassion was shown to the extreme in the Kingston Trial. (David C. Murray, Guelph, Ontario)

25

A SECRET DEAL

November–December 1971

MANY CITIZENS WHO had followed the murder trial in the news were outraged by the light prison sentences the Kingston Thirteen had received. It didn't make sense given the brutality of the attacks. But the country would soon learn that there had been more going on behind the scenes in the Kingston courthouse than anyone knew. On Monday, December 13, people across Canada woke to a headline in the *Globe and Mail* that read SECRET DEAL SETTLED KINGSTON TRIAL. RIOTERS' SENTENCES DECIDED IN CHAMBERS.

A picture of Ontario Supreme Court Justice William Henderson was on the front page and he was denying that he took part in any secret sentencing negotiations that ended the month-long trial. But Michael Valpy, a seasoned crime reporter with the *Globe*, had broken a story about the murder trial and subsequent convictions. Valpy had covered the entire trial and got to know several of the defence lawyers, but still, no one was willing to talk to him about the plea bargain deal without anonymity.[208] One lawyer said if his name was released, he would probably never be able to negotiate another deal with the Crown. Another defence lawyer echoed his sentiments and added: "We've got to live, you know." A third lawyer was angry at the implication they had done something unethical. He suggested that anyone who spoke to the press about the details of the case should be reprimanded for breaching solicitor–client privilege.

According to the lawyers who did talk to Valpy, informal discussions about reducing the charges of murder down to manslaughter began even before the trial got under way. Everyone knew it was going to be a difficult trial given the circumstances of the crimes, the number of witnesses, and the challenge of trying to prove who actually struck the fatal blows that killed the two inmates. And they knew early in the trial that the judge did not want to see the proceedings dragged out for months. At one point Justice Henderson had even remarked to the Crown in front of the defence lawyers that he didn't think they could prove a murder case.

On November 10, after only three witnesses had testified, the judge held a meeting with the lawyers in his chambers. In the closed-door discussions, the judge implied that the trial could be wrapped up within a few days if everyone could reach an agreement. But Mr. Sampson, the Crown attorney, insisted on calling more witnesses. He wanted all thirteen accused men to be implicated in the murders of Ensor and Robert.

Then, three weeks into the trial, the judge made two comments in front of the jury that the defence attorneys considered prejudicial towards their clients. He spoke about the courage of the inmate witnesses in coming forward to testify under the circumstances, and when one witness was describing the bloody scene in the dome, the judge remarked: "Never has so much been done by so few." The defence counsel considered making a motion for a mistrial. But then the judge suggested they all go to lunch. "There's nothing like companionship of other lawyers to change minds," said one lawyer who spoke to Valpy. It turned out to be an important lunch.

IN A NONDESCRIPT conference room overlooking the leaf-covered patio of the single-storey motel on the outskirts of Kingston, the entire legal team, sixteen men, from the city's most talked-about murder trial had gathered for a midday meal. Justice William Henderson, thirteen defence lawyers and two Crown attorneys were there to discuss the case. They were negotiating plea bargains, a process that was becoming more commonplace and acceptable every year in the overcrowded criminal courts. The out-of-the-way motel gave the judge and lawyers the space, convenience and, most importantly, privacy they needed to negotiate their deals.

At the beginning of the clandestine luncheon the defence lawyers were canvassed to see where each stood on recommending a guilty plea for his client. Eight of the lawyers said they were ready to go ahead, five were not. According to one of the defence lawyers present, the judge then asked the Crown attorneys if they were agreeable to a plea. When the men left the motel, they all agreed to meet the following morning, Friday, November 19, before the scheduled opening of the court at 10 a.m.

The next day, behind closed doors, each of the lawyers presented the judge with a sentence they thought was proper for their client. The Crown counsel had suggested a range of three to five years and all agreed. One lawyer later said he was there for less than three minutes. The judge asked him what sentence he was looking for. "I gave him the number of years and he said okay." The defence lawyers then took the sentence agreements to their clients. Most of the accused accepted immediately. Some of the lawyers also called Queen's Park to let the Attorney General know about the plea deals. Without the government's acceptance, no deal would go through. Allan Lawrence refused to give them any kind of commitment or guarantee he would not appeal the sentences. Because Mr. Lawrence would not come onside, the deal was almost abandoned. But they had the weekend to decide.

ON MONDAY MORNING, all of the lawyers involved decided to proceed with the plea deal and sentencing. When the trial resumed, the defence lawyers went through the motions of presenting their sentencing submissions to the judge in front of the jury and spectators. Each lawyer in turn spoke eloquently about his client's troubled background and then suggested a range of sentencing from four to five years. Crown attorney Newell agreed to the range and then Justice Henderson sentenced each of the accused. Before the prisoners were led out of the courtroom, defence lawyer Arthur Maloney stood up and said, "Never do I recall any case in my twenty-eight years of experience, a trial that was presided over with such dignity, impartiality, compassion and consideration as your Lordship displayed over the past four weeks."

The day had simply been an act for the public record. The script had already been written in secret, outside of the courtroom, and out of the public's view.

"I WAS NOT party to any deal," said Justice Henderson when news of the secret luncheon and subsequent meetings was published in the *Globe and Mail*.[209] He denied the defence lawyers' version of events about how they secretly decided on a plea bargain. It was not surprising that Justice Henderson denied his involvement, as it is clearly understood that a judge must remain impartial so he can objectively assess a proposed plea bargain to ensure it is fair and satisfies the principles of justice. Henderson would not agree to an interview but defended his actions in a phone conversation with a reporter from the *Toronto Star*. He said the lunch meeting at the motel had just been a courtesy. According to him, he had invited the lawyers to his farm in Amherstview several days earlier for a social evening and the lawyers were repaying his hospitality by taking him out to lunch.

Asked about the Friday morning meeting in his chambers, the judge said he could not recall exactly why the defence counsel had asked to meet with him. He went on to say that any discussions about sentencing happened between the Crown and defence lawyers. They did not involve him and he was not party to any bargaining on sentencing.

While a few of the defence lawyers claimed Justice Henderson was instrumental in negotiating the plea deal and sentencing, some of the others on the case backed him up and said he was not involved in the negotiations. According to Arthur Maloney, Justice Henderson was kept aware of what was going on, but he was not party to, nor bound to, anything that was discussed. Maloney added he had no assurance of what sentence the judge would hand down. "The case was terminated wisely and prudently," said Maloney.

"I'm rather amazed that anyone should find what occurred at the Kingston trial to be in any way improper or unusual," added lawyer Clayton Ruby.

To further justify the outcome of the trial, there was no shortage of arguments from some of the defence lawyers in favour of the negotiated settlement. They claimed there were significant considerations of cost, time and legal complexities of the proceedings. It was estimated the trial was costing forty thousand dollars a week.[210] And with respect to the trial itself, there were concerns about whether the accused should have ever been charged. According to a summary of the statements received by the police, fifty-seven inmates were identified as taking part in the beatings, but only thirteen were brought to trial. There was also questionable credibility of some of the witnesses, who appeared to contradict one another on who did the actual beatings and killings. With many more witnesses to be called, the trial could have lasted three or four more months and, according to the defence lawyers, the confusion imposed on the jury would have been immense.

Another consideration was how the accused would have survived a lengthy trial. Dave Shepley had attempted suicide by slashing his wrists with a razor blade in August.[211] He had received eighty-six stitches. Another inmate had been attacked by two of his co-accused, and a third convict had been transferred to a psychiatric hospital during the trial. This was a group of explosive, unstable men and, according to Warden Clark, there was a great deal of tension at Millhaven Institution, where most of the inmates from Kingston Pen were being held in segregation. Dr. D. Workman, the institution's physician, had even requested extra hospital staff to monitor the Kingston Thirteen.[212] "I am greatly concerned that one of these inmates will either maim himself or be a successful suicide," he wrote in a letter to the warden. "I feel the danger of something tragic happening is sufficiently high."

One lawyer expressed his personal views about the witnesses, saying he thought many of them were psychopaths. "They were all slashing their wrists. They would have emptied the penitentiary if the trial had continued."

A FEW DAYS after the secret negotiations and plea deals were exposed, former Conservative prime minister John Diefenbaker stood in the House of Commons to voice his concern about the light sentences handed down at the Kingston Penitentiary murder trial.[213] "Normally I do not believe in harsh sentences," he said. "But in this case there are fears in penitentiaries across Canada that the sentences are so light as to constitute an invitation on the part of inmates to follow the same course of action taken by those in Kingston." He reminded his fellow Members of Parliament of the unspeakable cruelty that took place on the last night of the riot and how the murdered inmates had been tortured before death. Diefenbaker, a seasoned defence lawyer who had fought to abolish the death penalty in Canada, asked Justice Minister John Turner whether there had been communication with the Ontario Attorney General's department to suggest that appeals should be launched. "Judges do make mistakes," he added.

Mr. Turner said the responsibility for appeals rested with Ontario Attorney General Allan Lawrence, but he understood that the Ontario minister did not intend to appeal the verdicts. The deadline for the appeal was December 22.

WHILE THE ONTARIO government was deciding whether to appeal the sentencing in the Kingston Penitentiary murder trial, the ordeal was far from over. There were lingering resentments, and most of them centred on money.

A more thorough review of the evidence would have been possible at the trial of the thirteen prisoners charged with the murders of two fellow inmates if members of the jury had been paid more, according to one of the jurors who sat through the trial. In an interview with the press, juror John Lux said most of the twelve jury members were extremely worried about how long the trial would last.[214] Paid ten dollars a day, Mr. Lux said the men discussed accepting the lesser pleas of manslaughter when many of them revealed their own economic hardships after serving on the jury for one month. Most of the jurors were behind on their finances and worried how long the trial would continue. One juror had applied for welfare to support his family. After the discussion carried on for some time, Mr. Lux said he asked: "Are we more concerned with our jobs than rendering a just verdict?"

"We all felt that we had to get out of it somehow, and this was the easy way out, an acceptable way out," said another juror. Moreland Green, a swimming pool salesman, told a reporter his personal finances were pretty grim after a month. He was pleased the trial was over but wondered if justice had really been done. Juror Alex McTavish said he felt the plea bargain shortened a long and costly trial, but also had some reservations. "I guess if I was an accused, I would hope that I had a good lawyer who could make a good bargain."

Unlike the jurors, the trial had not caused financial hardship for the thirteen defence lawyers. As per the legal aid fee schedule in 1971, each lawyer was paid $35 per hour while preparing their cases and $250 a day during the trial. The estimated legal aid bill for the trial was $150,000, which would translate to over a million dollars fifty years later.[215]

THE CITY OF KINGSTON, where the trial had taken place, was also claiming financial suffering. Every day of the month-long trial, the Kingston Police had stationed fifteen officers in the courtroom. Justice Henderson had requested the extra police presence, and in order to supply the personnel it had been necessary to call in off-duty officers, who were paid at the rate of time and a half. In addition, six Kingston detectives spent several weeks interviewing more than five hundred witnesses in connection with the deaths of the two inmates during the riot. In total, 658 man-hours had been accrued.

In a letter to Allan Lawrence, the Ontario minister of justice and Attorney General, the mayor of Kingston, E.V. Swain, claimed his city of fifty-six thousand citizens was forced to bear the unwarranted financial burden of the Kingston Penitentiary riot. The costs associated with the complex police investigation and the subsequent court appearances and trials were exorbitant. Since no other city in Canada had as many penal institutions within its immediate area, Kingston was in a unique situation and should be compensated. It did not seem right Kingston taxpayers were footing the bill for crimes committed in a federal penitentiary. The City of Kingston was requesting reimbursement in the amount of $22,096.78.

In his response to the mayor, Attorney General Lawrence politely declined the request. He stated the riot and trial were an extraordinary series of events that caused unusual expenditures at the federal, provincial and municipal levels of government. Therefore, in his opinion, each level should bear its own costs.

IN ALL FEDERAL PRISONS, staff read every letter coming in or going out. The only exception to the rule were letters to Members of Parliament after MPs complained that prison officials would add comments and notes to letters written by inmates. Solicitor General Goyer had agreed to stop the practice but urged MPs to "get the other side of the story" when receiving any grievances from prisoners. Although prison staff were no longer allowed to alter letters to MPs, everything else was closely monitored. Six months prior to the Kingston Pen riot, Acting Deputy Warden Chinnery intercepted a letter written by inmate #6709. Given its contents, he decided to forward a copy to his superiors in Ottawa right away.

In October 1970, inmate Bertrand Robert had written a letter to his lawyer, Mr. Dennis R. O'Conner of Toronto, asking for his assistance. He was intending to sue the federal government and the Penitentiary Service for the pain and suffering he had endured as a result of a knife attack in August 1970. Since Mr. O'Conner was handling the appeal of his conviction, Robert hoped he would be able to help him in this matter as well.

The letter was copied and sent to Paul Faguy, the Commissioner of Penitentiaries, to warn him of Robert's possible legal action. Robert never got the chance to sue the government or the Penitentiary Service, but now someone else was going to do it on his behalf.

The Canadian Penitentiary Service
Sir Wilfrid Laurier Building
Ottawa, Canada

Dear Sir:

Re: Bertrand Henry Robert (deceased)

*We have been retained by Patricia Robert, the ex-wife of
the deceased, Bertrand Henry Robert, who died on May
16th, 1971 as a result of injuries received in a riot at the
Kingston Penitentiary while he was serving a term there.
His former wife has instructed us to commence proceedings
against the penitentiary service for damages.*

    *We would be most grateful if you would supply us with
the style of cause to be used with respect to the penitentiary
service in an action commenced against it. Your immediate
attention to this request will be greatly appreciated.*

Yours truly,
Steele, Magee, Goodal and Punnett
Barristers and Solicitors
36, Fourth St.
Chatham, Ontario

BERTRAND ROBERT'S EX-WIFE wasn't the only party suing the federal
government. A 26-year-old inmate who claimed his skull was fractured by vengeful guards after the April riot was suing Solicitor
General Jean-Pierre Goyer and thirty-one other officials and
prison guards.[216] It was a historic lawsuit: the first time a prison
inmate was claiming damages against the Canadian federal government for mistreatment. In a written statement, the man said he

had been beaten with a blackjack and three-foot riot sticks when he arrived at Millhaven penitentiary after the Kingston Penitentiary riot. He was taken to the Canadian Forces military hospital, where he was treated for a fractured skull. "My pain and suffering has been so grievous, persistent and permanent to the extent that my enjoyment of life has been lessened and my life has been shortened," said the claimant. The lawsuit was asking for damages of $125,000. The inmate's name was William (Billy) Knight.

ON DECEMBER 10, crowds once again gathered at the Frontenac County Courthouse in Kingston to catch a glimpse of the infamous inmate who had instigated the Kingston Penitentiary riot but had got off on all charges.

"Was it you who started the riot at Kingston Penitentiary?" lawyer Stuart Willoughby asked the 28-year-old man sitting in the witness box.[217]

"That's right, sir," replied the cocky inmate. "I seized guard Terrance Decker, punched him once and held him."

"So it was you who grabbed the first hostage?" asked Willoughby.

"That's right, sir."

Billy Knight was having another day in court, but this time he was the one doing the accusing. He was testifying against two Millhaven guards charged with assaulting him. Willoughby was representing guards Grant Snider, a correctional officer since 1956, and Bernard Evans, a guard for four years. Evans and Snider were the first two correctional officers to stand trial since the preliminary hearing in July.

Knight told the court that when he and other prisoners arrived at Millhaven and got off the buses, they were met at the loading dock by guard Grant Snider. Knight said Snider struck him over the head with a blackjack club.[218] Knight testified that after he was struck, his head was bleeding profusely but he was forced to run a gauntlet of ten to fifteen guards along a prison corridor. He was struck multiple times before guard Bernard Evans grabbed him and knocked him to the floor and began punching him with his fists.

Medical evidence presented to Judge Gerald Smith and the twelve-man jury indicated that Knight had a vertical laceration on the back of his head that required six stitches.[219] He also had several bruises, a fracture on the left side of his skull and a possible hairline fracture close to the laceration.

The next witness, Knight's friend Norman MacCaud, gave a similar account of the beatings, stating the guards had harassed the prisoners by striking them with clubs and making them run a gauntlet on their arrival in April after the riot.

"He fell and bumped his head," said Bernard Evans when it came time for him to testify against the assault charges.[220] He told the court that William Knight came running down the corridor at Millhaven, bumped into him and fell backwards, striking his head against an iron barrier. He testified he went over and picked Knight up by the shirt and a scuffle ensued between the two men. As they struggled, Knight fell a second time and hit his head again. It was only after the second fall that Evans noticed blood coming from Knight's head.

Guard Grant Snider denied hitting Knight at any time, but he acknowledged using his billy club on several prisoners. He admitted to striking inmates on the buttocks to hurry them along, but Knight was not one of them. Snider said Knight was refusing to move quickly along the corridor, so he pushed him into the corridor leading to the cellblocks.

Millhaven warden Donald Clark testified he had given the guards orders that force was not to be used with the transferred prisoners. "Only if it was necessary to make them move quickly," added Clark. The warden was testifying under protection of the

Canadian Evidence Act because Billy Knight was suing him and thirty-three others, including Solicitor General Jean-Pierre Goyer, for damages he suffered in the attack at Millhaven.

In his summation to the jury, Crown prosecutor Clay Powell stated the obvious: most of the Crown witnesses had long criminal records and some were convicts of the worst kind. But he stressed the only way the judicial system could operate was to give every man the protection of law. "Even the worst criminal in a penitentiary is entitled to protection under the laws of our country."

The twelve-man jury deliberated for forty-five minutes before reaching their verdict. Guards Grant Snider and Bernard Evans of Millhaven Institution were found not guilty of assaulting William Knight during the transfer of prisoners from Kingston Penitentiary after the April riot.[221] Judge Gerald Smith made no comment on the verdict.

A total of eight Millhaven guards had been charged with a total of seventeen offences. The trials for the six other guards would begin in January 1972.

They too would be acquitted of all charges.

26
COOL HEADS

Kingston was a hellhole. It was an ancient prison run in an inhu-
mane manner. There was the old-style discipline. Someone hollering
at you from the time you got up in the morning to the time you went
to bed at night. "Straighten up that line. Get your hands out of your
pockets. Cut off those sideburns." Everyone was treated like a dog.
Their idea of prison was to put a man in a cage and lock the door.
And one day it just blew.

—inmate Pat Devlin, *Toronto Star*, December 21, 1976

April 15, 1972

ONE YEAR AFTER the Kingston Penitentiary riot, the *Globe and Mail*
Weekend Magazine ran a special anniversary story on the uprising.
It was written by Ron Haggart, the journalist who had been a key
member of the citizens' committee. Since the memorable events
of April 1971, Haggart had moved to the *Globe* from the *Toronto*
Telegram. He was now working in a different newsroom and there
were other stories to cover, including another prison riot.

On September 9, 1971, five months after the Kingston riot,
prisoners at the Attica Correctional Facility in Attica, New York,

revolted. Over twelve hundred inmates took control of the prison and forty-two staff were taken hostage. Seeking better living conditions and humane treatment, the prisoners wrote a manifesto of twenty-seven demands that included better medical treatment, improved sanitation, better food and an end to physical brutality. But after four days of taut negotiations, Governor Nelson Rockefeller, who had refused to come personally to the prison, ordered the state police to take back control of the prison. On Monday, September 13, 1971, tear gas was dropped into the prison yard and New York State police troopers opened fire. When the smoke cleared and the gunfire ceased, dozens lay dead. The final death toll was forty-three, including ten correctional officers and thirty-three inmates. Many more were wounded. It was later determined that nine of the officers and twenty-nine of the inmates had been killed by police bullets.

As one of the citizens who had spent hours trying to negotiate with the Kingston inmates, the prison administration and government officials, Haggart knew first-hand that the Kingston uprising could have resulted in a similar outcome. "Cool heads on both sides of the negotiating table had saved Kingston from the bloodshed of Attica," said Haggart. He was right.

In an intimate first-hand account, Haggart relived his experience in Kingston.[222] He took the *Globe and Mail* reader inside the penitentiary when over five hundred inmates seized Canada's notorious prison and held six prison guards hostage for four harrowing days. In his opening paragraph Haggart wrote: "This is Billy Knight, the man who started the April 1971 riot at Kingston and got away with it." A rare picture of Knight accompanied the headline. Although Haggart and Knight had spent hours together during the riot, Haggart had never fully understood why or how Knight had instigated the uprising. But a year later, from his prison cell, Knight agreed to speak to the newsman.

The arrogant former prison barber took credit for starting the Kingston riot and told Haggart the whole operation had been relatively simple. "Six men," said Knight, "were strategically placed among the first group of inmates to leave the gym that evening. Two men were needed to block escape routes from the dome, two to secure and hold the barred doors leading from the gym to the dome and two for physical support should the guards put up a strong resistance." Knight was proud to tell Haggart there were no weapons involved in the initial takeover other than hands. "I anticipated seizing the entire institution," a boastful Knight told the reporter. But his plans were thwarted when other inmates still in the gym did not move fast enough before guards realized what was happening and held them at gunpoint. As a result, the rioting inmates were confined to the main dome and the four cellblocks. They never gained access to other parts of the prison that could have aided in their revolutionary plans, such as the kitchen, hospital ward, administrative building and workshops.

Knight, the consummate convict-politician, claimed he instigated the riot to expose prison conditions. "Kingston was a living, breathing hell-hole and I chose to destroy it before it could destroy me," claimed Knight. The opening of Millhaven had also hastened the uprising, according to the inmate. "A few days prior to the riot they began transferring our best men—the ones who still had enough guts left to stand up and be counted." The prisoners at Kingston heard rumours about the security measures at the new super-max penitentiary. They would be spied on, listened to and watched twenty-four hours a day. "We knew we had to make our final stand at KP and make our grievances known to the public," said Knight. "We knew that once they got us into Millhaven, and once they screwed the lid down tight on us, any thoughts of rebelling in that place would be unthinkable."

Others had different theories as to why Knight started the riot. Barrie MacKenzie, who had taken over the negotiations for the prisoners when Knight failed to deliver any resolution, believed Knight's life had been threatened by another inmate and the riot was simply a diversion to get him transferred to another institution. Penitentiary officials thought Knight might have been conned by a couple of other prisoners who were planning an escape over the wall.

Regardless, Knight was the man who started the April 1971 riot at Kingston Penitentiary and got away with it. "I had a bellyful of bitterness, frustration and disgust that was slowly eating me alive," said Knight.

One year after the riot, Knight was living out the remainder of his original sentence ironically at Millhaven, the new super-secure penitentiary he had revolted against. Behind the electrified twenty-foot chain-link fence that surrounded the grey cement octopus, and somewhere deep inside the antiseptic facility, Knight was stuck in solitary confinement for his own protection. Some of his fellow inmates felt that Knight had instigated a rebellion that not only hastened their move to Millhaven but also had resulted in few concessions. They were still living in a hellhole, albeit one with fresher paint on the walls. And Knight had got away with it. There were some bitter feelings among the general population that he got off by giving information to the police. He was now considered a rat. "A lot of groundless suspicions," Knight told Haggart. "But of course I expect to pay my full pound of flesh in retaliatory measures for the part I played in rocking the boat."

The petty thief, who had already spent half his life in and out of prison, planned to further expose the horrors of prison life with a book, called *The Walking Dead*. He had instructed his lawyer, Barry Swadron, to send his 110-page handwritten manuscript to potential publishers. He wasn't a famous criminal, but he was now a famous inmate and he was sure people would want to read his memoir.

Knight eventually won $3,500 from his lawsuit against the federal government for the injuries he sustained during the attack by Millhaven guards—a far cry from the $125,000 he had sued for—and he planned to put the money to good use. He was fighting an adoption application his ex-wife had initiated. She was asking the courts to allow their two daughters, Sherry and Kelly, to be adopted by her current husband. Knight admitted he hadn't been around for his girls. In fact, he hadn't seen them in ten years, but when he got out of prison, he was planning to reconnect with them. And he wanted to help other kids as well. Knight was donating part of his settlement money to a group home for young delinquents. If someone had been there for him when he first ran afoul of the law, he said, maybe his life would have turned out differently. Just maybe.

LOOKING BACK ON THE RIOT, John Maloney, the Regional Director of Penitentiaries described Kingston Penitentiary as a "house of hate," and said he believed the inmates had wanted to inflict damage on the overcrowded, dank prison before it was closed. He told Haggart: "There is no doubt in my mind that if there had been a military assault on the cellblock, we would have had another Attica. And," he added, "It will be one of the happiest days of my life when they leveled that prison to the ground."[223]

A year after the riot Maloney admitted there had not been much movement on penal reform. The federal authorities had done little to improve the atmosphere of tension between inmates and staff in penitentiaries. And while it was becoming clearer that guards should be more involved in the rehabilitation process, the federal government was building institutions like Millhaven that were designed to reduce contact between staff and prisoners.

Maloney blamed the politicians. "They are after votes and building better prisons isn't going to get them votes."[224] Maloney said that politicians and the public forget that 98 percent of the people who go into prison return to society one day. "It's in society's best interest that they come out better able to cope than when they went in."

One former inmate who did get out had no intention of ever going back. Interviewed by the *Globe and Mail* a year after the Kingston riot, a former convict, identified only as George to protect his identity, said that as long as he could remember the riot, he would never set foot in another prison.[225] "It's nothing to do with going straight or wanting to make a go of it. I just can't go back to prison." George had spent a lot of time in and out of jail as a thief and bank robber, but what he witnessed during the riot changed him. Seeing the undesirables beaten made him physically sick. After it was all over, George said the men in the circle lay bleeding and battered on the dome floor. "They looked like they were all dead and the floor was full of blood," he recalled. "We just sat there waiting for daylight, waiting for the army to come in. We didn't care anymore." What shocked him and shamed him the most was that no one tried to stop the violence. "Those punks thought they were tough—kicking, beating and burning helpless, half-dead men—but they were cowards. Then I realized all of us who were watching, afraid to step in and stop it, were cowards too." That's when he knew he would never go back to prison.

For those former inmates of KP who were still behind bars, life had not got any easier.[226] They no longer had numbers on their prison uniforms, and they could grow their hair longer, but their daily routine was much the same. The inmates who had given evidence against their fellow prisoners during the murder trial had been placed in a special dormitory back in Kingston Penitentiary for their own safety.[227] But as the months passed, most were eventually transferred to other institutions because of the cost of maintaining the separate unit. "We're very cognizant of the danger to these people," said John Maloney. Most of the reintegrations had worked out well, but Maloney admitted some of the inmates, particularly those whose names had been leaked to the press during the trial, could never go back to a normal prison. Their testimony had marked them as rats for life.

FOR THE MEN who had been bound to chairs and beaten in a circle of torture on the last night of the riot, their lives had been forever changed. Many had lasting physical pain from their injuries, and their emotional scars would never go away. All of them had been transferred to other institutions, but most were still living out their prison terms in isolated dissociation ranges. The plea deal and light sentences in the murder trial against the Kingston Thirteen had ensured their fate if they were ever released into the general population of a federal penitentiary in Canada. Five of the undesirables who had survived, and prison guard Terry Decker, eventually applied to the Ontario Criminal Injuries Compensation Board for reparation related to their injuries.[228] Allan Saunders, who was serving seven years for bank robbery, told the tribunal he played dead after being struck over the head multiple times while he was chained to a chair in the dome. "Then we were dragged like hogs back to the cell area," he said. His wounds required eighty-seven stitches.

Another inmate named Leslie Zimmer testified that he suffered severe head injuries and most of his teeth were broken during the beatings.[229] He was in a great deal of pain, but it took over a month for him to be seen by a dentist. "I even tried to yank them out with a pair of pliers myself."

A third inmate, Robert Sheehan, who was in prison for a sexual offence, testified that he had sustained a fractured skull, a broken nose and multiple lacerations as a result of the beatings on the last night of the riot. The soft-spoken, slightly built convict said he was lying beside Brian Ensor when Ensor was killed. "I remember exactly the moment Ensor died," said Sheehan. "I think his last words were, 'Oh my God, I think I'm finished.'" Fighting back tears, Sheehan said, "I thought I was next."

After two days of testimony, the Criminal Injuries Compensation Board, which had been established in 1967 to provide monetary awards to crime victims, ruled the five inmates and the prison guard were not entitled to any compensation. In their decision, the board stated: "The inmates contributed to their injuries because they were in prison as a result of their own criminal behaviour."

The Ontario Supreme Court overruled the board's decision and ordered them to reconsider the application. The fight for any form of compensation would continue for years.

AS FOR THE PRISON that most of the Kingston Penitentiary inmates were transferred to after the riot, Millhaven proved to be far worse than Billy Knight or any of the rioting prisoners could have imagined. Canada's first super-max prison was a repressive series of concrete blocks with sliding doors and metal bars that blue-shirted guards locked and unlocked from behind bulletproof tinted glass. Guards with guns patrolled the corridors and workshops behind one-way glass, and others with high-powered rifles monitored prisoners during their daily exercise periods from observation towers. Specially trained dogs patrolled the perimeter of the prison, and tear gas could be pumped into all of the cells at the press of a button. Television cameras monitored every movement outside the cells and there was no social interaction between staff and inmates.

It didn't take long for Millhaven's new residents to decide they needed to leave. In December 1971, inmate Thomas William McCauley, who was serving time for attempted murder, armed robbery and burglary, cut through a fifteen-foot chain-link fence surrounding the prison and became Millhaven's first escapee.[230] He was caught soon after. Poor lighting in the prison was blamed for his escape.

Undeterred, McCauley and thirteen other inmates broke out the same way seven months later. Joining McCauley was Donald Oag, who along with his brother James had been among the inmates charged in the murders of Brian Ensor and Bertrand Robert. A massive manhunt was undertaken. Three hundred police officers and soldiers from CFB Trenton used aircraft, stopped trains and set up roadblocks. Extra tracking dogs and their handlers were recruited from police departments as far away as Buffalo. Two of the escapees were caught within hours, and eventually all were apprehended. It was Canada's largest prison breakout and, again, poor lighting was blamed.

Many years later, in 1990, a local band from Kingston called the Tragically Hip would immortalize the escape of the fourteen inmates from Millhaven in a song called "38 Years Old."[231] The band's lead guitarist, Rob Baker, had a unique connection to the penitentiaries in his hometown. He was the son of P.E.D. Baker, the Frontenac County judge who had presided over the arraignment of the Kingston inmates charged with murder and kidnapping. He had also presided over the arraignment of the thirteen Millhaven guards charged with assault.

Don Clark, the warden of Millhaven who asked the Members of Parliament to leave the institution when they wanted to investigate the alleged assaults on prisoners, was transferred to another prison the following year. Interviewed in 2012, Clark said Millhaven was poorly designed and not capable of functioning as a secure facility when it was hastily opened following the Kingston riot.[232] "The big problem," he said, "was the total political and architectural ineptitude in the planning of the place." In his opinion, it took years for Millhaven to become fully functional.

IN THE YEAR AFTER THE RIOT, Kingston Penitentiary underwent numerous renovations and repairs. Although it was slated to close in 1971, the Penitentiary Service reversed their decision and the archaic building was transformed into a new reception centre.[233] Inmates would spend six weeks in the Kingston Pen to be classified into maximum, medium or minimum security risks before being transferred to other prisons. Most of the ancient cellblocks had been repaired and turned into bright new living quarters with linoleum floors. The cost of the damage to Kingston Pen caused by the riot had been estimated at over one million dollars.

The radiator in the centre of the dome had been removed, and the hated brass bell that sat on top was never replaced. Each cell was now equipped with an individual lock in place of the ancient locking mechanism that had been destroyed during the riot. 1-D, the range where the undesirables had been tormented and left for dead on the last night of the riot, was boarded up. It would not be used again for many years.

FOR TWO DAYS after the Kingston Penitentiary riot ended, Ron Haggart sat in his dingy Kingston hotel room, punching away at his noisy typewriter to write a lengthy account of the prison standoff for the *Toronto Telegram*. The account of what he experienced inside the prison, while the rest of the country watched and waited outside, would earn the feisty reporter a National Newspaper Award.

Haggart began his story: "Inside Kingston Penitentiary I met Barrie MacKenzie. He is the bravest man I have ever known and he will hate me for saying so." MacKenzie was a hero according to Haggart, along with all the members of the citizens' committee. In the final hours of the riot they watched helplessly while MacKenzie put his life on the line by going back into the dome area and convincing the prisoners to surrender.[234] He didn't give up until he knew all of the kidnapped guards and inmates were safe. He was the last man out of the destroyed prison. Haggart wanted his readers to know that it was the actions of an inmate—not the government, not the prison staff or even the citizens' committee—that had prevented an all-out military invasion of the penitentiary that would have resulted in many lives lost. Barrie MacKenzie deserved to be recognized.

A YEAR LATER, no one other than Ron Haggart was still thinking about Barrie MacKenzie. The inmate had quickly disappeared from the headlines and news reports. The government never acknowledged his critical role in protecting the lives of the kidnapped guards and negotiating a peaceful end to the riot with Haggart. He was now just another con doing time, counting off the days until his next parole hearing. Maybe then someone would give him credit for what he had done at Kingston, but probably not. He wasn't writing a book or doing interviews. Sitting in his cell at Collins Bay, he had little to talk about because little had changed. "Well, at least they leave the TV on for an extra half-hour now, until eleven o'clock," he said.

AFTER KINGSTON

The depressing and dehumanizing life of the institution was the soil within which the violent seed was planted and grew.
—from the Report of the Commission of Inquiry into Certain Disturbances at Kingston Penitentiary during April 1971

April 24, 1972

ONE YEAR AFTER the Kingston Penitentiary riot, the commission of inquiry chaired by J.W. Swackhammer released its confidential report. The commission had been appointed soon after the deadly disturbance to determine the immediate causes of the riot, to identify if any penitentiary staff were at fault and to make recommendations so as to avoid similar events in the future. During their investigation, the four-man commission visited Kingston Penitentiary, Millhaven and several other federal penitentiaries. In addition, they interviewed 348 penitentiary staff and 211 inmates who had been in Kingston at the time of the riot. In camera hearings were conducted in Kingston and Toronto from June to September 1971.

The sixty-three-page document methodically outlined the events of April 14 to 18, 1971, and determined that Kingston Penitentiary was "hopelessly outdated and inadequate for the purposes for which it was being used in 1971." In addition, a steady curtailment of privileges and inmate programs over the previous five years had compounded the problems within the maximum-security institution. Inmates spent at least sixteen hours a day locked in isolation in their cells. Boredom and a sense of hopelessness were inevitable. The commission summarized the conditions of confinement that existed at the prison as "repressive and dehumanizing." It was a jungle-like existence in which the strong preyed on the weak and an insurrection was inevitable.

The commission determined the riot was not an isolated incident but part of an escalating series of violent institutional disturbances designed to bring public attention to long-standing grievances that had not been adequately dealt with by the Penitentiary Service.

In their report the commissioners stated,

We have noted a number of causes for Kingston's failure: the aged facilities, overcrowding, the shortage of professional staff, a program that had been substantially curtailed, the confinement in the institution of a number of people who did not require maximum security confinement, too much time spent in cells, a lack of adequate channels to deal with complaints and the lack of an adequate staff which resulted in the breakdown of established procedures to deal with inmate requests. These facts were established beyond doubt by the testimony heard by the Commission.

The Swackhammer inquiry also found that the relationship between guards and inmates at Kingston was exceedingly poor. Through interviews the commissioners conducted, they determined there were two distinct prison subcultures: the staff on the one hand and the inmates on the other. There was an antagonistic, bitter relationship of mistrust and repressive custodial attitudes that considered most inmates to be "scheming, unrepentant criminals." This prevailing belief resulted in more rigorous and restrictive control of the population. The commissioners concluded that the polarization between inmates and custodial staff inevitably led to the destruction and deterioration of the entire system within the facility. The commission recommended improved training for all prison staff to ensure a better understanding of the general rules of the institution and, most importantly, of the twin objectives of the penal system: rehabilitation and custody.

In their remarks, the members of the Swackhammer commission referred back to the Archambault Report of 1938, which suggested that the system within Canadian penitentiaries was "shrouded with absolute secrecy." This approach to corrections was used to mask unfairness, inequity and brutality from public view. To remedy this systemic problem, the authors of the Archambault Report recommended that a board of visitors, such as existed in England at the time, be created to provide independent oversight. In the thirty-four years since the Archambault Report, that recommendation had never been implemented.

As a result, the commission reported, the Canadian Penitentiary Service lacked a transparent and impartial outlet for inmate complaints. There was no effective system to air legitimate grievances; no recourse to review the actions or decisions of the prison authorities; and no mechanism to bring public attention to prison conditions. They found that the treatment prisoners received behind prison walls, far from the public eye, continued to be degrading and abusive.

Based on their findings, the commission tabled fifty-two recommendations designed to improve the operation of federal penitentiaries while providing rehabilitation to offenders. Key among their recommendations, they identified the need for an independent body to review and provide redress to legitimate inmate grievances.[235] As a result, on June 1, 1973, the new Solicitor General of Canada, Warren Allmand, appointed lawyer Inger

Hansen as the first Correctional Investigator for federally sentenced inmates.

The primary function of the Correctional Investigator would be to protect the human rights of prisoners and to conduct investigations related to the operations and activities of the Penitentiary Service and promote resolution. Prisoners would now have an independent body with which to file complaints about prison conditions or against authorities. Investigators would be given unrestricted access to federal prisons, where they could hold hearings, interview offenders, meet with staff and examine documents. The Office of the Correctional Investigator would also have a central role in reviewing policies and procedures of the Penitentiary Service to ensure that systemic issues were identified and appropriately addressed. Investigators could make scheduled or unannounced visits to penitentiaries.

But as an independent oversight agency, and consistent with the traditional role of an ombudsman, the office's recommendations would not be legally binding on the Penitentiary Service. The Correctional Investigator would be required to present their findings and recommendations to the Penitentiary Service. If the Service did not respond adequately, the Correctional Investigator could make a report directly to the Solicitor General. As required by legislation, the Office of the Correctional Investigator would publish an annual report to the Solicitor General, who in turn would be required by law to present each report to Parliament.

While the Swackhammer Report was seen as a step in the right direction, it was not well-received by some of the politicians who had been involved in the Kingston riot. In a seventeen-page review of the commission's findings, Paul Faguy, the federal Commissioner of Penitentiaries, said: "I find the report rather disappointing after five thousand pages of transcript, twenty-three volumes, one hundred exhibits and twelve months of research."[236] He recommended the report not be made public. Instead, he suggested sending out a press release outlining the highlights of the report.

The government did release the Swackhammer Report to the public, but it was later discovered that seven pages of the official report had been removed prior to publication. Those pages dealt with the commission's findings and comments related to the actions of four staff employed by the Penitentiary Service. In a letter to Prime Minister Pierre Trudeau dated February 28, 1973, Warren Allmand, the newly appointed Solicitor General, stated: "I propose to table the report in the House of Commons on March 1, 1973. A few changes which were necessary for the purposes of security and internal discipline of the Canadian Penitentiary Service have been made to the original report. I sincerely hope the publication of the report will enhance public understanding of the problems facing those working towards the rehabilitation of offenders."[237] The letter was marked Secret and was hand-delivered.

The pages omitted from the official report were extremely damaging.[238] They involved knowledge about senior staff at Millhaven Institution who had knowingly and purposely allowed the Kingston Penitentiary inmates to be beaten when they arrived at the prison. The Swackhammer commission determined that eighty-six inmates had suffered injuries at the hands of persons employed by the Canadian Penitentiary Service.[239] Although thirteen guards had been charged with assault but later acquitted, the commission found other staff not charged had been responsible for permitting the attack on the inmates. The names of those individuals were Patrick McKegney, Deputy Warden Howard S. Bell and Warden John D. Clark. It was suggested that McKegney and Bell be fired. With respect to Warden Clark, the commission found he had approved the issuance of riot sticks to his staff but took no steps to supervise the staff involved in receiving the Kingston prisoners. The commission recommended Clark be admonished for "being remiss in the performance of his duties." Patrick McKegney retired in 1972 and died four months later. Howard Bell continued working for the Penitentiary Service, and by the time the Swackhammer Report came out, Warden Clark had already been replaced at Millhaven and was now the director of the regional centre for Ontario at Kingston. Both Bell and Clark went on to have lengthy careers within the Penitentiary Service.

When questioned about the report's findings, Solicitor-General Allmand told the press he was shocked by the beatings suffered by the inmates but added that appropriate action had been taken by his department. No one was ever fired he said, but any guards with obvious punitive tendencies had been transferred to jobs where they couldn't do as much harm.[240]

AS THE STRUGGLE for penal reform and prisoners' rights continued, the 1971 Kingston Penitentiary riot would prove to be the seminal event of the decade. The 1970s would go down as the most violent in Canadian penal history, with sixty-nine major incidents in federal penitentiaries.[241] Prison riots, hostage takings and murders became almost routine. In 1974, Millhaven penitentiary was locked down after rioting inmates wrecked 166 cells in two days.[242] The uprising was eventually quelled by tear gas, and prisoners were locked in their cells twenty-three hours a day for the next four months. Millhaven became known as the prison of "last resort," the dumping ground for cons other prisons couldn't handle. "It is a place where you try to survive," said an unnamed employee interviewed by the *Toronto Star*. "That includes the cons, the guards and the brass who run the place."

In October 1976, at the hundred-year-old fortress in New Westminster, British Columbia, inmates rioted for a week, holding a young guard hostage for more than eighty hours. "This is not a normal riot," one of the inmates explained. "There has been no demand for escape. This is a movement."[243]

And the movement continued to spread. One week later in Quebec, 264 prisoners rioted and set fire to the main cellblock at the century-old Laval Institute before going on a prolonged hunger strike. Inmates threatened to mutilate themselves unless prison conditions were improved. The prison originally built for 300 was bursting with 650 inmates at the time of the riot. The warden of Laval eventually asked the army to step in and remarked, "There is a war going on here and my staff are not trained to fight a war."[244] The government responded by saying it would not tolerate prison disturbances and would move quickly to dispel them, with the RCMP, with the army, with tear gas, and with anything else needed to convince inmates "there is nothing to gain by this type of action."

But another riot at Millhaven, in October 1976, finally resulted in a House of Commons subcommittee review of custodial practices at federal prisons. The committee, comprising eleven federal MPs, called the conditions in Canadian prisons a national disgrace. As for Millhaven, it was there that they found some of the worst cases of abuse and staff brutality towards inmates. "Millhaven's early history was marked by the use of clubs, shackles, gas and dogs often in combination. As former inmates of Kingston Penitentiary said: 'Kingston of 1971 hasn't gone away, it's just moved down the road.'"

Prisoners across the country were demanding better living conditions and basic human rights, but they were still subject to the rules and regulations of a closed correctional system where underpaid and bitter guards continued to enforce barbaric rules and punishment. The Commons report noted that in forty-two years between 1932 and 1974 there were a total of sixty-five major incidents in federal penitentiaries, yet in just two years—1975 and 1976—there were sixty-nine major incidents, including thirty-five hostage takings, one in which a prison guard was murdered.[245] The report found a near-total breakdown of order and authority within the penal system.

In a major study of prison conditions in Canada, University of British Columbia law professor Michael Jackson said the prisoner uprisings were part of a larger emerging pattern in society in which people on the lowest rungs, whose lives were controlled by the system, were saying, "Look, we're people too."[246] Prisoner discontent was a civil rights movement, according to Jackson.

While visiting prisons and talking to inmates, Jackson also found that prison disciplinary hearings chaired by wardens and their deputies were highly dysfunctional, kangaroo courts where prisoners were generally presumed guilty. "The rule of law is absent in Canadian prisons," he said. "Wardens are the modern equivalent of lords of the manor, governing their own fiefdoms in which they are the law." Jackson also reported that rehabilitation programs and educational opportunities were almost non-existent, and inmates and staff were locked in a cycle of violence and blame. Canada's federal prisons were in a perpetual state of tension, and inmates were taking out their pent-up rage on the facilities and the people who ran them. "We can't affect the politicians and we can't seem to affect the public," said a Millhaven inmate. "So, all we can do is destroy the system."[247]

Finally, in 1977, a parliamentary subcommittee on the penitentiary system was formed. Chairman Mark MacGuigan stated: "A crisis exists in the Canadian penitentiary system. It can be met only by the immediate implementation of large scale reforms."

Echoing previous committees and studies, the MacGuigan Report criticized the "warden's court" system of adjudicating disciplinary matters, in which wardens and their delegates made decisions, as lacking both independence and impartiality. In response, it was recommended that independent persons external to the institution be appointed to uphold the appearance of justice and to ensure that disciplinary hearings were fair and equitable.

Although the newly established Office of the Correctional Investigator had recommended in the annual report of 1973–74 that disciplinary courts be directed by external chairpersons, nothing had been implemented. The establishment of the Independent Chairperson (ICP) system to adjudicate disciplinary proceedings in federal prisons finally took place in 1977.

What followed over the next few years was a concerted effort to modernize correctional law, and in 1982 the Supreme Court of Canada affirmed under the Charter of Rights and Freedoms that citizens' rights also applied to inmates behind bars. The rights afforded to all Canadian citizens did not stop at the prison gates, and therefore prisoners should not be subject to cruel and unusual punishment.

Fifteen years after MacGuigan's report to Parliament, the 1992 Corrections and Conditional Release Act was signed into law. The Act completely replaced the Penitentiary and Parole Acts that had previously governed the operations of the Correctional Service of Canada and the National Parole Board. The legislation embraced a culture of respect and human rights within the correctional system. The Act stated that offenders retain the rights and privileges of all members of society, except those that are necessarily removed or restricted as a consequence of the sentence, and that correctional decisions should be made in a forthright and fair manner.

While new legislation afforded prisoners the same human rights as any Canadian citizen, those working on the front lines had difficulty putting equality at the centre of their day-to-day jobs. Prison guards exposed to the realities of everyday life in a federal prison expressed cynicism about the ideals of justice and the rights of prisoners.

In 1993, Kingston Penitentiary inmate Robert Gentles suffocated to death while being sprayed with mace and forcibly removed from his cell. And one year later videotape emerged of eight female inmates in segregation at Kingston Prison for Women being forcibly removed from their cells by riot squad guards wielding batons and shields. The women were stripped naked, searched, hand-cuffed and dressed in paper gowns. When portions of the video were leaked to the media and broadcast by the CBC ten months later, it ignited a national outcry and led to a commission of inquiry that condemned the culture of Corrections Canada and its actions.[248] The Commissioner, Justice Louise Arbour, con-cluded that Corrections Canada failed at all levels to respect the spirit and the letter of the law. In her report she stated:

> A guilty verdict followed by a custodial sentence is not a grant of authority for the state to disregard the very values that the law, particularly criminal law, seeks to uphold and to vindicate, such as honesty, respect for the physical safety of others, respect for privacy and for human dignity. The administration of criminal justice does not end with the verdict and the imposition of a sentence. Corrections officials are held to the same standards of integrity and decency as their partners in the administration of criminal law.

Shortly before the release of her report, the Commissioner of the Correctional Service resigned. In a letter to over ten thousand employees of Canada's prison system, John Edwards acknowl-edged that the events at Kingston Prison for Women were symptoms of a far wider problem and that there was a major crisis in Canada's correctional system.[249] At its root, Edwards claimed, were a set of conflicting attitudes and mixed messages that existed both inside and outside the prison service. These contradictory approaches expected corrections to punish and rehabilitate while treating prisoners fairly and keeping them under control. The Commissioner's frankness was unique in a long-standing culture embedded in secrecy and one that was usually allowed to hide its abuses behind prison walls.

In 2007, the Conservative government under Prime Minister Stephen Harper appointed a new task force to review Canadian corrections. Their report, called "A Roadmap to Strengthening Public Safety," concluded that prison culture was heading in the wrong direction, having elevated the rights of offenders over those of the victims. The task force recommended a back-to-basics approach in corrections, and the government implemented a host of legislative and policy changes designed to tackle crime, hold offenders accountable and make communities safer.

At the same time, the government enacted significant budget cuts that affected the ability of the correctional system to uphold its mission "to contribute to public safety by actively encouraging and assisting offenders to become law-abiding citizens, while exercising reasonable, safe, secure, and humane control." Overcrowding in penitentiaries became commonplace, with double bunking a widespread phenomenon. Suddenly two inmates were sharing one cramped cell the size of a small bathroom. This resulted in more inmate violence and attacks on correctional staff. Reduced access to meaningful programs, along with other cost-cutting measures like charging inmates for the use of penitentiary phones, heightened prisoners' levels of frustration, creating conditions of further unrest within the prisons.[250] And the fastest-growing portions of the inmate population—Indigenous prisoners and the mentally ill—were further marginalized by a lack of programs addressing their specific needs.

And while the tough-on-crime strategy and new legislation such as Bill C-10, the Safe Streets and Communities Act, were meant to make neighbourhoods safer, front-line workers maintained that the strategy had the opposite effect of setting the community up for danger by keeping people in prison longer without effective programming and transitional supports to assist with community reintegration.[251] In 2011 the Harper government announced plans to spend $158 million on prison expansion in Alberta, Saskatchewan, Quebec and Ontario.[252] The government also stated it would spend $2 billion over five years to absorb an increase in the number of prisoners due to stiffer sentencing provisions they had imposed with new legislation. Critics of the plan asked why the government was spending billions more on locking people up when crime rates were going down. Once again, federal corrections was moving backwards from a philosophy of upholding human rights and prisoner rehabilitation towards a culture of warehousing inmates—similar to the atmosphere of the 1970s when Kingston Penitentiary exploded.

IN 2015, THE LIBERALS defeated Stephen Harper's Conservative government. Forty-four years after the 1971 Kingston Penitentiary riot, when then Prime Minister Pierre Trudeau was on his honeymoon, another Trudeau was back in charge of the federal government. Prime Minister Justin Trudeau inherited a criminal justice system shaped by a fear-driven ideology and a decade of punishment-oriented policies. There were too many people in jail. Trudeau's government promised to blow up much of the Conservative agenda, be more transparent and move the Correctional Service of Canada away from its long-standing default position of secrecy.

One of the best-kept secrets of Canada's correctional institutions was the use of solitary confinement to manage prisons. Four decades after the inmates of Kingston Penitentiary revolted, demanding more humane treatment, prisoners were still being locked in isolated cement cells for up to twenty-three and a half hours a day without meaningful human contact.

At the time of its inception, in the nineteenth-century penitentiary, solitary confinement was intended to be a more civilized form of punishment since it left no physical marks on the body. It was supposed to inspire penitence in the criminal's heart, but according to Charles Dickens, who visited Kingston Penitentiary in 1842, solitary confinement buried men alive. Though he believed the prisons' architects thought they were acting humanely, Dickens wrote: "Very few men are capable of estimating the immense amount of torture and agony which this dreadful punishment, prolonged for years, inflicts upon the sufferers." In the late 1800s, eight inmates at Montreal's Saint-Vincent-de-Paul Penitentiary took part in a riot after the prison's tobacco supply was cut off. A Quebec judge shipped them off to Kingston Pen because it boasted "new facilities for solitary confinement, a punishment fit for inmates known for starting trouble."

In the 1930s, the *Globe and Mail* reported that one man had been kept in solitary confinement for twenty-three years at Kingston Penitentiary.[253] The cruel and inhumane practice continued well into the twenty-first century, and it has been estimated that tens of thousands of inmates have spent years locked away in solitary confinement across the country. A lack of independent oversight also meant prison wardens acted as both investigator and adjudicator in decisions about placing an inmate in solitary confinement and deciding how long they would remain there.

But then stories began to leak out from behind the solid steel doors of the segregation units across the country:

On October 19, 2007, Ashley Smith died of self-strangulation after spending 1,047 days (almost three years) in federal solitary confinement.

On August 13, 2010, Edward Snowshoe died in federal solitary confinement after 162 days.

On December 6, 2016, Adam Capay was removed from a provincial jail after spending 1,636 days (four and a half years) in solitary confinement with twenty-four-hour lighting.

The United Nations' Standard Minimum Rules for the Treatment of Prisoners, also known as the Mandela Rules, considers more than fifteen consecutive days in segregation to be torture.

In one of his first acts as prime minister, Justin Trudeau instructed his cabinet to implement recommendations concerning solitary confinement and the treatment of prisoners with mental illness arising from the coroner's inquest into the death of Ashley Smith.[254] The coroner's jury concluded that the Correctional Service should limit solitary confinement to fifteen consecutive days and a total of sixty days in a calendar year.

In 2017, the Liberal government introduced a bill that would place new restrictions on indefinite solitary confinement in federal prisons. Bill C-56 stated that an inmate could not spend more than twenty-one days in solitary confinement, and eighteen months after the bill's passage the number of days would drop to fifteen, the threshold recommended by the Mandela Rules and the Ashley Smith inquest. The bill also created a new position, that of an external reviewer to examine all cases where a prisoner's placement in solitary exceeded those of the new limit. But prison reform advocates said the bill did not go far enough in protecting vulnerable prisoners and ensuring independent oversight. The Canadian Civil Liberties Association filed a lawsuit against the federal government, alleging the laws governing solitary confinement were unconstitutional and violated a prisoner's rights under Section 7 of the Charter of Rights and Freedoms that relates to the right to life, liberty and security of the person. An Ontario Superior Court judge agreed and gave the Liberals one year to overhaul the laws.[255]

In January 2018, the British Columbia Supreme Court also declared the federal solitary confinement policy unconstitutional after the British Columbia Civil Liberties Association and the John Howard Society launched a lawsuit against the government.[256] The federal government appealed the decision. Later that year, Public

Safety Minister Ralph Goodale announced Bill C-83 would end the practice of segregating federal prisoners who pose risks to security or to themselves. Inmates who do pose risks would instead be moved to new "structured intervention units," where they would get better access to programming, interventions and mental health care. Under Bill C-83, prisoners transferred to structured intervention units would be permitted to spend four hours a day outside their cells, during which time they would be guaranteed a minimum of two hours to interact with others. Inmates in these units would be visited daily by health professionals and see patient advocates.

Bill C-83 was passed by Parliament on June 21, 2019. Ralph Goodale, Minister of Public Safety and Emergency Preparedness, issued the following statement:

> Correctional institutions must provide a safe and secure environment for staff and inmates, which assists with the rehabilitation of offenders, reducing the risk of re-offending and keeping our communities safe. Once in effect, Bill C-83 will abolish administrative and disciplinary segregation in all federal correctional institutions, increase mental health services and Indigenous supports, and bolster independent oversight in the Canadian correctional system—all backed by $448 million in new investments.

Bill C-83 was instantly panned by a number of human rights organizations that said the bill offered only a cosmetic rebranding of solitary confinement.

In 1973, based on recommendations in the Swackhammer Report, the office of the federal Correctional Investigator was created to provide independent oversight of the Correctional Service of Canada through accessible and impartial investigation of individual and systemic concerns in federal penitentiaries. Forty-five years later, newly appointed federal ombudsman Dr. Ivan Zinger wrote in his inaugural report: "The culture and infrastructure of corrections has hardened. While I recognize that safety and security of both staff and prisoners is paramount, beyond a certain threshold security measures can be counterproductive, hindering rehabilitation and reintegration efforts. These have not been progressive changes for the profession." Zinger blamed the current prison culture on issues that sounded eerily similar to those that Billy Knight and the prisoners' committee had identified during the April 1971 Kingston Penitentiary riot. Zinger blamed overly restrictive environments, too few programs for offenders, disruptions in routine, too much time locked up, a poor and outdated infrastructure, and inadequate food for generating inmate dissatisfaction and dissension. "Prisoners," he had previously written, "are sent to prisons *as punishment, not for punishment.*"

The federal ombudsman also stated, "If tension is allowed to build in a prison context, it can easily boil over into acts of individual or collective violence."

Finally, Zinger made mention of another issue that has pervaded Canada's prison system ever since the first inmate stepped foot in Kingston Penitentiary in 1835. He called for more openness in correctional services. "It is my belief that transparency in corrections leads to greater accountability, better performance and improved public safety results."

On April 15, 1971, a cocky prison barber named William (Billy) Knight told reporters that the inmates in Canada's oldest prison were "sick of being zombies." He wanted the entire world to come to the infamous Kingston Penitentiary and take a look inside. He wanted them to see how the forgotten were treated and how they lived. Fifty years after the Kingston Penitentiary riot, and after five decades of government policy shifts and bureaucratic fumbling on penal reform, we are still waiting to take a look inside.

WITNESSES TO A RIOT

THE REPORTERS

Ron Haggart

Immediately following the riot, Ron Haggart wrote a lengthy account of the events for the *Telegram* newspaper, which won a National Newspaper Award. A year later, he wrote a feature story for the *Globe and Mail's Weekend Magazine*. Speaking about the physical nature of the 130-year-old prison shortly after the riot ended, Haggart said: "The brutal and harsh mid-nineteenth century ideas of penology are perpetuated by the existence of that building."

Mr. Haggart eventually moved on to broadcast journalism, helping to launch CITY-TV. Then, in 1974, he was invited to become a senior producer for a new CBC magazine show called *The Fifth Estate*. There, he mentored a new generation of journalists, encouraging them to push the boundaries of traditional reporting.

Ron Haggart died in August 2011 at age eighty-four. After his death, the Canadian Journalists for Free Expression cited his critical role during the Kingston Penitentiary riot in awarding him its prestigious Vox Libera Award.

In 2013, Kelly Haggart published her father's writings about the riot in a book entitled *Cool Heads at Kingston Pen*. It is an important historical account of Haggart's personal experience during the riot, and although he gave credit to others, the book is a lasting reminder of the critical role he played in resolving one of Canada's worst prison riots.

Henry Champ

Henry Champ never forgot his impromptu visit to Kingston Penitentiary in the midst of the riot. He was the only reporter allowed into the dome and cellblocks to meet with the inmates. He had never been inside a prison before and later said he found it very depressing. "The idea of there being such a place like that was something I would have never comprehended."

The CTV news correspondent went on to become the network's bureau chief and was a familiar face on other news programs such as *W5*. Later he moved to the United States, where he became a news correspondent for NBC News. In 1993 he returned to Canada to become a news anchor for CBC *News: Morning*. He retired from the CBC in November 2008 after serving as the Washington correspondent for CBC Newsworld. Henry Champ died in 2012 at the age of seventy-five.

THE LAWYERS

J. Desmond Morton

The feisty Irish law professor didn't let a heart attack stop him from taking part in a hastily convened committee to deal with rioting prisoners in 1971. Nor did his precarious health prevent him from entering that same destroyed prison to meet face to face with hundreds of inmates when they asked for his help. He then stood at the gates of another prison, Millhaven, one month later and demanded to meet with prisoners who had been beaten by guards.

Professor Desmond Morton was well-known for his outspoken opinions on many aspects of criminal law in Canada. After the 1971 riot he never backed down from expressing his frustration and anger towards government officials. He blamed the federal Solicitor General, Jean-Pierre Goyer, for prolonging the riot until two prisoners had been killed and many others injured. And he blamed the same man for the beatings suffered by the Kingston prisoners when they got off the buses at Millhaven. "Can it be that fundamental human rights do not apply to prisoners in Canada?" he once asked. Professor Morton died in 1989 at the age of sixty-two.

William (Bill) Donkin

Bill Donkin was the Ontario director of legal aid for York County (Toronto) when he was asked to join a citizens' committee to negotiate with rioting prisoners at Kingston Penitentiary. He was appointed Master, Supreme Court of Ontario in 1980. Mr. Donkin died in 2008.

Aubrey Golden

After his experience during the Kingston Penitentiary riot, Aubrey Golden said that he had a new understanding of the tension that builds up inside a prison. "It heightened my sensitivity towards sending people to jail," he said.

Mr. Golden practised as a general counsel in a wide variety of civil and criminal cases until 2002. For the past twenty years, Mr. Golden has turned his legal experience and skills to the field of mediation. Golden co-authored the book *Rumours of War* with Ron Haggart and previously wrote a column on legal issues for the *Toronto Star*. He was also a regular commentator on CBC current affairs programming on issues involving constitutional reform, collective bargaining, public affairs and censorship.

Golden Mediation is located in Toronto and practices in a broad range of areas, including employment law, environmental disputes, public interest, defamation, and Aboriginal and general human rights cases.

Arthur Martin

Goldwyn Arthur Martin was one of Canada's most prominent criminal lawyers. As an outspoken opponent of capital punishment, he represented many accused of murder and was successful in keeping all of his clients from the gallows. He believed prisoners should be rehabilitated and people should not be sent to prison just for retribution. After the KP riot, Mr. Martin said he felt strongly that the days of the large, multi-purpose penitentiary were numbered. "Violent and dangerous prisoners should be housed in small, secure institutions with adequate medical and psychiatric staff," he said.

Arthur Martin lectured at Osgoode Hall from 1942 to 1966 and was appointed to the Ontario Court of Appeal in 1973. He became an officer of the Order of Canada in 1991 and a Companion in 1997. He died in 2001 at the age of eighty-seven.

THE GUARDS

Kerry Bushell

Kerry Bushell will never forget his twenty-fifth birthday, when he and five other guards were huddled in a cold, damp prison cell praying they would make it out of Kingston Penitentiary alive to be reunited with their families. A few months after the riot, Kerry left the Penitentiary Service and established a new career as an instrument technician with Ontario Hydro. Kerry has given a few interviews about his ordeal and appeared in a 2013 documentary about Kingston Pen. Kerry and his wife, Elaine, who were newlyweds in 1971, are now retired and live a quiet life in southern

Ontario. Kerry still cherishes the gold wedding band he got back after the riot.

Edward Barrett

When the riot broke out, senior keeper Ed Barrett handed over his wallet to an inmate and said, "When this is all over, I want my wallet back intact." He got it back with everything still inside. Barrett, who had never missed a day of work prior to the riot, died of a heart attack seven months later, in November 1971. He was fifty-seven years old.

Terry Decker

Terry Decker, who was the first guard attacked by Billy Knight and his gang, returned to his job at Kingston Penitentiary but tried to avoid working directly with inmates for several months. He then transferred to Millhaven, where a prisoner he was transporting stabbed him in the knee. Decker eventually worked his way up the ranks in the Correctional Service and became a keeper at Collins Bay. In a 1985 interview he reflected on the riot and said the experience had a profound and lasting effect on him. He battled depression and alcoholism for years. But he did not harbour any bitter feelings towards the inmates. He felt the experience had made him a more empathetic and compassionate person. Terry Decker retired from the prison service in 1987 and died in 2003. He was fifty-nine years old.

Douglas (Dad) Dale

Doug Dale took one month off after the riot but never returned to Kingston Pen. He was transferred to Millhaven, where he worked in the maintenance department, away from inmates. He never talked about his experience in the riot. When he retired, he volunteered at the Penitentiary Museum.

Donald Flynn

Donald Flynn went back to work at Kingston Penitentiary shortly after the riot but had difficulty readjusting. "I couldn't stand KP because of the hell I went through," he told a reporter years later. "The first night shift back on duty, I was put in the same area where I was taken hostage." The following year, Flynn transferred to Millhaven but still had issues with his nerves. He said his move to Millhaven was like "going from the fire into the frying pan." He took early retirement in 1979 and volunteered at the Penitentiary Museum across the street from Kingston Pen. Donald Flynn died in 2010.

Joseph Vallier

Joseph Vallier, who was forty-seven at the time of the riot, had only been on the job for six months when he was taken hostage. The day after the riot, the father of five told a reporter from the *Kingston Whig-Standard* that he and the other guards were convinced they would be killed. He said they were told repeatedly that they would be thrown over the railings on the fourth floor of the dome. But despite the threats, he said the inmates never mistreated them.

THE PRISONERS

Barrie MacKenzie

Barrie MacKenzie, the inmate hero of the Kingston Penitentiary riot, was paroled in 1972, but he was not able to stay out of prison for long. His parole was revoked in 1976 for not maintaining employment and it was later discovered he had murdered an acquaintance in Windsor, Ontario. In 1983 MacKenzie's ex-wife implicated him in the 1975 unsolved murder. He was convicted on January 25, 1984. Charles Saunders, one of the other inmates on the prisoners' committee during the KP riot, was also convicted on the same murder charge. MacKenzie was released from Collins Bay Institution in 1990. His whereabouts remain unknown.

William (Billy) Knight

Knight sued the federal government, including the Solicitor General, for the injuries he sustained from the guards at Millhaven. Knight won the suit and received $3,500 in compensation. He paid his lawyer $1,500 and gave $1,000 to start a group home for juveniles in Surrey, British Columbia.

After spending almost a year in segregation at Millhaven, Knight was transferred to British Columbia Penitentiary to serve out the remainder of his sentence. While out on day parole in 1975, he took off and travelled back to Chatham, Ontario, where his parents lived. While at large he stole a car and robbed a Sunoco gas station at gunpoint. He then kidnapped and raped a fifteen-year-old girl who was working at the gas station. Knight's older brother, Robert, was his accomplice.

He was recaptured in Windsor and sentenced to sixteen years. He was transferred back to Millhaven in October 1975. Once again he was put in protective custody. Knight was not able to operate in the general population in any of the prisons in Ontario. In November 1976 he was transferred to Saskatchewan Penitentiary. While in Saskatchewan, Knight slashed his Achilles tendon with a razor blade. He survived the attempted suicide. He did not mix well in the general population and was once again put in protective custody.

A classification officer reviewing his file stated: "Knight is a very demanding individual who can strongly display his rather volatile character. He is an unpredictable person who has developed an extremely questionable reputation throughout his exposure to the corrections system. Wherever he goes, trouble follows." A parole board member once said: "Knight could charm you out of your teeth, gold fillings and all."

In 1978, he requested a transfer to a Quebec prison, but he never made it. Billy Knight died while in custody at Saskatchewan Penitentiary on December 10, 1978. His manner of death was not released. He was thirty-five years old.

Dave Shepley

The inmate who led the attack on the undesirables had been in prison since 1965. He was eventually released from Kent Institution, a maximum-security facility in British Columbia, on May 12, 1981. Shepley was arrested two months later in Coquitlam, BC, after an alleged break-in and assault. It was rumoured that he later died of a drug overdose.

Brian Beaucage

In 1974, Brian Beaucage was released from prison on mandatory supervision, but he found himself back behind bars the following year for assault. He bounced in and out of prison for the next ten years.

In January 1987, Beaucage was shot three times in the chest in the parking lot of a nightclub in Ottawa. He survived the attack, but four years later he was murdered with an axe in a house on Lansdowne Avenue in Toronto. A London, Ontario, police officer told the *Toronto Star* that Beaucage was a well-known motorcycle gang member with a violent past who "lived by the sword and died by the sword." His lawyer told the same paper that Brian was not a typical inmate. "He was quite bright, but he lived life on the edge." Beaucage was forty-three years old when he died and had spent seventeen years behind bars.

Wayne Ford

Wayne Ford had just turned twenty when he started a life sentence at Kingston Penitentiary in July 1966 for killing his mother. Released from prison in 1975, he was determined to turn his life around and never see the inside of a jail cell again. He succeeded. For several years he worked as a Lifeline worker, going into prisons to help offenders get their lives back on track. The Conservative government of Stephen Harper eventually shut the program down. Today, Wayne lives a quiet life in western Canada. He still reports to a parole officer once every three months.

Robert Robidoux

In 1983, 31-year-old Robbie Robidoux was released on mandatory supervision after serving eight years for manslaughter in the death of Brian Ensor. Later that same year Robidoux threatened to kill a family of three with a kitchen knife. Robidoux had been living with the family of a physiotherapist who met him while he was in the Saskatchewan Regional Psychiatric Centre. Robidoux pleaded guilty to the attack and was sentenced to seven more years in prison. The judge in the case stated that Robidoux "had failed to correct his behaviour" and ruled him to be a dangerous offender. But the judge also said he was "cautiously optimistic" that Robidoux could be rehabilitated. The judge was right.

Robbie Robidoux had been in and out of foster care, institutions and prisons from the time he was seven. He has now been out of prison for over thirty years.

Roger Caron

In 1978, Roger Caron, a grade six dropout, won the Governor General's Award for his first book, *Go-Boy!*, a prison autobiography detailing his twenty-four years inside some of Canada's worst jails and penitentiaries. The experiences he wrote about were a harsh indictment of the country's penal system. The book described how, from the time he was first incarcerated at sixteen, Caron was whipped, stabbed, clubbed, tear-gassed, raped and subjected to years in solitary confinement.

Paroled in 1978, he continued to write and speak about his prison experiences. Caron's second book, *Bingo!*, published in 1985, was his first-hand account of living through the 1971 riot.

The former bank robber known as "Mad Dog" became a poster boy for prison rehabilitation and was once described by Prime Minister Pierre Trudeau as a "great Canadian." But his literary fame could not keep him away from his former high-risk lifestyle. In 1990 Caron was arrested for robbing a department store and was sentenced to eight more years in prison. Released in 1998, he was sent back to prison three years later when he was caught with a gym bag containing a loaded gun, a knife, a wig and duct tape. When asked what he was doing, Caron told the police officer: "I was going to do a job, obviously." Stricken with Parkinson's disease, Roger Caron died in 2012 at the age of seventy-three.

THE WARDEN

Arthur Jarvis

Arthur Jarvis was the warden of Kingston Penitentiary from 1968 to 1972. Interviewed in 1996, at age eighty, he still had a copy of the letters he had sent to his superiors on January 14, 1971, warning of the high degree of tension in the prison. The letters detailed serious problems in the prison, including overcrowding and understaffing. Jarvis got no response to his letters. A subsequent government inquiry into the causes of the riot commended Jarvis for his attempts to warn the Penitentiary Service about the impending prison revolt. Arthur Jarvis joined the Canadian Penitentiary Service in 1938 and retired in 1974.

Arthur Jarvis passed away in 2002 at the age of eighty-seven. A Correctional Service of Canada honour guard from Kingston Penitentiary paid tribute to the prison's former warden at his funeral.

THE POLITICIAN

Jean-Pierre Goyer

When the Kingston Pen riot ended, the men on the citizens' committee blamed Solicitor General Jean-Pierre Goyer for the uprising's brutal end. They believed if Goyer had negotiated in good faith with the prisoners, the riot would have ended peacefully, without bloodshed. Goyer was also criticized for refusing to allow Members of Parliament into Millhaven to investigate the prisoner beatings that occurred after the transfer from Kingston. In addition, Goyer had to defend his position when he insisted that the Swackhammer inquiry into the causes of the riot be held behind closed doors.

But, surprisingly, historical documents consider him the "architect of prison reform." After the Kingston riot, Goyer said reform was desperately needed and it was the federal government's intention to upgrade the quality of prison life to preserve human dignity. "Rehabilitation rather than punishment must become the goal of the Canadian penal system," he said. "Criminal justice must be synonymous with social justice and let us not forget that the offender is a citizen and a human being." But he also said he was not going to carry out prison reform if prisoners did not behave themselves. "I'm not going to take the risk of moving into reform if the inmates are not going to behave like responsible people."

Goyer became a Member of Parliament in 1965 and was appointed Solicitor General by Pierre Trudeau in 1969. It was thought that the intelligent protege of the prime minister would go far in national politics. But he repeatedly found himself defending his policies and there were constant demands for his resignation. After the 1972 federal election he became Minister of Supply and Services, and he eventually resigned from cabinet in 1978. He was done with politics and returned to his law practice in Montreal. Jean-Pierre Goyer died in 2011 in Montreal. He was seventy-nine.

NOTES

CHAPTER ONE

1 "1971 NHL Stanley Cup Playoffs Summary," Hockey Reference, www.hockey-reference.com/playoffs/NHL_1971.html.

2 Roger Caron, *Bingo!* (Toronto: Methuen Publishing, 1985), 101.

3 Michael Cobden, "Kingston prisoners often 'break down and scream,'" *Toronto Star*, June 12, 1971, 18.

4 Information on William (Billy) Knight's early life is contained in his personal manuscript, *The Walking Dead, 1971*.

5 *Report of the Commission of Inquiry into Certain Disturbances at Kingston Penitentiary during April 1971*, April 24, 1972, 11.

6 Michael Enright, "The halls of anger," *Maclean's*, March 21, 1977, 32.

7 Donna Barnett, "The jail guard: a prisoner without bars," *Kingston Whig-Standard*, November 19, 1975, 11.

8 As told to me during interviews with former correctional officers.

9 I learned about the tavern through conversations with former penitentiary staff and residents of Kingston.

CHAPTER TWO

10 "Kingston: Canada's Penitentiary City," www.stoneskingston.ca/penitentiary-city.

11 Frederick Edwards, "This is Kingston," *Maclean's*, February 1, 1941, 18.

12 Bryan Palmer, "Kingston Mechanics and the Rise of the Penitentiary, 1833-1836," *Social History/Histoire Sociale* vol. 13, no. 25 (1980): 10.

13 Dennis Curtis et al., *Kingston Penitentiary: The First Hundred and Fifty Years* (Ottawa: Canadian Government Publishing Centre, 1985), 39.

14 Jennifer McKendry, "The early history of the Provincial Penitentiary, Kingston, Ontario," *Society for the Study of Architecture* (SSAC Bulletin) 14:4 (1989): 97.

15 Roger Caron, *Go-Boy!* (Toronto: McGraw-Hill Ryerson, 1978), 131.

16 Emma Reilly, "The 'pen' of Kingston past," *Queen's Journal*, October 14, 2005, www.queensjournal.ca.

17   Curtis et al., *Kingston Penitentiary*, 18.
18   Stevie Cameron, "Big Moments in the Big House," *Globe and Mail*, September 30, 2013, 3.
19   Curtis et al., *Kingston Penitentiary*, 38.
20   "History of the Canadian Correctional System," Correctional Services Canada, https://www.csc-scc.gc.ca.
21   Austin Campbell, "House of Hate," *Maclean's*, October 15, 1933, 32.
22   Reilly, "The 'pen' of Kingston past."
23   Nancy Weston, "Ontario's prisons: the inside story," *Globe and Mail*, November 27, 1997, 26.
24   Don Townson, "Kingston's sadistic Warden Smith," *Maclean's*, September 24, 1960, 81.
25   Curtis et al., *Kingston Penitentiary*, 42.
26   Peter Hennessy, *Canada's Big House: The Dark History of Kingston Penitentiary* (Toronto: Dundurn Group, 1999), 28.
27   Curtis et al., *Kingston Penitentiary*, 43.
28   Alessandra Iozzo, *In the Best Interests of the Child?: The Industrial School System in Late Nineteenth and Early Twentieth Century Ontario* (Ottawa: Faculty of Graduate Studies and Research, Carleton University, 2000).

CHAPTER THREE

29   Farrell Crook, "Public called least important on prison information scale," *Globe and Mail*, June 18, 1971, 11.
30   Ontario Provincial Police report on the death of Brian Ensor, from Chief Inspector R.A. Ferguson, Criminal Investigation Branch, May 6, 1971.
31   Reilly, "The 'pen' of Kingston past."
32   Caron, *Go-Boy!*, 36.
33   Brian Stewart, "Not a country club," *Maclean's*, April 9, 2001, 34.
34   Hennessy, *Canada's Big House*, 100.
35   Daily prison routine as reported in the *Report of the Commission of Inquiry*, 13.
36   Cobden, "Kingston prisoners," 18.
37   Ibid., 18.
38   Hennessy, *Canada's Big House*, 101.
39   Curtis et al., *Kingston Penitentiary*, 147.
40   *Federal Corrections Magazine* Vol 3, #4 (October/November 1964), 14.
41   Memorandum to the Solicitor General, November 2, 1966, 2.
42   John Hawes and Norman MacCaud, "For the sake of argument we're denying prisoners the right to learn," *Maclean's*, November 1967, 49.
43   "New wardens appointed," *Federal Corrections Magazine* Vol 6, #2 (April–June 1967).
44   Allan Dickie, "Two Kingston convicts seize 3 hostages negotiations begin," *Toronto Star*, January 8, 1971, A1.
45   Internal memo written by warden Arthur Jarvis, Re: Abduction of officers Marsden, Turner and Bramley, Jan 11, 1971.
46   *Report of the Commission of Inquiry*, 14.
47   "Suicides last year in federal jails," *Gazette* (Montreal), February 19, 1971.

48 Telegram to Prime Minister Pearson, April 28, 1967.

49 "New Millhaven complex: it's the fear of the unknown," *Kingston Whig-Standard*, April 17, 1971.

50 Ron Haggart, "This is Billy Knight, the man who started the April 1971 riot at Kingston Penitentiary and got away with it," *Globe and Mail*, April 15, 1972, A1.

CHAPTER FOUR

51 Details of the attack on the guards as recounted in police documents written by Chief Inspector R.A. Ferguson, Ontario Provincial Police, Criminal Investigation Branch, May 6, 1971.

52 *Windsor Star*, April 15, 1972, 87.

53 *Maclean's*, March 1, 1933, 13.

54 Hennessy, *Canada's Big House*, 91.

55 Jim Cole, "Kingston Penitentiary: A piece of Canadian history with a long record of brutality," *Toronto Star*, April 19, 2012.

56 "Beating back," *Maclean's*, May 15, 1933.

57 "Schools for crooks," Ralph Allen, *Maclean's*, May 15, 1946.

CHAPTER FIVE

58 Frank Croft, "What it's like to be in a prison riot," *Maclean's*, October 15, 1954, 116.

59 H.L. Jones, "Convicts leave pen in shambles," *Lethbridge Herald*, August 16, 1954, 1.

CHAPTER SIX

60 Eyewitness statement of Edward Francis Patricks, written by Detective Sergeant C. St. Remy, Kingston Police, April 1971.

61 Paul Hunter, "Life after life," *Toronto Star*, May 4, 2013, IN2.

62 Caron, *Bingo!*, 115.

63 "Kingston Penitentiary: a chronology," *Kingston Whig-Standard*, April 19, 2012.

64 Marilyn Dunlop, "Kingston pen: turmoil doesn't show," *Toronto Star*, April 17, 1971.

65 Recorded in an internal document written by A.H. Bird (Assistant OPP Commissioner) to Eric Silk (Commissioner of the Ontario Provincial Police), April 21,1971.

66 Andrew Salwyn, "Five hundred prisoners riot at Kingston: six hostages held," *Toronto Star*, April 15, 1971, 1.

CHAPTER SEVEN

67 Michael Valpy, "Diary of a misspent life: The pedophile who faces a lifetime behind bars," *Globe and Mail*, December 9, 1972, 7.

68 Paul King, "The prisoners who live in fear of death," *Toronto Star*, January 31, 1976, F1.

69 Anne Steacy, "Treating sex criminals," *Maclean's*, July 18, 1988, 46.

70 Michael Valpy, "Laws on sexual offenders put pathetic men in jail for life, professor says," *Globe and Mail*, February 3, 1972.

71   Ibid.
72   Interview with Robbie Robidoux, May 6, 2017.
73   Letters to the editor, "Ugliness in Kingston," *Globe and Mail*, April 20, 1971.
74   *Federal Corrections Magazine* Vol 3, #4 (October/November 1964), 18.

CHAPTER EIGHT

75   Arthur Jarvis, "Summary of events and action taken during the disturbance at Kingston Penitentiary April 14–18, 1971."
76   Jordan Press, "Location, 'mystique' set facility apart," *Ottawa Citizen*, April 20, 2012, 4.
77   Robert Sutton and Peter Van Harten, "Kingston prisoners hold 6 guards: threaten to cut off fingers," *Toronto Telegram*, April 15, 1971, 1.

CHAPTER NINE

78   Jarvis, "Summary of events and action taken."
79   Sheldon MacNeil,"Inmates are tired of being zombies," *Kingston Whig-Standard*, April 15, 1971, 3.
80   Conversation between prison officials and inmates during first press conference was recorded in an internal government memo written by Commissioner of Penitentiaries Paul Faguy, April 15, 1971.
81   Sheldon MacNeil, "Last chance for us," *Kingston Whig-Standard*, April 15, 1971, 1.
82   Conversation between prison officials and inmates during first press conference.
83   "Citizens' group barters with defiant convicts," *Toronto Daily Star*, April 16, 1971, 1.
84   In an internal government document written by Commissioner of Penitentiaries Paul Faguy he states, "For a number of reasons we should not consider Ron Haggart, Tommy Douglas or any representatives of the Civil Liberties Group." Document dated April 15, 1971.
85   "Four days of fear for stoolies," *Toronto Telegram*, April 19, 1971.
86   Anne MacLennan, "Hostage's wife: 'I'm very concerned, but I'm not getting emotional,'" *Kingston Whig-Standard*, April 16, 1971, 1.
87   "Henry Champ dies at age 75," *Brandon Sun*, September 23, 2012.

CHAPTER TEN

88   Henry Champ, "Newsman finds 'pure democracy' in prison chaos," *Toronto Telegram*, April 16, 1971.
89   Robert Taylor, "KP revolt termed 'spur-of-the-moment' affair," *Kingston Whig-Standard*, April 16, 1971, 1.
90   "Journalist delighted in controversy," *Toronto Daily Star*, August 29, 2011.
91   Hawes and MacCaud, "For the sake of argument," 49.
92   "Prisoner died in fire he set jury says," *Toronto Daily Star*, March 5, 1970.
93   Internal government memo: list of prisoners' demands written and copied to Paul Faguy, Commissioner of Penitentiaries, and J.-P. Goyer, Solicitor General, April 16, 1971.

94   "It's the do-gooders who caused this, guard says," *Kingston Whig-Standard*, April 16, 1971, 21.

95   Telegram to Mrs. K.G. Bushell from Department of the Solicitor General, April 16, 1971.

96   John Kirkpatrick, "More troops are flown into city," *Kingston Whig-Standard*, April 17, 1971. 2.

97   Don Dutton, "False move could cost six lives, guard warn," *Toronto Daily Star*, April 16, 1971, 3.

CHAPTER ELEVEN

98   Duncan Thorn, "Inmate-writer will work on film version," *Kingston Whig-Standard*, April 16, 1971, 12.

99   Documentation of this secret conversation between the acting prime minister and the Solicitor General was found in a memo marked "Kingston Penitentiary," *Cabinet Conclusions*.

100 "Hope of release for pen hostages," *Toronto Telegram*, April 17, 1971.

101 Kirkpatrick, "More troops are flown into city," 3.

102 Kelsey Merry and Robert Sutton, "Negotiators take demands to Ottawa," *Toronto Telegram*, April 16, 1971.

103 "Troops with riot clubs and gas masks circle cell block at Kingston," *Toronto Star*, April 17, 1971.

104 "Troops in KP second time in 17 years," *Kingston Whig-Standard*, April 16, 1971.

105 Ibid., 2.

106 Dunlop, "Kingston Pen: turmoil."

CHAPTER TWELVE

107 Ron Haggart, "Behind the bargaining," *Toronto Telegram*, April 21, 1971, 17-24.

108 "Hope of release for pen hostages," *Toronto Telegram*, April 17, 1971.

109 Ibid.

110 Sheldon MacNeil, "There is nothing left says off-duty KP guard," *Kingston Whig-Standard*, April 17, 1971, 2.

CHAPTER THIRTEEN

111 "Pickets were moved by police," *Kingston Whig-Standard*, April 19, 1971, 17.

112 "The last day," *Kingston Whig-Standard*, April 19, 1971.

113 "40 demonstrators ask for negotiations with rioters," *Toronto Star*, April 19, 1971.

114 Haggart, "Behind the bargaining," 17-24.

CHAPTER FOURTEEN

115 Vincent Devitt, "Convict held in prison deaths saved 2 from beating, court told," *Toronto Star*, November 9, 1971, 42.

CHAPTER FIFTEEN

116   "Children treated like animals, placed on hot stove, trial told," *Globe and Mail*,
      May 27, 1970, 10.

CHAPTER SIXTEEN

117   Wilf Kealey obituary, www.yourlifemoments.ca, February 17, 2010.
118   "After the Kingston Riot, *Time Magazine*, May 3, 1971, 11.
119   Dennis Bell, "Many questions unanswered," *Kingston Whig-Standard*, April 19,
      1971, 2.
120   "Jailer cleans up in tin cans," *Toronto Star*, April 19, 1971.
121   Ibid.
122   John Scott, "Kingston cellblock a shambles: Undesirables wing shows evidence
      of violence committed," *Globe and Mail*, April 24, 1971, 11.
123   Sheldon MacNeil, "OPP join in probe of riot," *Kingston Whig-Standard*,
      April 21, 1971, 6.

CHAPTER SEVENTEEN

124   Rae Corelli, "Riot at Kingston ends, one dead, 11 injured," *Toronto Star*,
      April 19, 1971, 1.
125   "Torture in ruined cellblock is cited by prison officials," *Toronto Telegram*,
      April 19, 1971, 1.
126   Stan McDowell, "Mutilation report denied," *Toronto Star*, April 23, 1971, 27.
127   Stan McDowell, "Inquest may bring murder charges," *Toronto Star*, April 20,
      1971.
128   Ibid.
129   Ibid.
130   Statement of the Solicitor General in the House of Commons, April 19, 1971.
131   "Kingston prisoner called hero of riot saved guards' lives," *Toronto Star*, April
      20, 1971, 1.
132   Rae Corelli, "Ottawa blamed for prisoner's injuries in Kingston riot," *Toronto
      Star*, April 20, 1971, 3.
133   "Goyer mishandled his role in prison riot, negotiator says," *Toronto Star*,
      April 20, 1971.
134   Ibid.
135   Corelli, "Ottawa blamed," 3.
136   Desmond Morton, "What really happened in Kingston," *Globe and Mail*,
      April 21, 1971, 7.
137   Report of Inspector J.W. Kealey, Kingston Police Department regarding
      disturbance at Kingston Penitentiary, May 18, 1971.

CHAPTER EIGHTEEN

138   "Inquiry opens Monday," *Kingston Whig-Standard*, June 5, 1971.
139   "Howard protests against order to depart during NDPers' unannounced
      Millhaven visit," *Kingston Whig-Standard*, May 19, 1971.

140 "MPs' formal inquiry into penitentiary," *Prince Albert Daily Herald*, April 6, 1970.
141 "The inquiry into KP: reasons for secrecy," *Kingston Whig-Standard*, May 19, 1971.
142 "New jail treats men like cattle: professor," *Toronto Star*, April 20, 1971.
143 *The Advance Newsletter* Spring 1971.

CHAPTER NINETEEN

144 Memorandum to the Director, Criminal Investigation Branch, Ontario Provincial Police, May 7, 1971.
145 Memorandum from Attorney General Allan Lawrence to E. Silk, Commissioner, Ontario Provincial Police, Re: Kingston Investigation, April 29, 1971.
146 Memorandum to The Director, Criminal Investigation Branch, Re: Murder of Brian Ensor, Kingston Penitentiary, May 6, 1971.
147 Don Dutton, "Guard: ultimatum broke rioters' will," *Toronto Star*, April 20, 1971.
148 Government of Canada, brief on claim by Leslie Zimmer and Julius Martiz, March 27, 1973.
149 Letter to John Hodgson, vice-president of Canadian Bar Association (Ontario), from Ian Scott, counsel for the Commission of Inquiry, May 21, 1971.
150 Letter to J.P. Goyer, Solicitor General, May 12, 1971, 71.
151 "KP riot: open probe asked," *Kingston Whig-Standard*, May 26, 1971, 2.
152 See note 29.
153 Sheldon MacNeil, "Prisoners silent over reasons for hunger strike," *Kingston Whig-Standard*, May 13, 1971, 2.
154 John Doig, "Millhaven hunger strike to be probed, Turner says," *Toronto Star*, May 13, 1971, 3.
155 Gerard McNeil, "KP Riot—charges flying," *Kingston Whig-Standard*, May 19, 1971, 3.
156 "Robert was afraid he'd be killed," *Kingston Whig-Standard*, May 19, 1971.
157 J.D. Morton, "The continuing enigma of Millhaven," *Globe and Mail*, November 19, 1971.
158 Bruce Dawson, "Convicts to stand trial," *Kingston Whig-Standard*, July 8, 1971.
159 "Convict says he set fire to self to protest solitary confinement," *Globe and Mail*, June 30, 1971, 4.
160 Government of Canada memorandum, Re: Collin's Bay: Swallowed Glass, May 17, 1971.
161 Rae Corelli, "Bid fails, convict to stay in solitary," *Toronto Telegram*, June 26, 1971, 10.
162 "Goyer gives up plan for oppressive jail," *Globe and Mail*, May 12, 1971, 2.
163 Memorandum to A.F. Lawrence, Minister of Justice from H. Graham, Ontario Provincial Police, May 27, 1971.

CHAPTER TWENTY

164 Thomas Claridge, "Eleven moved from direct contact with Millhaven inmates: Goyer," *Globe and Mail*, May 29, 1971, 4.

165   Ibid.

166   Copy of letter received by the Honourable Robert Stanbury, Member of Parliament, Scarborough, from Mrs. Norma Agnew, May 3, 1971.

167   Internal government document marked Highly Confidential containing list of names of charged guards. Memo sent to Solicitor General Goyer, from information obtained in a phone call from Millhaven warden Clark advising, "Summons charging our officers are being issued by the OPP today," May 27, 1971.

168   "Prison guards submit pleas of not guilty," *Globe and Mail*, June 4, 1971, 27.

169   Bruce Dawson, "Troops on alert for possible prison duty," *Kingston Whig-Standard*, July 19, 1971.

170   Confidential memorandum to the Solicitor General from acting executive assistant J.R. Cameron, June 2, 1971.

171   "12th guard faces charge of assault," *Globe and Mail*, June 16, 1971, 8.

172   Sheldon MacNeil, "Prison wardens will be asked to provide more information," *Kingston Whig-Standard*, June 18, 1971.

173   "Shackled prisoners clank into court to face murder charge," *Belleville Intelligencer*, June 5, 1971.

174   "Punishment before trial court told," *Toronto Star*, June 9, 1971, 3.

175   "Kingston inmates say they sleep on slabs," *Toronto Star*, June 5, 1971, 86.

176   Psychological Report on William David Shepley, Department of Psychology, Millhaven Institution.

177   Mike Norris, "Special report: A horrendous scene," *Kingston Whig-Standard*, April 9, 2011, 2.

178   "Hearings under way," *Kingston Whig-Standard*, July 13, 1971.

179   Bruce Dawson, "Judge Klein firmly in control of opening session," *Kingston Whig-Standard*, July 13, 1971.

180   "Kingston convicts' scuffle at court," *Toronto Star*, July 16, 1971.

181   Michael Valpy, "Lawyers fail to get 13 out of solitary," *Globe and Mail*, July 17, 1971.

182   "Carried from court, prisoner threatens to kill if ever freed," *Globe and Mail*, July 7, 1971, 9.

183   Department of Justice, Crown attorney John Sampson, August 12, 1971.

CHAPTER TWENTY-ONE

184   Letter to the Honourable John Turner, Minister of Justice, August 12, 1971.

185   "Communication and the prisons," *Kingston Whig-Standard*, July 27, 1971.

186   Morris Duff, "Beaten after riot," *Toronto Star*, July 20, 1971, 10.

187   Ibid.

188   Bruce Dawson, "Convict claims he and 11 others beaten on arrival at prison," *Kingston Whig-Standard*, July 20, 1971.

189   "Guards deny assault charge," *Globe and Mail*, February 3, 1972, 9.

190   "12 guards charged," *Kingston Whig-Standard*, July 20, 1971.

191   Michael Valpy, "Millhaven guards ordered to trial on assault charges," *Globe and Mail*, July 22, 1971, 4.

192   Bruce Dawson, "Five plead guilty to reduced charges; Knight discharged," *Kingston Whig-Standard*, August 18, 1971, 1.

CHAPTER TWENTY-TWO

193   Memorandum to the Director of the Criminal Investigation Branch, Ontario
       Provincial Police, August 30, 1971.

CHAPTER TWENTY-THREE

194   Letter to the editor, "The horror of the prison code continues," *Globe and Mail*,
       October 9, 1975, 6.
195   Michael Valpy, "Trial of thirteen begins in prison slayings," *Globe and Mail*,
       October 29, 1971, 4.
196   Bruce Dawson, "Murder hearings underway," *Kingston Whig-Standard*, July 13, 1971.
197   "Kingston inmate's face masked by blood, prison official testifies," *Globe and
       Mail*, November 3, 1971.
198   Vincent Devitt, "Ex-inmate links 7 to prison beatings at murder trial," *Toronto
       Star*, November 4, 1971, 4.
199   Michael Valpy, "Armed during prison beating, witness admits," *Globe and Mail*,
       November 18, 1971, 13.
200   Vincent Devitt, "Inmate faked death in 'pile of bodies' and says he watched
       convict being beaten," *Toronto Star*, November 10, 1971, 2.
201   Devitt, "Convict held in prison deaths saved 2."
202   Vincent Devitt, "Toast in blood 'made up,' lawyer suggests at trial," *Toronto
       Star*, November 11, 1971, 40.

CHAPTER TWENTY-FOUR

203   David Pike, "12 at Kingston guilty of manslaughter," *Toronto Star*,
       November 23, 1971, 42.
204   Letter to the editor, "A most disturbing trial," *Globe and Mail*, November 30,
       1971, 6.
205   Letter received by Attorney General Allan Lawrence regarding sentencing of
       Kingston inmates in deaths of Brian Ensor and Bertrand Robert, December 1, 1971.
206   Rae Corelli, "Mini prisons proposed to replace penitentiaries," *Toronto Star*,
       November 24, 1971, 1.
207   Letter received by Allan Lawrence, Attorney General, December 6, 1971.

CHAPTER TWENTY-FIVE

208   Michael Valpy, "Secret deal settled Kingston trial," *Globe and Mail*, December
       13, 1971, 1.
209   "Lawyers confirm deal on sentences," *Toronto Star*, December 13, 1971, 12.
210   "The arguments for a bargain: confusion, tension and $40,000 a week," *Globe
       and Mail*, December 13, 1971.
211   Memorandum to the warden of Millhaven Institution, August 20, 1971.
212   Internal memo, Government of Canada, August 19, 1971.
213   Letter to the editor, *Globe and Mail*, December 27, 1971, 6.
214   Letter to the editor, "Judges and juries and misplaced economy," *Globe and
       Mail*, December 22, 1971, 6.

215 Rae Corelli, "Lawyers for convicts bill Legal Aid $150,000 for trial," *Toronto Star*, March 10, 1972, 1.

216 Rae Corelli, "Kingston inmate sues Goyer for $125,000," *Toronto Star*, October 19, 1971,68.

217 "Convict tells court he started riot at Kingston," *Toronto Star*, December 10, 1971, 10.

218 "Gauntlet description repeated at Millhaven guards' trial," *Globe and Mail*, December 11, 1971, 10.

219 "Prisoner had head wounds, trial told," *Globe and Mail*, December 14, 1971.

220 "Inmate struck head in fall, guard states," *Globe and Mail*, December 15, 1971, 8.

221 "Two guards are acquitted of jail assault," *Globe and Mail*, December 16, 1971, 2.

CHAPTER TWENTY-SIX

222 Haggart, "This is Billy Knight," A1.

223 "After the Kingston Riot," *Time Magazine*, May 3, 1971, 11.

224 Cobden, "Kingston prisoners."

225 "Reforming a con," *Globe and Mail*, May 9, 1972, 14.

226 "Riot trial witness now being transferred," *Globe and Mail*, January 12, 1973.

227 Ibid.

228 "Inmate beaten in riot needn't get award, court rules," *Globe and Mail*, November 20, 1974, 35.

229 Judi Timson, "Four Kingston prisoners recall six hours of terror," *Toronto Star*, July 19, 1972, 1.

230 Rae Correlli, "6 of 14 escaped convicts surrounded near Kingston," *Toronto Star*, July 11, 1972, 1.

231 John Bowen, *Kingston Life* 14, no. 5 (July/August 2012).

232 Ibid.

233 "Kingston penitentiary takes on new look as reception centre," *Toronto Star*, September 4, 1971, 91.

234 Ron Haggart, "The convict who saved Kingston," *Toronto Telegram*, April 20, 1971, 1.

AFTER KINGSTON

235 Government of Canada memorandum, Re: Recommendations of the Swackhammer Report, March 8, 1973.

236 Government memo written by Paul Faguy, Commissioner of Penitentiaries, n.d.

237 Letter to Prime Minister Trudeau, February 28, 1973.

238 Internal government memo written to Dalton Bales, Minister of Justice and Attorney General for Ontario, from Jean-Pierre Goyer, Solicitor General, November 22, 1972.

239 "Guards beat 86 prisoners after 1971 riot, probe finds," *Globe and Mail*, March 2, 1973.

240 "Cons truncheoned after riot," *Ottawa Citizen*, March 2, 1973, 23.

241 "Penal system needs large-scale reforms," *Toronto Star*, June 8, 1977.

242 Ibid.
243 "Riot in cell block Canada," *Maclean's*, October 18, 1976.
244 Ibid.
245 "Prisons are a national disgrace; can we really improve them?" *Gazette* (Montreal), June 14, 1977.
246 Michael Jackson, *Justice behind the Walls* (Vancouver: Douglas & McIntyre, 2002).
247 "Memories of Kingston hold seeds of riot at Millhaven," *Globe and Mail*, November 25, 1974.
248 "Infamous prison for women strip search video debuts online," *cancrime.com*. March 2, 2011.
249 Kevin Marron, "Secrets behind the walls," *Maclean's*, April 15, 1996.
250 Meagan Fitzpatrick, "Inmates to pay more for room and board," CBC News, May 9, 2012, www.cbc.ca/news/politics/inmates-to-pay-more-for-room-and-board.
251 John Edwards, Willie Gibbs, and Ed McIsaac, "Jails don't keep people out of jail," *Globe and Mail*, January 5, 2012.
252 Jim Bronskill, "Critics say Harper government throwing prison expansion money away," *Toronto Star*, January 10, 2011.
253 Monika Warzecha, "Solitary horrors: the grim history of solitary confinement and its modern-day comeback," *National Post*, April 13, 2016.
254 Patrick White, "Ottawa draws line on solitary at 15 days," *Globe and Mail*, June 20, 2017.
255 Patrick White, "Canada's solitary confinement laws are unconstitutional, Ontario judge rules," *Globe and Mail*, December 18, 2017.
256 Adrian Wyld, "B.C. court upholds ruling that struck down solitary confinement law," *Globe and Mail*, June 24, 2019.

ACKNOWLEDGEMENTS

WRITING IS A SOLITARY ENDEAVOUR, and for an introvert like me it is the most rewarding form of work. I don't mind the lost hours searching through historical archives or struggling to focus in front of the microfiche machine. And writing into the wee hours of the morning is my happy place. But this book is about much more than just me and my laptop, and there are many voices within these pages that I am indebted to.

First of all, I would like to thank my editor, Janice Zawerbny. She has been my champion. Without her unwavering support and early interest in the manuscript, this book might not have found its perfect home with Biblioasis literary press. Janice asked publisher Dan Wells to read the first few chapters of an obscure story about a 1971 prison riot, and I'm so glad he did. It's not easy to get a non-fiction title published in Canada these days, particularly for a first-time writer such as myself, but Dan Wells and his amazing team in Windsor decided to take a chance. And for that I am very grateful.

This book began as a rough proposal for the Master of Fine Arts in creative non-fiction at the University of King's College in Halifax, Nova Scotia. At the beginning of the two-year program I nervously stood in front of a group of other novice writers and top-notch instructors to pitch this story. I had no idea what it would take to write a book, but I knew this was an important story and it was the one I wanted to tell. Thankfully, I was in the right place to begin this journey. Thank you to my mentors Kim Pittaway, Harry Thurston and Tim Falconer. Your guidance was invaluable. And thank you to Dean Jobb and Stephen Kimber, who offered great advice, support and some much-needed humour.

I have also been fortunate to have other mentors along the way, celebrated Canadian writers for whom I have developed a tremendous appreciation and respect. Thank you to fellow Celt Ken McGoogan, who actually got me into this crazy adventure of writing a book, and thank you to Shaughnessy Bishop-Stall, whose guidance and support gave me the confidence I needed to craft a much stronger narrative two thousand words at a time. I'm also grateful to researcher Joel Kropf who mined Library and Archives Canada for parole records, government papers and other documents. His expertise and knowledge was invaluable.

To piece together a story that took place fifty years ago in a prison, I needed a lot of help. And when many doors closed in my face, others opened with kindness and patience. I am grateful to have met Erin Murphy, a retired corrections officer from Kingston. Erin was very supportive of this project and introduced me to a number of fellow officers who had amazing stories to tell. I appreciate their trust and candour. I want to acknowledge all of the dedicated men and women of the Correctional Service of Canada past and present, who work in an opaque, bureaucratic system, but who do make a difference every day.

I am also appreciative to Kerry Bushell and his wife Elaine. As the last surviving guard held hostage in the riot, I know that reliving these memories has been difficult for Kerry. I hope, fifty years on, this book offers him some closure on what was a terrifying ordeal.

How do you research and write a book when you actually have a full-time job? I hadn't really thought about that before I began, but the answer lies in having a supportive business partner. Thank you to Maria Armstrong, my dearest friend, and colleague for almost thirty years. You kept the lights on while I ran off to be a writer. I owe you.

And to my sons Aedan and Conor, thank you for listening to all of my crazy prison stories and for being who you are. Many of the inmates I have written about were barely older than you are now, but they lost their way, often due to circumstances beyond their control. Poverty, violence, racism and other systemic injustices often reflect the faces of those who reside in our prisons. You are kind and thoughtful young men and I know you will always stand up for others less fortunate and offer a helping hand to those in need.

Finally, I would like to thank my husband, Oliver. He has never wavered in his support for this book even when my boxes of research took over the dining room table or when he had to go to bed alone because I just needed to finish what I was writing. His objective comments on early drafts kept me on track and he is forever my grammar king. Neither of us knew what we were getting into five years ago when I said I was going to write a book, but we made it! Thank you for believing in me and thank you for your love.

And to Zuffy and Daisy, my beautiful four-legged companions lost along this journey, you are forever in my heart.

CATHERINE FOGARTY is a storyteller. She is the founder and president of Big Coat Media, with offices in Toronto, Los Angeles, Vancouver, and North Carolina. An accomplished television producer, writer and director, Catherine has produced award-winning lifestyle, reality and documentary series for both Canadian and American networks.

Catherine is the executive producer of the Gemini nominated series *Love It or List It*. In addition to that franchise, Catherine has produced several other lifestyle and documentary series including *Animal Magnetism* (W Network), *My Parents' House* (HGTV), and *Paranormal Home Inspectors* (Investigative Discovery Canada). Catherine also produced and directed *I Don't Have Time for This*, an intimate documentary about young women with breast cancer.

Originally trained as a social worker, Catherine studied deviance and criminology. She worked with numerous at-risk populations including street youth, people with AIDS, abused women, and social services.